A DREAM OF JUSTICE

TIMBERLINE BOOKS

STEPHEN J. LEONARD AND THOMAS J. NOEL, EDITORS

The Beast
BEN B. LINDSEY AND HARVEY J. O'HIGGINS

Bound by Steel and Stone: The Colorado-Kansas Railway and the Frontier of Enterprise in Colorado, 1890–1960
J. BRADFORD BOWERS

Colorado's Japanese Americans: From 1886 to the Present
BILL HOSOKAWA

Colorado Women: A History
GAIL M. BEATON

Denver: An Archaeological History
SARAH M. NELSON, K. LYNN BERRY, RICHARD E. CARRILLO, BONNIE J. CLARK, LORI E. RHODES, AND DEAN SAITTA

Denver Landmarks and Historic Districts, Second Edition
THOMAS J. NOEL AND NICHOLAS J. WHARTON

Denver's Lakeside Amusement Park: From the White City Beautiful to a Century of Fun
DAVID FORSYTH

Dr. Charles David Spivak: A Jewish Immigrant and the American Tuberculosis Movement
JEANNE ABRAMS

A Dream of Justice: The Story of Keyes v. Denver Public Schools
PAT PASCOE

Enduring Legacies: Ethnic Histories and Cultures of Colorado
ARTURO J. ALDAMA, WITH ELISA FACIO, DARYL MAEDA, AND REILAND RABAKA, EDITORS

Frank Mechau: Artist of Colorado, Second Edition
CILE M. BACH

The Gospel of Progressivism: Moral Reform and Labor War in Colorado, 1900–1930
R. TODD LAUGEN

Helen Ring Robinson: Colorado Senator and Suffragist
PAT PASCOE

The History of the Death Penalty in Colorado
MICHAEL L. RADELET

The Last Stand of the Pack, Critical Edition
ARTHUR H. CARHART WITH STANLEY P. YOUNG; ANDREW GULLIFORD AND TOM WOLF, EDITORS

On the Plains, and Among the Peaks; or, How Mrs. Maxwell Made Her Natural History Collection
MARY DARTT, EDITED BY JULIE MCCOWN

Ores to Metals: The Rocky Mountain Smelting Industry
JAMES FELL

Season of Terror: The Espinosas in Central Colorado, March–October 1863
CHARLES F. PRICE

The Trail of Gold and Silver: Mining in Colorado, 1859–2009
DUANE A. SMITH

A Tenderfoot in Colorado
RICHARD BAXTER TOWNSHEND

A DREAM OF JUSTICE

The Story of *Keyes v. Denver Public Schools*

PAT PASCOE

UNIVERSITY PRESS OF COLORADO
Louisville

© 2022 by University Press of Colorado

Published by University Press of Colorado
245 Century Circle, Suite 202
Louisville, Colorado 80027

 The University Press of Colorado is a proud member of
the Association of University Presses.

The University Press of Colorado is a cooperative publishing enterprise supported, in part, by Adams State University, Colorado State University, Fort Lewis College, Metropolitan State University of Denver, University of Alaska Fairbanks, University of Colorado, University of Denver, University of Northern Colorado, University of Wyoming, Utah State University, and Western Colorado University.

∞ This paper meets the requirements of the ANSI / NISO Z39.48-1992 (Permanence of Paper).

ISBN: 978-1-64642-289-0 (hardcover)
ISBN: 978-1-64642-493-1 (paperback)
ISBN: 978-1-64642-290-6 (ebook)
https://doi.org/10.5876/9781646422906

Library of Congress Cataloging-in-Publication Data

Names: Pascoe, Pat, author.
Title: A dream of justice : the story of Keyes v. Denver Public Schools / Pat Pascoe.
Other titles: Timberline books.
Description: Louisville : University Press of Colorado, [2022] | Series: Timberline books | Includes bibliographical references and index.
Identifiers: LCCN 2022031531 (print) | LCCN 2022031532 (ebook) | ISBN 9781646422890 (hardcover) | ISBN 9781646424931 (paperback) | ISBN 9781646422906 (epub)
Subjects: LCSH: Keyes, Wilfred, 1925–1999—Trials, litigation, etc. | Denver Public Schools—Trials, litigation, etc. | Noel, Rachel, 1918–2008. | Segregation in education—Law and legislation—Colorado—Denver. | School integration—Law and legislation—Colorado—Denver. | Educational law and legislation—Colorado—Denver. | Noel, Rachel, 1918–2008. | School board members—Colorado—Denver—Biography. | Civil rights workers—Colorado—Denver—Biography.
Classification: LCC KF228.K49 P37 2022 (print) | LCC KF228.K49 (ebook) | DDC 344.73/0798—dc23/eng/20220831
LC record available at https://lccn.loc.gov/2022031531
LC ebook record available at https://lccn.loc.gov/2022031532

Cover illustration from Benton-Pascoe campaign literature. Courtesy of the author.

To the unsung heroes of desegregation

Contents

Foreword

THOMAS J. NOEL

The University Press of Colorado's Timberline Series welcomes Pat Pascoe's book to its offerings which feature much of the best scholarship on Colorado. Pat, an author, and former state senator, who holds a PhD in English, brings her writing skills, meticulous research, and personal knowledge to one of the most contentious, consequential, and often overlooked struggles in Colorado's history—the long battle to integrate the Denver Public Schools.

History books often wallow in the past, but this timely tale is still being played out in the ongoing endeavor to make good public education accessible to all students. Pat became heavily involved when her husband, Monte, a prominent attorney and civic activist, ran for the Denver school board on a pro-integration platform in 1969. On the board he hoped to join other integrationists including his close friend and fellow lawyer Edgar Benton, and Rachel Noel, who in 1965 became the board's first Black member.

In the early 1960s Noel had been frustrated when school administrators opened Barrett Elementary School on the west side of Colorado Boulevard in Northeast Denver. Black students, including Noel's daughter, who had

https://doi.org/10.5876/9781646422906.c000a

been crossing the Boulevard to attend predominantly white Park Hill Elementary, were then assigned to Barrett where pupils academically lagged a year behind those at Park Hill.

Prompted by the Civil Rights Movement, the Barrett experience, and the 1968 assassination of Dr. Martin Luther King, Jr., Noel and Ed Benton wrote the Noel Resolution calling for integration of the Denver Public Schools. The board approved the resolution in May 1968. A year later, on May 20, 1969, after a heated election campaign, voters overwhelmingly rejected Monte Pascoe's attempt to be elected to the board and they also dumped Ed Benton who ran for re-election. In their places citizens put Frank Southworth and James Perrill, advocates of neighborhood schools and opponents of busing.

Faced with a new board hostile to meaningful integration, the pro-integrationists successfully sued the school district in a case titled *Keyes v. School District No. 1* (Denver public schools) filed in 1969. One of the many merits of Pat's book is its careful, clear chronicling and explanation of the legal arguments and court rulings which ultimately led to a landmark U.S. Supreme Court decision in 1973.

Federal Judge William Doyle implemented court-supervised integration appointing Pat and others to the Community Education Council to oversee desegregation orders. She was an excellent choice because she understood integrated schooling. Earlier she had taught in an East Palo Alto California high school with a large Black population. In Denver Pat and Monte enrolled their two older children in a school with a large number of Black students.

To effectively integrate the schools, Doyle mandated busing of white and Black students. Many white parents vehemently objected to having their children moved from largely white neighborhood schools to schools with children of color. Some left Denver to avoid busing. The city's suburbs, fearful that Denver would expand its school district by annexing land, successfully supported an amendment to the Colorado State Constitution that made it extremely difficult for Denver to annex more territory. Deep community divisions led to the bombings of school buses, bombings of homes, school riots, and threats against Noel, Benton, Pascoe, and Doyle. Anti-busers such as Southworth and Perrill were also targeted as fringe elements in the community engaged in a potentially deadly mini-Civil War.

The Pascoes and many others suffered in their crusade to assure all students good educations. Yet Pat and Monte, who died in 2006 at age seventy-one, never regretted that they fought for the sake of Denver's Black and Latino children. Reviewing the decades-long struggle, she writes: "Desegregation would be difficult, but it was far less painful than the poverty engendered by segregation resulting in lower achievement, lower lifetime income, poorer health, and shorter life span."

Preface

EDMOND NOEL AND ANGELA NOEL

It is indeed an honor for us, as Rachel B. Noel's two children, to write this preface for Pat Pascoe's *A Dream of Justice: The Story of* Keyes v. Denver Public Schools. The roots of Pat's insightful account trace to the 1968 Noel Resolution, which aimed to end segregation in Denver's public schools and was written by our mother and her fellow Denver Public Schools (DPS) board member Ed Benton. Pat painstakingly details what happened at the ground level in Denver from the start of the *Keyes* case to its end twenty-seven years later. She describes the brave attempts to provide equal educational opportunity for all of Denver's schoolchildren—and the brazen efforts to deny them. This is history told through its events and its people, who saw a historic responsibility and took it on. In her research and writing, Pat verifies Denver's role in the Civil Rights movement of the 1960s and 1970s and in subsequent generations' challenges and possibilities.

What are some worthy lessons to be gleaned by people of goodwill? For one, considerable progress in matters of social justice in all aspects of American life can happen when white liberals and Black, Brown, or other

https://doi.org/10.5876/9781646422906.cooob

minority allies work together to oppose whites' hatred and bigotry and the institutions that foster and sustain those sentiments.

To be sure, our mother's efforts to rally the Black community against inequities in Denver's schools were complemented by effective alliances she forged across the racial divide. Ed Benton's role was similarly and singularly important. As white liberal political candidates, he and his fellow 1969 board candidate Monte Pascoe (and their families) were targeted and stood tall against whites' unabashed bigotry and hatred, the extent of which surprised Denver's white and Black citizens alike.

We may have wanted to believe back then that an insignificant percentage of white people held these racist beliefs and that even those who did would follow the law. Today's Donald Trump era has shown that we were wrong and that the percentage of white racists is large enough not only to threaten our educational institutions and more but, in fact, to endanger our very way of life.

And so, what to do? In his "Letter from Birmingham Jail, April 16, 1963," Dr. Martin Luther King Jr. said, among many other things, "We will have to repent in this generation not merely for the hateful words and actions of the bad people but for the appalling silence of the good people."[1] Rachel and Edmond Noel, Ed and Stephanie Benton, and Pat and Monte Pascoe (and many others Pat discusses) would not be silenced. It remains to be seen whether today's silent white liberals will step up to the challenge.

As important as her sounding alarms about past misdeeds, Pat has also captured a view of the optimism of earlier times. It is important to recognize that the Noel Resolution was not proposed in the acrimony of 2016 through 2022 but instead in the righteous sorrow following Dr. King's assassination in 1968.

Elections of then emerging black politicians, like Rachel Noel, at the local and state levels in the mid- to late 1960s continued that hope and pushed for change. Even after the deflating Benton-Pascoe school board election loss, Pat describes the fervent belief that the *Keyes* case legal fight, based on *Brown v. Board of Education*, could succeed and bring permanent change through legal enforcement of *Brown's* promise.

Keyes illustrated the inadequacy of the United States Supreme Court's appetite for enforcement since 1954, but it was also a harbinger of the immense white backlash against integration in our schools. That backlash continued through the election of President Barack Obama and escalated with the emergence of unprecedented levels of racism and whites' bigotry under former president Donald Trump—from police brutality to diminished voting rights to the rise of organized, well-funded, public-facing white hatred groups and the nearly successful insurrection attempts at the US Capitol. America saw the KKK march in Washington, DC, in the 1920s; will we see that again? Today, this faction of American hatred is not the least bit hesitant. Fortunately, neither is Pat Pascoe.

Will a "still-too-silent" unknown percentage of white people rise up and join their Black, Brown, and other allies to help save the soul of the country, as happened with the Civil War in the mid-1800s and the Civil Rights movement in the mid-1900s? Will it take until the mid-2000s, and will that be too late? The time to decide and determine is now.

The Greatest Generation won a world war and passed the Civil Rights legislation of the mid-1900s, but it will take an even greater generation to turn back Trump and his followers, save our democracy, and fulfill America's true promise. For today's children and tomorrow's, the stakes could not be higher. For today's children and tomorrow's, the battle must be won.

Acknowledgments

So many people helped me gather information for this book, but I can only name a few of them. First, my friend Edgar Benton answered many questions throughout the years of writing this book. I am also indebted to Janet Bardwell and Andrew Bardwell, the children of George Bardwell, who shared their memories and records. Robert Connery was very generous with his time and his ample files on the early history of the *Keyes* case. And Michaela Barnes shared a memoir of her late husband, Craig Barnes. Edmond (Buddy) Noel, the son of Rachel Noel, was also a great source.

As always, the librarians at the Western History section of the Denver Public Library were helpful, as were the librarians in the archives at Norlin Library at the University of Colorado. Samantha Hager assisted me with records at the Colorado Department of Education. I also received help from the staff of the Denver Public Schools.

Marcia Bishop explained the desegregation index, and LaDonne Bush was very helpful regarding the legal records of the case. Thank you to my editor David Horne for finding mistakes I needed to correct. I am grateful for the assistance of Charlotte Steinhardt, Rachael Levay, and the rest of the staff at the University Press of Colorado. All remaining errors are, of course, my own.

I also want to thank the people who allowed me to interview them because they thought this story was important.

I especially appreciate my courageous husband, Monte Pascoe, and my children, Sarah, Ted, and Will, who were always supportive.

All those who struggled to make desegregation work are unsung heroes.

A DREAM OF JUSTICE

Introduction

My husband, Monte Pascoe, and I, along with many other families—white, Black, and Hispanic—were deeply involved in the effort to desegregate School District No. 1, also known as Denver public schools. Although I offer just one white person's perspective among many, which comes with the knowledge that I carry unconscious bias, I believe this story should be told and that people living today should understand the kind of community we all had hoped to create.

Monte's family moved from Iowa to Denver when he was in third grade, and his family was deeply attached to Montview Boulevard Presbyterian. In addition to attending services, his father, Don, served as an elder, and his mother, Marjorie, was a member of many church groups. They were compassionate—the kind of people who tried to help anyone who needed it.

In the Boy Scouts, Monte earned every possible honor: God and Country, Eagle Scout, Order of the Arrow. Monte learned the importance of team-work in sports, which he began participating in when he was nine years old. At East High School, he was a star athlete, playing football, basketball,

https://doi.org/10.5876/9781646422906.c000c

and track and playing in the national East-West football game after being named a high school all-American. During his senior year, Monte was part of the state championship mile relay. Monte earned a scholarship to Dartmouth, where he won the Barrett Cup as the outstanding senior, and he was awarded another scholarship, this one to Stanford Law School. His sense of justice developed further as he learned more about the inequities in our legal system.

I grew up in a small town in Wisconsin. My mother was widowed when I was eighteen months old and my sisters were three and seven years old. I don't recall any Black people in my town, but after my mother transferred to St. Louis with the civil service when I was twelve, I learned that much of life in that city was segregated. There were identifiable Black or white schools and swimming pools, but the buses were mixed. The schools and the church I attended in Clayton, just outside of St. Louis, were almost completely white. A teacher at Clayton High School, under the auspices of the National Conference of Christians and Jews, organized monthly meetings of student representatives from all the high schools in the metropolitan St. Louis area, which necessarily included schools that were nearly all Black. As one of those representatives, I had my first experience talking with young Black people. We met monthly and, among other things, went to the art museum together. A few of us visited an all-Black high school, where I experienced the discomfort of what it feels like to be in the minority. Later, when my mother was transferred to Colorado, I went to Aurora High School and the University of Colorado, both almost entirely white at the time.

Monte and I were married the summer after we graduated from college, and we lived in Menlo Park, California, while he attended Stanford Law School. I taught in a high school with a large Black population in East Palo Alto, but because I taught average English classes, I had few Black students, who were mostly in remedial classes—suggesting the disadvantages of the elementary schools in Black neighborhoods. When Monte graduated from law school in 1960 we returned to Denver, where he started his law practice. We soon had our first child. Then our relatively peaceful lives were disturbed by cataclysmic national events.

One shock after another tore up America in the 1960s, a rapidly changing background for the beginning of desegregation efforts. The first came shortly after the inauguration of President John F. Kennedy: the thirteen-day

Cuban Missile Crisis of October 1962. We all feared that Russian missiles in Cuba, armed with nuclear bombs, would destroy cities in the United States. Kennedy announced an embargo on materials for the missile sites, which was effected by surrounding Cuba with US Navy ships. Finally, Kennedy and Russian premier Nikita Khrushchev agreed that the missiles and the missile sites would be destroyed. In return, Kennedy secretly agreed to remove American missiles in Turkey. The nation was greatly relieved that nuclear war was averted.

But anti-Black racial violence increased in the United States. In June 1963, Medgar Evers, the National Association for the Advancement of Colored People's (NAACP's) Mississippi field secretary, was fatally shot in his driveway by a segregationist. In September, four Black girls were killed in a bomb attack at the Sixteenth Street Baptist Church in Birmingham, Alabama, which shocked many white and Black Americans.

President Kennedy's voice in the civil rights debate was silenced in November 1963 when he was assassinated in Dallas, Texas.

Despite the violence, Martin Luther King Jr. came to Denver the following January. He spoke at Montview Boulevard Presbyterian Church to a thousand people, some standing outside in the falling snow and listening to him through loudspeakers. His visit became a catalyst for movements already under way in Denver.[1]

In June 1964, three civil rights workers in Mississippi—a local Black man, James Early Chaney, along with two fellow white volunteers, Andrew Goodman and Michael Schwerner—went missing. A widely publicized FBI investigation led to the discovery of their bodies in an earthen dam. The men had been working with the Congress of Racial Equality (CORE) to register Black voters.

After Kennedy's assassination, the violence against civil rights workers, the march on Washington, and continued ongoing violence across the country and particularly in the South, the impetus for the Civil Rights Act grew until it passed on July 2, 1964, followed by the key Voting Rights Act on August 6, 1965. These laws aroused hope and expectations among minority groups, yet there were no immediate changes in living and voting opportunities.

Closer to home, our family experienced our own tragedy. After having two healthy children, Sarah in 1960 and Ted in 1963, our beautiful baby Donald

Kirk, born in 1967, struggled for three weeks in the hospital and died. In later years we determined that he probably had cystic fibrosis, but that wasn't recognized at the time. This was the most difficult loss we had ever experienced. When I told six-year-old Sarah that God had decided to take our baby, she said, "I think God's a meany!" In her child's way, she expressed what we were feeling. Our family sorrow and the nation's losses seemed to be all of a piece. We were blessed with another little boy, Will, in 1968, but he was born with cystic fibrosis, a genetic disease that challenged him throughout his life.

The nation's violence was far from over. Martin Luther King Jr. was assassinated on April 4, 1968, setting off violence in many cities in the North and the South. His assassination directly gave rise to the efforts to desegregate Denver Public Schools because it inspired Rachel Noel and Ed Benton to write a resolution calling for the integration of the entire school system.

In 1968, Robert F. Kennedy was assassinated after winning the California Democratic primary. We had driven to Colorado Springs that night to meet Vice President Hubert Humphrey, who was planning to speak at the Air Force Academy graduation, because Monte was advancing the trip. However, after the assassination, Humphrey immediately flew back to Washington. Later in the summer, amid growing protests over the Vietnam War, there was chaos at the 1968 Democratic National Convention in Chicago, where Monte coordinated the Colorado Humphrey delegation.

Denver was famously known as a sleepy little cow town in the 1960s, where night life closed down by 8 p.m. Most of the important levers of power were held by white men, including those in the city and state government. There was little interaction between whites and Blacks and Hispanics outside of the employment world, and even that was limited. Racial or ethnic groups lived in the silos of different neighborhoods, and they attended different schools, churches, and social events. White people were often unaware of the racism experienced by Blacks and Hispanics.

This was the January 1969 setting in which Monte decided to join incumbent Ed Benton and run for the Denver school board on a pro-integration platform. He believed citizens would be willing to change old patterns and ways of thinking to ensure that minority children had the equal educational opportunity they deserved, leading, in turn, to a better society in which the talents and contributions of people of all races and ethnic and religious backgrounds could be appreciated and celebrated. Desegregation would be

difficult, but it was far less painful than the poverty engendered by segregation, which resulted in lower achievement, lower lifetime income, poorer
health, and a shorter life span. Schools were not the only locus of racism in
our society, but school integration was a necessary first step in dismantling
systemic racism.

My involvement in desegregation came as a school monitor and member
of the Community Education Council established by Judge William Doyle
to oversee his desegregation order in *Keyes v. School District No. 1* [Denver]
filed in 1969. In the spring of 1969, before the first court order, our two oldest children, Sarah and Ted, open-enrolled at Hallett Elementary School—a
majority Black school—for the 1969–1970 school year because we wanted
to demonstrate that integration could work and could also provide Black
and white children with a better education. At the end of that year, they
returned to their neighborhood school, primarily because we expected that
the court orders to implement desegregation would happen the following
year—though in fact it took far longer. By fall of 1969 the United States
Supreme Court had already upheld and ordered implementation of the integration of northeast Denver schools three days before school started. We
were optimistic that the plaintiffs would win the lawsuit and that the court
would soon order the desegregation of all of Denver's schools. Then our
support would be needed for the integration of our neighborhood school,
Dora Moore. We had no illusion that Denver could be desegregated through
the kind of open enrollment we had experienced at Hallett, where only
38 percent of the school was white in 1969–1970.

All three of our children attended Denver public schools, including Dora
Moore Elementary School, Byers and Morey Junior High Schools, and East
High School.

We firmly believed, and I still believe today, that the community should
provide equal educational opportunity in integrated schools to every child
of every race and ethnicity.

During the years in which the lawsuit continued, Monte served twelve
years on the Denver Water Board and twelve years on the Colorado School
of Mines Board, was appointed by Governor Richard Lamm to head the
state Department of Natural Resources, and ran for mayor of Denver. He
was state chair of the Democratic Party and a delegate to two national
Democratic conventions. All of his adult life he practiced law, except when

he was director of the Department of Natural Resources. After his sudden death in 2006, Denver's mayor created the annual Monte Pascoe award for civic leadership.

During the same period, I earned a PhD in English literature at the University of Denver, was a delegate to two national Democratic conventions, and was elected to the first two of three four-year terms in the Colorado State Senate. At the time I was elected to the senate, I was the sixth woman and the eleventh Democrat among the thirty-five senators. Eventually, I served as Democratic caucus chair and chair of the education committee. I focused on full funding for education, particularly preschool, as well as a bill to ease the transition to English in achievement tests for bilingual children and another to make mental health treatment available to schoolchildren. Among the sixty-plus bills I sponsored were many designed to remove inequities in the law, for example, laws that impoverished divorcées, penalized spouses of those on Medicaid, or disadvantaged LGBTQ partners. I passed a bill establishing an organ donor registry and another that guarantees freedom of the press for students. My first year in office—several years before the Columbine school shooting and before the federal ban—I sponsored a bill to ban the sale of assault weapons. Nearly every year after that, I sponsored gun control legislation, none of which passed. I was always allied with the two Black members of the senate with whom I served, whether with Regis Groff to fight against capital punishment or condemn apartheid in South Africa or Gloria Tanner and her resolution on preserving Dearfield, a Black pioneer settlement.

A word about the organization of the book: I tell the story of the struggle to desegregate the Denver Public Schools, from the implementation of the court orders in 1969 and 1974 to the end of court supervision twenty-six years later, in 1995. It begins with the citizen studies that exposed the inequities of segregated schools. Then the desegregation battle begins with Rachel Noel's proposal to integrate the entire school system, followed by the momentous pro-integration campaign of Ed Benton and Monte Pascoe for the school board in 1969. When anti-busers won that election and reversed the integration plan for northeast Denver, the *Keyes* case was filed. The book follows the case through briefs, transcripts, and decisions as it moved through the courts several times until the United States Supreme Court decision in 1974.

Many people assert that we tried integration and it didn't work. That simply isn't true.

Even when begrudgingly implemented by the school district, for as long as it was in effect, desegregation provided more opportunity for minority children and raised the achievement of Black and Hispanic children without lowering the achievement of white children. This is the proof.

1

Separate and Unequal

When Monte and I looked for our second house, we were concerned about the quality of the neighborhood schools. We looked in Park Hill, where Monte had grown up and attended Park Hill Elementary School, Smiley Junior High School, and East High School, but we found that we could not afford the houses we wanted in that area. We liked Park Hill in part because it was an integrated neighborhood with many white and Black residents who believed in an integrated society. In 1966 we bought a house at 744 Lafayette in south Capitol Hill.

Our new school, Dora Moore Elementary, was reputed to be good. Reputation was all we could judge by, because Denver school achievement scores were not published until several years later. Dora Moore was mostly white, likely contributing to its perception as a "good" school. Racial percentages in schools were not reported until after the Voorhees Report in 1964 (see below). We were unaware of the fact that despite the 1959 Colorado Fair Housing Act, there was still a lot of redlining, which prevented Black people and families from buying in certain neighborhoods and steered buyers into

https://doi.org/10.5876/9781646422906.c001

segregated neighborhoods.[1] We later learned much more about the great gap between achievement in largely Black or Hispanic schools and that in largely white schools.

A word about terminology: the school district, when it did begin to count members of different races and ethnicities, used the terms *Negro*, *Hispano*, and *Anglo*. It wasn't always clear whether Anglo included Asian American and Native American, though they were sometimes grouped as "other." The school district itself used different terms over the course of the lawsuit. In this book I have used Black, Hispanic, and white in conformity to common modern usage except when I am directly quoting a person who used other terms. At the same time, I realize that Hispanic refers to an ethnicity rather than a race and that racial designations can be varied and artificial categories.

When I use the term *minority*, I do not mean to suggest that the contributions of Blacks or Hispanics were minor but that their numbers were smaller than the numbers of white students. In 1969 the Denver schools were roughly 70 percent white, 17 percent Hispanic, and 13 percent Black, according to the Benton-Pascoe campaign. Public school population percentages are different than the percentages of the total population of the city.

Many Denver citizens were proud of their schools in the early 1960s, perhaps because they did not know the extent of the schools' inadequacies. The national Civil Rights movement encouraged local citizens and local school boards to look more closely at matters of race, which in Denver led to several citizen study committees.

The Voorhees Report

The first among the citizen reports commissioned by the Denver Board of Education was the "Report and Recommendations to the Board of Education, School District Number One, Denver, Colorado" by a special committee chaired by James D. Voorhees, which became known as the Voorhees Report. The committee was created in June 1962 after Superintendent Dr. Kenneth Oberholtzer presented a plan in February of that year proposing a new junior high school at Thirty-second Avenue and Colorado Boulevard. The Black community reacted strongly against building this school because it would have been segregated as a Black school.[2] At board meetings in March,

April, and May, citizens urged the board to consider racial and ethnic factors in setting boundaries.

School board member Edgar Benton, first elected to the board to fill a vacancy in 1961, recalled that the first time he became aware of potential segregation by board action was when attorney Don Hoagland, president of the Urban League, came before the board to object to the junior high school at Thirty-second and Colorado. The eastern attendance boundary at Colorado Boulevard was at the edge of the school grounds, which was the effective eastern limit of a mostly Black neighborhood; just beyond the boundary, across Colorado Boulevard, was a neighborhood with a mostly white population.[3]

Benton was orphaned at age eighteen months, his father having died of tuberculosis and his mother of a complication from childbirth shortly after his sister was born. He was raised by a grandmother who lived in what he referred to as a shed. His attendance at Colorado College was nearly accidental; a state employment officer refused to accept his application for a job and sent him instead to the director of admissions at the college. He later attended Yale Law School and became a successful lawyer, representing Shell Oil for most of his career. In the course of his studies and career, he became a champion of education and an eloquent and effective speaker for the cause of equality.

Benton was no doubt influential in the board's decision to form a citizens' committee to study the issues raised by the junior high siting. During the time of the committee's deliberations, many violent national events were catalysts for action to end racial discrimination. There was also a new member of the school board with the 1963 election of Allegra Saunders, a state senator, and Benton was reelected as well.

The Voorhees Report laid the groundwork in many areas for the plaintiffs in the *Keyes v. School District No. 1* desegregation case, filed in 1969, which shaped the desegregation of Denver schools for the next twenty-six years. The thirty-two-member citizens' committee included three future school board members: Voorhees, Rachel Noel, and Bernard Valdez, as well as Thomas Faxon, Mrs. Donald C. McKinlay, Minoru Yasui, and others. What they learned in the committee probably affected their positions years later, when some of them became members of the board. The committee studied five functions of the public schools: (1) administration and organization; (2) buildings,

equipment, libraries, and supplies; (3) curriculum, instruction, and guidance; (4) pupils and personnel; and (5) school-community relations—in other
words, every element of education that affected student opportunities.[4] In
the report it was clear that the committee's ideal was that the schools should
be substantially equal. The committee found that minority schools were
unequal, to the degree that Denver public schools (DPS) was not complying
with the 1896 United States Supreme Court decision *Plessy v. Ferguson*, which
had approved separate facilities for minority groups as long as they were
equal, let alone with the 1954 ruling in *Brown v. Board of Education*, which
stated clearly that segregated schools are inherently unequal.

The committee found that citizens lacked information about DPS as a
whole beyond their own neighborhoods. It found a breakdown in communication, especially between the district and minority neighborhoods.[5] In
addition, in some areas of the city there was a strong feeling of unequal
treatment, as suggested in the introduction to the committee report:

> There is in Denver wide belief among the racial and ethnic minorities that
> the schools to which their children go are in some way unequal. In addition,
> however, there is the fact that there is not available to many children . . . the
> democratic experience of education with members of other races and groups
> with which they will have to live and compete. The responsibility to eliminate
> or reduce this result where possible and to compensate for it where elimina-
> tion is not possible by the removal of prejudice . . . must be the responsibility
> of the school to its pupils.[6]

The committee's findings made clear that the separate facilities and the education offered were not equal in any of the five areas of its study.

In the second area—buildings, equipment, libraries, and supplies—the
committee found gross discrepancies. Though it did not divide its findings
into predominantly white schools and predominantly Black or Hispanic
schools, the committee did observe that the shortages and inadequacies
appeared most frequently in the older parts of town where most of the
minority schools were located. The report found that twenty of the total
eighty-nine elementary schools had no cafeteria, three schools had no gymnasium space, and ten used converted classrooms or basement space for gyms.
Eight had no auditoriums. Fourteen elementary schools, many of them with
lower socioeconomic and/or minority students, had no libraries, and many

libraries were used as classrooms. The number of library books per pupil varied from 13.1 per student to 3.2 per student. The report added that "students who do not have the opportunity to use an organized library until after they leave the sixth grade have not received equal educational opportunities in the field of library services." Library books could not be checked out in quantity (no more than one book) in some schools. That was the case in one junior high on double sessions, with one group of students in the morning and a different group of students in the afternoon: there were simply not enough books for the number of students. The committee recommended that an organized library be provided in every elementary school.[7]

Swimming was offered only at high schools that had a pool. Inclusion of swimming pools in the construction of new high schools had been inconsistent. Landscaping and outdoor maintenance were lacking at some schools.[8]

The committee recommended the sharing of facilities and the gradual replacement of old facilities. It believed priority should be given to the provision of libraries, then lunchrooms, gyms, and auditoriums, in that order.[9]

There was a feeling in some unnamed parts of the district, the report noted, "that in some instances the nature of site selection and the type of construction in new schools reflect the socio-economic standards of the area in which the school is located."[10]

In the third area—curriculum, instruction, and guidance—the committee found that middle-class parents used the preschool opportunity more than lower-income parents. This may have been because the service was only offered one day a week. During the session, parents met in one room while the children attended preschool in another room. Lower-income mothers often worked and needed full-time preschool or childcare. Without recognizing this problem, the report said more parents should be encouraged to take the preschool offering.[11]

Lives of minorities were seldom portrayed in textbooks or other reading materials, the committee observed; few stories or pictures represented minorities. The committee recommended that DPS pressure publishers to provide material about people from diverse racial and ethnic groups. In addition, it wanted to continue an allocation of funds to provide language arts materials for low achievers, especially in disadvantaged neighborhoods. In a similar vein, the committee recommended supplemental experiences for pupils in disadvantaged areas, such as excursions, speakers, and exhibits.[12]

Counseling for the non-college bound, many of whom were minorities, was found to be lacking, while guidance for the college bound was found to be generally adequate. In minority schools there was a need for "more understanding and a real concern for these youth and their futures." Some of the minority students believed "some counselors lack empathy and believe that, since the minority youth may not in all probability be going to college, minimum guidance in planning for the future is given." In the lower socio-economic areas, "Counselors need more training for greater understanding of various racial, economic, and social backgrounds."[13]

The committee noted that the district had no program for the "emotionally handicapped" and limited opportunities for vocational education, and it called for curriculum expansions.[14]

In the area of pupils and personnel, there was clearly a pattern of assigning teachers by race. The committee reported that the percentage of teachers on probationary status, and thus less experienced, in schools in disadvantaged areas might have been higher than the overall percentage of such teachers in the district. Worse, the committee was convinced "that race has been relevant in the assignment of teachers," not with the objective of integrating the races but with the objective of keeping Black teachers in predominantly Black schools. There was at that time at least one Black teacher in each senior high school, but at Manual, a largely Black high school, there were eleven. Nine of thirteen junior high schools had one or more Black teachers, but the predominantly Black Cole Junior High had thirty-three. The report recommended that minority teachers be assigned throughout the district,[15] but the district had limited control over reassignment due to the contract with the teachers' union. Current teachers had preference in moving to schools with openings, so teachers were rarely reassigned.

In the same area of pupils and personnel, the Voorhees committee urged the district to create a program of in-service human relations training by the end of the current year, using resources within and beyond the community. Though the committee thought all personnel should take such training, the district should start with teachers in "culturally disadvantaged" schools.[16] Teachers should have had such training in college, but few of them did, according to the committee report.[17]

The committee defined "culturally disadvantaged" children as students for whom:

Conversation in the home is conducted in a language which doesn't resemble
that of the classroom.

The child's community doesn't contain many examples of success.

Teacher attitudes handicap the child.

There is a lack of sufficient exposure to experiences outside the immediate
environment.[18]

The committee found an overlap in culturally diverse and economically disadvantaged children, on the one hand, and membership in racial or ethnic minorities, on the other.[19]

More minority teachers should be hired, the committee said, especially for minority schools. Further, the administrative group hiring the teachers should include representatives of minority groups.[20] There were no Blacks and very few members of other minority groups in the headquarters of the Denver public schools. This created the impression "that democracy may be preached but is not practiced in the Denver Public Schools." The committee also recommended that the administration's policy be to assign principals to schools regardless of their race or ethnic backgrounds.[21]

To build a closer relationship between teachers and "culturally disadvantaged" children, the committee suggested that class size be reduced, teacher's aides be employed, and teachers' administrative duties be reduced or eliminated.[22]

In its study of school-community relations, the committee found that *de facto* segregation existed in Denver, especially "in regard to Negro citizens." Though the school system did not create the pattern of residential segregation, that pattern was imposed on the schools and affected education. The committee recommended that:

> The Board of Education should develop and adopt a policy statement based
> on the belief that school and community are inseparably joined in developing
> effective leadership for a free society. Such a statement should recognize that
> fulfillment of this function depends in part upon the opportunities children
> have during their school years to become acquainted with children and adults
> from a variety of racial and ethnic groups . . . The statement should call for
> increased activity by schools to develop acceptance of and appreciation for
> minority groups through wholesome interracial experiences which in turn
> create wider community acceptance and appreciation of minority groups.[23]

The committee recognized that eliminating inequalities arising from racial and ethnic factors was an area of special sensitivity in school-community relations.[24]

In its recommendations, the committee approved continuation of the neighborhood school as opposed to busing children to magnet schools or for the purpose of integration, which it did not mention, while noting that the neighborhood school should never be used "deliberately as a device to contain or restrict any ethnic or racial group." In a very important observation, it tentatively recognized that in the past, actions of the board had contributed to segregation:

> The Committee feels that in adhering without obvious deviation to the principle of establishing school boundaries without regard to racial or ethnic background, the Board and the administration have concurred, perhaps inadvertently, in the perpetuation of existing *de facto* segregation and its resultant inequalities in the educational opportunity offered. The Committee believes that the broadened educational experiences resulting from a heterogeneous school population are of positive value to all pupils, regardless of background, and that ways should be found which are educationally sound to create such experiences.[25]

Thus, without quite admitting it, the committee gingerly recognized that both the board and the administration contributed to segregated and unequal education. Indeed, some of the policies appeared to deliberately segregate Black students. It was likely difficult, especially in a tumultuous national scene of racial conflict, for the mostly white committee to recognize and admit that segregation was not limited to the South.

In the future, the board should consider racial, ethnic, and socioeconomic factors in establishing boundaries and locating schools, the committee advised. However, it said that transportation of pupils for the sole purpose of integrating school populations was impractical. Thus, it did not support the only means by which the Denver schools could have become integrated, perhaps in response to public opinion. The report included a poll of Denver residents on the subject of busing, which asked how they felt about busing if they were promised that no one school would have mostly minority children. To the proposal of busing elementary children, 21 percent of the residents said yes and 64 percent said no. On busing junior high students, 25 percent said yes and 59 percent said no. On busing senior high students, 27 percent said yes and 56 percent said no.[26]

The committee recommended eliminating "optional" attendance areas, which were used by white parents to flee schools with growing Black populations. However, it recommended limited open enrollment to schools at 90 percent capacity or less, on a first-come, first-served basis. The committee did not propose open enrollment for the purpose of integration, however.[27] Voluntary open enrollment later became a tool for limited integration when the district required that each volunteer pupil improve the racial balance, both in the school they were leaving and in the school where they open-enrolled. In the 1969–1970 school year, our two older children open-enrolled at Hallett School, along with 229 other white students (as of February 1970) whose parents believed in integration.[28] In the 1969 Benton-Pascoe campaign, racial balance was defined as 70 percent white, 13 percent Black, and 17 percent Hispanic—the approximate overall proportions of population in the system. Racial balance was defined differently by the plaintiffs and the defendants in the lawsuit.

The Voorhees Report observed that "the people of Denver are still communicating" and that Denver had two major assets: effective leadership and a framework of public opinion that had not yet polarized into opposite camps. Though Denver continued to have effective leaders, public opinion certainly became polarized, especially in the school board election of 1969.[29]

In response to the evidence of deep disparities exposed by the Voorhees Report, the board of education passed Policy 5100, Equality of Educational Opportunity, on May 6, 1964, just two months after the report was submitted. "All children within the district are entitled to a good education," it declared. And "barriers of prejudice, discrimination, and ignorance impede equality." Most telling was its comment on neighborhood schools: "The continuation of neighborhood schools has resulted in the concentration of some minority racial and ethnic groups in some schools. Reduction of such concentration and the establishment of more heterogeneous or diverse groups in schools is desirable to achieve equality of educational opportunity. This does not mean the abandonment of the neighborhood school principle, but rather the incorporation of changes or adaptations which result in a more diverse or heterogeneous racial and ethnic school population, both for pupils and for school employees."[30]

Though the language was emphatic and directive, it did not lead to any changes. The district's inaction was commented on later in Judge William E. Doyle's injunction preventing the district from canceling the 1969 integration plans. He noted that "following the finding of the Study Committee Report, the Board adopted Policy 5100 which called for changes or adaptations which would result in [a] more diverse or heterogeneous racial and ethnic school population. However, during the years following the adoption of Policy 5100, although there was debate, there was no effective effort in the way of implementation."[31] National events continued to illustrate the need for change. On July 2, 1964, President Lyndon B. Johnson pushed the Civil Rights Act through the US Congress as a kind of homage to John F. Kennedy. This was followed the next year by the Voting Rights Act.

On March 7, 1965, marchers in Selma, Alabama, were clubbed by state troopers and three people were killed as a result. James Reeb, a Unitarian minister who had traveled to Selma to participate in nonviolent protest, was attacked on March 9, 1965. The Black hospital could not treat him, and the white hospital refused to do so. After doctors at a Birmingham hospital performed brain surgery, he went into a coma and died two days later.

In May 1965, John Amesse, Rachel Noel, and Jim Voorhees were elected to the school board. This eventually resulted in a majority interested in positive action to integrate the schools, as Amesse and Voorhees became persuaded that the schools were segregated.

In 1966, the report that came to be known as the Coleman Report documented the lack of equal educational opportunity for minority children in America.[32]

The Berge Report

Though no positive steps toward integrating the schools were taken immediately after the Voorhees Report, another citizens' study committee was formed, resulting in what became known as the Berge Report after its chairman, attorney William G. Berge,[33] who was later elected to the school board and ironically became part of the segregationist faction. When such a committee was suggested, Edgar Benton argued against forming yet another study committee. When Jim Voorhees said the board couldn't take action without additional study, Benton replied, "We don't need more study; we need more courage."[34]

This new advisory committee's charge was to determine whether the neighborhood school policy, Policy No. 1222-C, should be applied to the location of new schools or additions to schools in northeast Denver.[35] The overcrowding of schools there had reached a critical point, as there was an overpopulation of 1,497 pupils in 1966. Twenty-eight of the twenty-nine mobile units added to schools in the district were in northeast Denver, which gave the appearance of an effort to keep Black students in the predominantly Black schools.[36] A study by University of Denver professor George E. Bardwell showed that the Black population in Park Hill had grown from 0.3 percent in 1950 to 37.1 percent in 1966.[37]

The district's problem, as identified by the committee, was to provide equal educational opportunity through integration of the schools. It suggested such methods as boundary changes, transportation of pupils, new construction, educational parks, and open enrollment in secondary schools. The proposal was limited to schools in northeast Denver, though the committee foresaw the possibility that these methods might be needed anywhere in the district.[38]

The study members still refused to see any intent to segregate on the part of the board or the administration, in spite of evidence to the contrary. They said, "Objective evidence is nonexistent that the Board of Education or the school administration of the Denver Public Schools deliberately intended to create such 'de facto segregation' in certain schools within the district."[39] The committee's "philosophy" statement said, "We hold that desirable education for our children can best take place in a school system that is actively involved in furthering the racial and cultural integration of our school community."[40]

In its interim report in June 1966, the committee endorsed the neighborhood school policy but urged the achievement of more heterogeneous schools. It called for immediate implementation of compensatory education at Smiley and Baker Junior High Schools and urged that a new junior high in northeast Denver create a heterogeneous community to be built on a site large enough to later accommodate an educational park. The committee recommended expansion of the busing of pupils out of Stedman Elementary School and endorsed the proposed bond election. It had specific recommendations for various schools, including a Children's Academy of the Arts, to which children would be bused twice a week. It believed the schools should voluntarily promote racial and ethnic integration of the community, but while the committee approved of busing to relieve crowding and provide opportunity, it said that "forced busing of pupils for the sole purpose of achieving integration should not be involved in any suggested solution."[41] Thus, the committee set up a conflict between its lofty goal and the only actual means of achieving it.

In Judge Doyle's first ruling in the *Keyes* case, he mentioned the Berge committee: "Finally another Study Committee was appointed for the purpose of examining existing conditions and recommending specific procedures and guidelines to be taken. At this time there was a proposal to build an addition to the Hallett School and, indeed, it was built over the protest that it would result in intensified segregation. The final report of the second Study Committee was filed on February 23, 1967. The report of the Committee also noticed the intensified segregation in the northeast schools and recommended that there be no more schools constructed in northeast Denver."[42] Later, in his testimony in the *Keyes* case trial, Berge was asked about the results of this study committee:

> Berge described work of an advisory council on equality which he chaired
> before his election to the board in 1967. Under questioning by Craig Barnes,
> he said he didn't recall that the council examined any of the specific acts
> which the plaintiffs charge were segregating steps such as boundary changes
> in 1956 involving East and Manual High Schools. He said two of the rec-
> ommendations of the council were carried out, (1) a cultural arts program
> providing part time integration for elementary children and (2) the superior
> schools programs at Smiley and Baker. They were unsuccessful in seeking
> land around Lowry for an educational center.[43]

Despite these two citizens' study committees having pointed out the gross inequities of the educational experience of some children in Denver, little or nothing was done to improve the situation or even to meet the requirement of separate but equal schools. Some members of the school board, however, were about to take the first steps toward integrating the schools.

2

The Noel Resolution

In 1968, national events continued to take the public by surprise. Senator Eugene McCarthy of Minnesota nearly won the New Hampshire primary against President Lyndon B. Johnson, whose support for the war in Vietnam had made him very unpopular. McCarthy received 42 percent of the vote to Johnson's 49 percent. This led to Robert F. Kennedy entering the race on March 16 and Johnson's surprise announcement on March 31 that he would not run for reelection. Monte, who had served as the advance man for several of Vice President Hubert Humphrey's trips, went to Washington around the beginning of May for Humphrey's announcement that he would enter the presidential race.

In Denver, even after two local studies had revealed the unequal education provided to minority children, there were few changes in the schools in spite of the efforts of two board members, Ed Benton and Rachel Noel. One national event provided the impetus that led to change: the assassination of Martin Luther King Jr. on April 4, 1968. When Ed Benton heard on the radio that King had been assassinated, he immediately called board member

https://doi.org/10.5876/9781646422906.c002

and friend Rachel Noel. She was not home, so he spoke to her husband, Dr. Edmond Noel, and told him the devastating news. There was a silence as Dr. Noel grasped the enormity of what Benton had said. Then Benton said, "I'm coming over." By the time he arrived, Rachel had returned home. The three of them leaned together in a group hug and wept.[1]

Anyone who knew Rachel Noel, the first Black member of the Denver school board, understood that she was a good human being, and she was one of the most influential public volunteers I have ever known. Craig Barnes recalled Rachel Noel's quiet moral courage: "You couldn't be in her presence without being uplifted, by being touched and moved in the spirit. What we saw was this dignity of character. She never said come work with me . . . come fight for civil rights, come fight for school integration. She just said with the softest voice possible, this is not right. This is not right."[2] When I asked Rachel's son, Buddy (Edmond F. Noel Jr.), the secret of Rachel's success, he replied,

Ed Benton. She wasn't alone. There was one other person with enough backbone to speak up. Jim Voorhees came on board later. She was alone in that she had to speak up . . . [She] couldn't be pushed around into inappropriate language or behavior. [She] came from the South where women are refined . . . Her grandfather was a lawyer. Her father was a lawyer and tried a case over voting rights. Her grandfather had a school named after him in 1895, which was rebuilt and rededicated in 1971. My mother had a certain Southern gentility. She didn't raise her voice, use coarse language, smoke, carry on. That threw off the men around the table. Men on each side smoked cigars at board meetings. She never mentioned it, though it bothered her.[3]

Rachel described her family history in a recorded interview:

My Bassette grandfather was born in slavery . . . He talked to his children about it, but not his grandchildren . . . He wanted to look to the future . . . He believed education was the pathway . . . The family gathered at my grandmother's house in the country. In 1971 an integrated school was named for my grandfather in Hampton, Virginia, because he was a leader. He founded a savings and loan association [for Black people] which was the oldest in Virginia. My mother was from Whitville in the mountains . . . I went to Hampton Institute [a private Black college]. Then I went to Fisk and later worked at a Settlement House in Southeast Washington.[4]

She said that on the school board, "Mr. Benton's voice [was] most concerned. They complemented each other. He could not speak as I could, being a black person."[5]

In the immediate aftermath of King's assassination, Ed and Rachel decided that the school board should pass something more than a commemorative resolution. Instead, they believed they needed to take some positive steps to effect integration. Initially, Rachel wanted Benton to co-sponsor the resolution, but he convinced her that it must come from her as the only Black person on the board.[6] Here is Rachel's description of the process:

> [I] educated the other members of the board about black people. John Amesse told me I had made him understand what it meant to be segregated. After that he supported me. Mr. Benton was sensitive . . . but we had to have four votes [to pass the Noel Resolution]. I was planning a resolution on Martin Luther King . . . Mr. Benton did the last writing . . . I did not present it in conference ahead of time, as Benton told me not to. He was my guiding hand.[7]

The resolution, number 1490, was initially presented to the board at a volatile meeting at South High School on April 25, 1968. It was laid on the table for consideration in two weeks' time. As passed on May 16, 1968, it was four pages long, single spaced. It referred to Policy 5100, Equality of Educational Opportunity, passed May 6, 1964, by the board, in which the Denver Public Schools (DPS) recognized that "the continuation of neighborhood schools had resulted in the concentration of minority racial and ethnic groups in some schools and that a reduction of each concentration and the establishment of an integrated school population is desirable to achieve equality of educational opportunity."[8] Denver Public Schools Policy 5100 had had little effect. In contrast, the Noel Resolution, as it became known, directed the superintendent to submit to the board, no later than September 30, 1968, "a comprehensive plan for the integration of the Denver Public Schools," which was to be adopted no later than December 31, 1968.

That was just part I of the resolution. Part II described at length the feelings of distrust in the community regarding the motives and actions of the board. It mentioned the failure of the board to communicate the financial needs of the schools. After referring to King, it asked for evidence that equal educational opportunity existed in the schools. Then it called for a timetable to reduce concentrations of minority racial and ethnic groups in the schools

FIGURE 2.1. "Rachel Noel at DPS board meeting," ARL 117, Denver Public Library, Denver, CO.

and the integration of the populations. Human relations and sensitivity training for teachers and administrators were called for, as was consideration of the study of minority groups. Transportation was to be considered too. The school administration was required to report on all the requests in part I and part II by September of that year. Obviously, this request was very demanding and included many features that aroused public opposition.[9] (See appendix A for the full text of the Noel Resolution.)

The public began organizing and writing both for and against the Noel Resolution as soon as it was introduced.

Letters against the Noel Resolution

In the two weeks before the resolution came up for a vote, board members received a huge volume of letters both for and against the resolution. Opened

FIGURE 2.2. Ed Benton and Rachel Noel, "School Board Member Edgar Benton Speaks." He defended the resolution of member Mrs. Rachel Noel. *Denver Post* via Getty Images, May 7 and 8, 1968.

and laid flat, the letters to Ed Benton in opposition measured 2½ inches in height while the stack of favorable letters was slightly smaller. I was able to read them when Benton loaned them to me in 2013.[10] Most of the letters in opposition began something like this: "We carefully chose to buy a house in close proximity to schools so that our children could walk to elementary school, junior high, and high school. We pay very high taxes to support our neighborhood schools." This was usually followed by a variety of arguments against what the public perceived as massive cross-town busing, though the Noel Resolution only called for the creation of a plan by September 1968. The arguments against busing included the time on the bus (which the writers assumed would be two hours a day), the cost of buses and fuel, the difficulty children would have participating in activities, the difficulty parents would have attending parent activities, and the distance of the mother from the school if a child became ill (most mothers did not work). Many families, like ours, did not have two cars, which added to the concerns. Some parents in southwest Denver had already endured years of busing because the newer areas there had no schools.

The letters revealed a number of public misconceptions, with the first about the school board. Many writers believed each school board member represented a particular part of the DPS district (in fact, at that time they were all elected at large); that school attendance boundaries had been set in stone some time in previous history and never had been and never would be changed; that their taxes were earmarked for their particular neighborhood school; that the board was controlled by threats and pressure from local, vocal minority groups (our school board "should be run by responsible people, not by schoolchildren, hippies, and minority groups"); and that some board members thought they knew better than the majority what was good for them.

Then there were misconceptions about conditions in Denver and the DPS. Here is a typical comment: "Integration would best be achieved by each individual family moving to the neighborhood of its choice socially and economically." This ignored the fact that it was often economically impossible for a minority family to move into a better neighborhood and was also prevented by discrimination, despite the Colorado Fair Housing law.

Another comment: "Our schools are not segregated now, and whoever says they are is badly mistaken." To the contrary, the studies of two citizens' committees made it clear that there were identifiably inferior Black schools and superior white schools.

Many letters claimed that the writer had nothing against minority people; in fact, the writer said he or she had grown up with them, lived near them, or attended church with them. Yet there were also writers who clearly did not know many "Negroes" and feared sending their children into "their" neighborhoods. There was discussion of "them," revealing racist stereotypes and tropes. Some posited ideas that "colored people," "like the Jews," should pull themselves up by their own bootstraps, never acknowledging the systemic racist structures that prevented many families of color from equal employment and housing. Others feared violence. For example:

> The rioting and threats of violence in the predominantly negro [sic] neighborhoods cause us to fear for the safety of our children if they should be bussed into these areas.

> There is a record of violence at both Smiley and East. [My son] is a seventh grader. He is blond, blue-eyed, and small for his age . . . I would be afraid to send him to school with big Negro boys.

> It's too bad, that there are people in this country that are willing to turn this country over to people that don't want to work! I feel as part of the majority, that this country isn't going to be turned over to the minorities!!

> They live and behave in North Denver just as they would if they resided in an under-privileged area. It appears . . . that some people, white included, do not have the desire to improve their way of life regardless of their surrounding or how much is done for them.

Still another writer suggested that these issues could be resolved by demonstrating how minority groups could develop self-pride: "Show them how picking up or cleaning up their house, street or alley makes a better place, no matter how poor." She continued by suggesting that they be taught to garden.

On the subject of integration itself, there were many comments, some disingenuous in their support but some very sensitive to the difficulties of the effort. A common position was "integration—yes; busing—no." While allowing the writer to deny any racism, this tactic ignored the fact that it was impossible to achieve comprehensive school integration without busing. Similarly, some called for voluntary integration, though this had not led to much integration in the past.

"Let the minority child attend our neighborhood school," some said. This one-way busing would require minority children to bear the full burden of integration and, while it would appear to support integration, would be patently unfair.

The focus on integration undeniably stirred up racial tensions in the community, as one writer noted: "Even the thought of forced integration arouses feeling and generates friction that normally would not have existed, and for which one can only blame the members of the Board who, through fear or false pride, have allowed this situation to develop." Another writer opposed to integration focused on the perceived feelings of the students: "There will be resentment on both sides. Minority groups will be resentful and have chips on their shoulders because they will feel unwanted . . . White children may resent the intrusion. The white children in minority schools will feel unwanted."

Finally, many suggested that minority school buildings should be improved and that they should have better teachers and the same materials as white schools. This stance essentially advocated for a return to *Plessy v. Ferguson's* separate but equal provision that was negated by the Supreme Court's *Brown v. Board of Education*[11] decision, which ruled that separate schools for minority children were inherently unequal.

The letter writers threatened various actions if the integration went forward, including moving out of Denver, enrolling their children in private schools, refusing to pay their school property tax, running for the school board, and filing a lawsuit against the school board.

Some schools sent surveys to the board showing overwhelming opposition to busing. These surveys were used as evidence that the board was not following the wishes of the majority, therefore proving that the board was not truly representative. The letters revealed a fundamental misunderstanding of our constitutional form of government, which gives officials elected by the majority the responsibility to govern but constrains them by the US Constitution as interpreted by the courts. This constraint includes the Fourteenth Amendment, which guarantees equal protection of the law to all. The United States Supreme Court would ultimately find in the *Keyes* case that the Denver school board violated this amendment.[12]

Letters in Favor of the Noel Resolution

The letters to Ed Benton in favor of the Noel Resolution often began with praise for him and for his position in favor of integration of the schools, and the writers urged him to run for reelection in May 1969.[13] For some, the revelation of the virulent racism in the city came as an unpleasant surprise: "It was a truly frightening experience for me to attend the PTA meeting held at Abraham Lincoln High School on May 9 and to observe the degree of bigotry and narrow-mindedness exhibited by many of my neighbors in southwest Denver." The PTA had stirred up feelings opposed to busing, including asking every parent to write a note to the board and to fill out a questionnaire indicating whether they were for or against busing for racial balance.

On the other hand, there were some dire predictions of events if the schools were *not* integrated. Robinson G. Lapp, the executive director of Metro Denver Fair Housing, wrote, "In our generation this country must end segregation [or] else segregation will end this country as a democracy. When you have a chance to be part of the solution and not [of] the problem, the chance should be taken. I urge you to rise to that opportunity." Some letter writers predicted the kind of violence that had been seen in other cities if the Denver schools were not integrated: "As I view our troubled times, read the Kerner Report and other material I feel that the alternatives before us and our future are quite clear. We will either move ahead and get on with the business of putting meaningful action into the words of our Declaration of Independence, i.e., 'all men are created equal'; or we will move even further apart, creating more hatred and separateness, and possibly fighting the civil war [all] over again. With more blood letting, destruction and the possible death of *our* [original emphasis] children and grandchildren." In another version of this fear: "It is clear that the United States will become a nation whose citizens, of whatever origin, will be accepted into the mainstream of life; or it will become a country torn apart by frustration and fear. We have a microcosm of this situation in Denver. We are grateful that you see it so clearly."

How did some of the following writers, who appear to be mainly white, come to be supporters of integration? For many, support stemmed from firsthand experiences with minority people, whether at work, at church, at home, or in their childhood. Here is the comment of one doctor and his wife: "Moreover, we are gradually learning that we can live in an integrated environment, that it can be a rewarding and gratifying experience. To those of us who work together with Negro physicians, nurses, technicians, scientists, clerical assistants, etc., nothing seems more unjust, more demeaning and indeed more embarrassing than to deny these people's equal educational opportunity." Another couple remembered the segregation of the South and had no wish to extend it: "Mrs. ___ and I were born, raised, and educated in North Carolina and Virginia . . . We don't wish to return to the 'South' and certainly don't want the 'South' to come to us . . . Only integration can accomplish the American principle of equal opportunity for all, arrest the national trend toward self-destruction, and preserve for ourselves and our children a strong and prosperous environment." A child psychologist said it was his opinion that "segregation in the schools in any form is extremely harmful from both an academic and emotional standpoint." Another family said they had experienced the gradual deterioration of racially unbalanced schools their children attended.

According to some parents, their children's integrated education was superior to a segregated one: "Our children's school is 70 percent white, 30 percent black. We feel that our child is receiving a superior education—both intellectually and socially—because of this fortuitous racial composition." They believed the demographics of the school approximated the world the children will have to live in.

The pro-integrationists had a lot of faith in the beneficial effects of integration: "I am equally sure that when black and white children go to school together, both end up with fewer hostilities and fears of each other, both learn to live together and work together." Another writer said, "The issue is higher than the false issue of busing. The heart of America is being eaten out by fear, anxiety, and guilt . . . and White America must face the fears in order to survive. I urge you to support the Noel resolution as a step toward educating the children of Denver for the world in which they live." Some writers recognized that real integration would require busing: "I must say that there does not appear to be any alternative to compulsory cross-bussing if we really intend to carry out, in practice, the objectives expressed in the Noel Resolution." Parents who were members of the American Baptist Foreign Mission Society complained that Ellis Elementary School was too white. They said, "Even a school as fine as Ellis, with its excellent principal and faculty, cannot possibly prepare our sons to live in a city of many races and cultures as long as it is kept segregated from these other groups."

Some letters pointed out the dire need for more classroom space, so at the same time the board was trying to integrate the schools, there were areas with serious shortages. Parents in southwest Denver had waited for the construction of schools for years while their children were bused. In northeast

Denver, Smiley and Gove Junior High Schools were overcrowded and increasingly largely Black. East High was also gaining minority enrollment. Smiley was moved from double sessions to single sessions, but a group of Smiley parents called "the Drastic Action Committee" determined that the junior high was an inferior institution of learning. They demanded equal materials, equipment, and books. They called for a racial balance matching the city as a whole and a stable teaching force with adequate sensitivity training. Busing only Black students, they said, would be unacceptable.

Gove asked for four new temporary buildings for vocal music, science, industrial arts, and home economics. The school's Human Relations Committee listed the reasons for the anger of minorities there:

Failure of schools to recognize and meet their needs

Constant confrontation with some teachers too often untrained in working with minorities

Lack of identity due to almost total omission of minority history and contributions

Failure to encourage potential student leaders among minorities

Dearth of minority teachers

Irrelevance of curriculum to students' needs.

There were other serious school needs in the new Montbello neighborhood. Wyman Elementary School parents asked for a new building before the scheduled replacement in 1972–1977. They had no lunchroom, no auditorium or suitable gymnasium, only two lavatories for grades 1–6, and a 1902 coal furnace.

Groups in Support of the Noel Resolution

According to a humorous poem sent to Ed Benton celebrating the passage of the Noel Resolution, these supporters appeared at the May 16 school board meeting:

Rabbi Goldberger

Jesse Wagner

Jules Mondschein

Young man from Regis

American Friends

Urban League

Folks from Montview Church

Professor Perdew

NAACP

Psychologists of Colorado

Human Relations gents from Southwest and Southeast Denver Social Action
   Group

Citizens for One [Community]

Student speakers

Black Educators

DU School of Social Workers

B'hai

Bear Valley—"while their friends can all come in, they cannot come out!"

Our Savior's Lutheran Church, Archie L. Madsen, Pastor

Letters of support for the Noel Resolution came from the following groups:

League of Women Voters of Denver

American Friends Service Committee

Moore School (survey—for voluntary busing)—Marjorie Priester

Gilpin [Elementary School] faculty

ACLU

Montview Boulevard Presbyterian Church Session

Bruce Avery, pastor, East Denver Church of God

Smiley staff

Metro Denver Fair Housing Center

Rev. Thomas M. Rauch, S.J. Regis College

Denver Classroom Teachers Association, which said that all schools would be
   closed and picketed on May 16, the day of the vote, unless the two members
   who voted to table the resolution announced that they would vote for it. It
   was signed by Neal F. Breaugh, ED, DCTA

Park Hill Action Committee, Fred Thomas, chair; the sponsoring churches were
   virtually all the churches in Park Hill

Executive Committee of Denver County Democrats, Hugh Burns, chairman

KLZ Editorial

Christ Methodist Church

Citizens for One Community, who urged immediate response to citizens who support the Noel Resolution or they would initiate additional picketing

The League of Women Voters document urging quality integrated schools was signed by:

League of Women Voters
Core City Ministries
North West Denver Community Relations Council
White Buffalo Council
Denver East Central Human Relations Council
Metro Program Board of the Colorado Council of Churches
NAACP
Religious Council on Human Relations
Church Women United
Colorado Commission on Civil Rights
Speak Out on School Integration
Citizens for One Community
South West Denver Human Relations Council
Black Educators United
Clearing House for Concerned Citizens
Metro Denver Fair Housing Center
South East Denver Human Relations Council
National Council of Negro Women
American Friends Service Committee
Denver Federation of Teachers
Metro State College

Persuading Voorhees and Amesse

The two additional votes needed on the board to pass the resolution were most likely to come from James D. Voorhees and Dr. John Amesse, who were elected to the school board in 1965. Amesse told Rachel Noel that she had educated him about what it meant to be segregated, and after that he supported her.[14] By the time Amesse retired from the board, he was fully convinced that integration was necessary. He "presented an emotional appeal to the 'concerned and informed citizens of this city of hope.' Based on achievement test results, the children of 50 Denver schools are not receiving adequate education. He said 'Argue pro and con as you will . . . but the fact is that segregated education is inferior in Denver. Obviously, Denver can't abide this blight of educational inequality.' "[15]

To win over Voorhees and Amesse, George E. Bardwell, a University of Denver mathematics professor, asked to meet with them to present the convincing evidence he had developed about the effects of racial segregation in Denver. The extensive analysis and maps and charts prepared by Bardwell and Paul Klite, a doctor and professor at the University of Colorado Medical School, would be persuasive again in the later court case. Bardwell spent many hours, over a number of years, working at the University of Denver computer analyzing every aspect of the Denver public schools and printing out endless statistics at a time when computers were just beginning to be used for statistical analysis.

Voorhees said Amesse called him and told him he had something to show him. Voorhees recalled that meeting:

We went out to some motel on East Colfax, and [George] Bardwell . . .
was out there with this map. And there it was—right there—race and low
achievement—segregation and low achievement.

[John] said, We've got to do something about this.

John and I were sort of in the middle. It was our conversion. I really think
it had more to do with that map than anything else because that was [the]
physical evidence of what Rachel had been talking about.

Voorhees also cited the influence of Fred Thomas and two Black ministers. Supporters of the Noel Resolution included Denver mayor Tom Currigan, the Denver Classroom Teachers Association, the Denver Chamber of Commerce, and business, civic, union, and neighborhood organizations.[16]

The clear evidence of the correlation between the proportion of the minority population and low school achievement would not have been possible without the district's first public release of school-by-school test scores in May 1968.[17] Prior to 1968, no individual school scores had been published. In the past the scores had been interpreted by the district to make them seem better than they were. This is a description of the process: "Prior to the achievement testing all pupils in these grades were given tests of academic aptitude from which IQ scores were derived. The interquartile distribution of IQ scores makes possible analyses of accomplishment in relation to ability, or comparisons of the attainments of above average, average, and below average group[s] with each group's expected level of achievement."[18] Then they could say about third grade students: "Pupils at the median level of ability achieved at or above expectancy on five of eight tests. Achievement of pupils in the below average group did not reach expectancy on any test. The attainment of the above average group of pupils was particularly good with expectancy being either reached or exceeded on every test."[19] In other words, in a kind of circular explanation, they proved that the results of the achievement test were consistent with the results of the IQ test, which were, arguably, dependent on the child's achievement.

In fifth grade, the scores revealed that the achievement of the below-average group was below expectations. In junior high schools, the average scores were at or above expectations for all groups. In the high schools, pupils in the average, below-average, and above-average groups scored above expectancy and above national norms.[20] In other words, if you expect less, you can be happier with lower scores. We don't know exactly what Bardwell's map showed, but a table from the DPS publication reported that when the national average score was at the 50th percentile, the composite minority school percentile was at the 22nd percentile in grade 5, the 30th percentile in grade 9, and the 28th percentile in grade 11; that is, 70–78 percent of students in the country would score higher than they did.

In contrast, in schools that were over 90 percent white, the scores were at the 66th percentile in grade 5, the 73rd percentile in grade 9, and the 74th percentile in grade 11.[21]

Voorhees said in later testimony in the federal district court that he had changed his opinion on the subject of race and education in his years on the board. He said that test data released the previous fall showed "direct correlation between concentrations of poor children, minority children and low achievement."[22]

The Noel Resolution Passes

The Noel Resolution passed by a vote of five to two on May 16, 1968, with Noel, Benton, Voorhees, Amesse, and Allegra Saunders voting for it; William G. Berge and Stephen J. Knight III voted against.

Benton said that when the Noel Resolution was adopted, "all hell broke loose" and he remembers receiving death threats. He recalled: "One night I had a phone call at 3:30 in the morning. This gruff male voice said, 'There's a man in the park behind your house with a gun and he's going to kill you.' To which I said, 'I'm sorry, you have the wrong number!' There was a stunned silence and he hung up."[23] The police came, but they did not find anyone with a gun in the park.

The Gilberts Plan

The passage of the Noel Resolution required a number of initiatives by the school administration, the most important of which was a comprehensive plan for integrating the entire school system. Superintendent Robert D. Gilberts presented the plan to the board in October 1968 to be considered for adoption in December, though apparently it was available at least a month before then. It was an elaborate plan for reorganizing Denver's entire school system in four phases over ten years. It proposed sending minority students out of their neighborhoods to integrate primarily white schools, but there were no plans for transporting white students to minority schools. The administration clearly thought of desegregation as a minority problem. In the elementary school busing plan, minority children at Smith would go to eight white schools, Phillips children to three white schools, and Stedman children to eleven white schools (to which they were already being transported).[24] The plan had the advantage of keeping neighborhood elementary schools intact for white students while providing some integration at central locations within each complex.

Gilberts divided the city into twelve elementary school complexes; four junior high complexes, which seemed largely administrative; and one model high school complex. He supported the model-school complex, in part because he thought citizens would accept the plan. This was the plan's core: "The Model-School Complex, a subsystem of the city and school system, links together large groups of students of varying socio-economic, racial-ethnic, and religious backgrounds on one or more interrelated sites . . . The complex focuses on innovation, research and development, evaluation of educational change and diffuses tested educational improvements to the whole system . . . School organization within the Model-School Complex can contribute significantly to integration."[25] The idea was that students would go to one school in each complex a few days a week or for part of a day.

Many of the older minority schools were to be razed in whole or in part, including the older part of Dora Moore, our neighborhood elementary school, which today has Historic Landmark status. Each complex would have involved the public in creating its own curriculum.[26]

Integration at the junior high level, similarly, "will be accomplished primarily through transportation of pupils from crowded inner-city schools." In fact, Cole, a majority Black junior high, was to be phased out.[27] High schools would be integrated through open enrollment if the applying student improved the integration level of the receiving school. There were similar open enrollment plans for elementary and junior high students beginning in the spring semester of 1968–1969. Manual was to become a college high school in joint operation with a state college. After the construction of a new high school in west Denver, the present West High School would become the complex center for all high schools.[28] Transportation for open enrollment and special programs would be provided by the district. The district would organize further student exchanges with other school districts in the metropolitan area.[29]

Gilberts admitted the existence of rather severely segregated schools in the district: "At the present time there are 24 elementary schools, 5 junior high schools, and 4 senior high schools which have less than 10% Negro and Spanish-American pupils. In contrast, there are 8 elementary schools, 2 junior high schools, and 1 senior high school having more than 50% Negro, and 18 elementary schools and 2 junior high schools having an enrollment of over 50% Spanish-American pupils."[30] The plan also addressed integration of faculty, sensitivity training, necessary changes in curriculum, other educational innovations, and extensive capital development needs.

In the rationale section of the plan, Gilberts tried to explain away the schools' failure to educate children from a lower socioeconomic class:

> Certain schools have become saddled with a disproportionate amount of responsibility for what is really a nationwide problem of society, as well as a metropolitan and local community problem. These are the schools where shifts in residential housing patterns have resulted in a concentration of racially isolated minorities with limited education and low incomes . . .

Test scores show that our city's public schools are doing an outstanding job in educating those children who eagerly come to school motivated by their families to learn. However, there is evidence that the schools are only partially successful with those children who reside in areas where there are lower levels of income and of education. And this is the problem . . . It is only recently that the public has realized the enormous concentration of intellectual and financial resources required to overcome the effects of [a] limited socio-economic background.[31]

Benton received a flood of letters after the Gilberts reorganization plan was introduced. Some supported the plan, but most who mentioned it insisted that it fell short of truly integrating children in the schools. One writer urged the board to "redraw the Gilberts plan[s'] complex boundaries to provide more integration and to balance socio-economic groups, too." Gilberts was faulted for failing to educate people about integration from May 16 to October 1, 1968, which would have prepared them for his plan. The League of Women voters said DPS needed a plan with timetables and ongoing evaluation. One writer said the Gilberts Plan didn't do what the Noel Resolution called for: "Full racial integration now—in the best schools we can provide—is what we need; it is what we must have; what we want; what we will insist on. We dare not settle for anything less."[32]

Another writer said, "The complex boundaries, as now drawn, fail to provide adequate integration in those areas of greatest need." The boundaries could be redrawn, he said, to increase integration. New buildings should stabilize many areas of the city, but authorities should consider remodeling existing structures. Voluntary busing didn't do enough. One writer called it sheer fantasy. Another set of parents said time was running out for any meaningful integration in society, and in most cities it was already too late. They recommended modifying the Gilberts Plan to provide for complete integration or giving minority groups autonomy in running their own educational facilities.[33]

Minority leaders were also unhappy with the plan. Rev. Jesse Wagner, the Black co-chair of Citizens for One Community, said Gilberts didn't obey the board's directive to come back with a comprehensive integration plan for the entire district and added that he had overstepped his authority by deciding what the city would accept. The plan, Wagner said, would lead to "black schools for black children in black neighborhoods run by black people." He called for dynamic leadership from downtown, not "biased paternalism."[34]

Black leader Fred Thomas, chair of the Park Hill Action Committee (PHAC), was also critical of Gilberts's presentation. He thought Gilberts was more concerned about a possible white exodus than about creating programs that would keep whites in the district. Rachel Noel was also disappointed. Both Knight and Berge applauded Gilberts's avoidance of massive "cross-busing." Berge said, "The way I interpret Bob's program is that it's going to be done on a very reasonable, realistic, go-slow, let's-get-the-community-behind us basis."[35]

Benton, Noel, and Voorhees wouldn't comment on the plan until they had read it. Amesse said Gilberts did an "admirable job of generalizing for a plan that takes community feelings into account as well as the necessity of integration as indicated by the Noel resolution." Ramon Navarro, president of Mexican-Americans for Progress, didn't like the plan. Integration wouldn't work, he said, "until Anglo, Negro, and Hispano people get rid of their bigotry and begin to look at each other as brothers and sisters." Rodolfo (Corky) Gonzales agreed that busing minority youngsters out of their neighborhoods wasn't the answer. "The real answer is to create our own awareness of our own self-identity," he said.[36]

In September the board heard twenty-seven pro-integration speakers. Militants talked about separatism. Many people, including Fred Thomas and Esther Nash, did not want that, preferring integration and quality education. Sen. George Brown believed Gilberts had paid more attention to separatists than to others. Superintendent Gilberts disagreed.[37]

The PHAC said Gilberts's plan would not integrate the schools. Thomas, who was co-chair of the PHAC education subcommittee, said, "We're sick of gradualism. I want integration because I don't trust the power structure. With integration I know that if your kids are getting a good education, my kids will too." Others noted that in the Gilberts Plan, the burden for integration fell on the Black children.[38]

Paul Klite, along with George Bardwell and Martha Radetsky, presented an alternative to the Gilberts Plan. It divided the city into six, not twelve, clusters, with division lines running mainly north and south across racial residential lines. The schools in the clusters would have no white enrollment below 54 percent. Three thousand more students would be bused than prior to the integration plan, a total of 13,990 students, equally divided between majority and minority students. Their plan could be implemented immediately and was not tied to a bond issue. In contrast, Rev. Wagner said the Gilberts Plan was lacking the one ingredient essential for a quality education—integration.[39]

Bardwell spoke to the board about the Gilberts Plan. In 1964, DPS was 69 percent white, 13 percent Black, and 18 percent Hispanic. Using his computer skills, he projected Denver's school population in 1970, when elementary schools would be 59 percent white, 17 percent Black, and 24 percent Hispanic. He said there would be 900 fewer total students in the elementary schools. In September 1968, a suggestion was made to use a segregation index, which Bardwell created. The index represented the percentage of children, white and minority, attending segregated schools. He said there had been a decrease in the segregation index in elementary schools from 1964 to 1970. If nothing was done, he said, the segregation index would decline to 64.4 by 1970. Under the Gilberts proposal, he said, this index would decrease to about 49.5 by 1970, but mostly by requiring minority families to transport children. The Gilberts proposal would attack segregation so gradually that time would run out before the benefits of a majority white, yet integrated system could be realized.[40]

Bardwell said that under Klite's proposal for six complexes, the index would be reduced to 9.8 by 1970; that is, only 9.8 percent of Denver's students would still be in segregated schools. Desegregation might attract whites back to the city, as it had in Evanston, Illinois, and Berkeley, California. He provided an illustration that showed the great variation in the percentage of minority children in the various clusters. Using census data, he showed that the Gilberts twelve-cluster plan also showed greater variation in average income among the clusters, with a range of $3,800. Klite's six-complex plan had a variability of $2,200.[41]

In the last half of 1968, Denver was in turmoil due to the uncertainty created by the continually changing plans for the schools. Mayor Tom Currigan, who was supportive of integration, resigned on December 7. In January 1969 the school board adopted Resolution 1520 relating to East High and Smiley Junior High, the first of three resolutions to begin integrating schools in northeast Denver. Integrating these two schools necessarily involved many other schools. Parts of the East district were assigned to South and George

Washington High Schools. Parts of the South and George Washington High Schools areas were assigned to East. An area from Hill Junior High was assigned to Smiley, and 850 students from Smiley were assigned to other junior high schools. Passions on both sides of the issue were intense.

That same month my husband, Monte, decided to join incumbent Ed Benton and run for the Denver school board on the Benton-Pascoe pro-integration platform.

3

The Benton-Pascoe Campaign

The Benton-Pascoe campaign was a watershed event for racial relations in Denver, the culmination of a movement that had begun in Park Hill. Each side in the campaign had very different views on the issue. Virtually every civic organization, including Black and Hispanic groups, endorsed one side or the other. The passionate advocacy even led to threats of violence before the May 20, 1969, election.

The Wellspring of the Movement—Park Hill

The impetus for the effort to integrate Denver Public Schools came from a dedicated group of Black and white people who worked together to integrate homes and schools because they believed integrated schools and society would benefit both Black and white children. Later, a few Hispanic leaders were added as well, though fewer Hispanic children lived in northeast Denver's Park Hill. By the time the Noel Resolution passed, Park Hill leaders felt they had been on a nine-year campaign to create an integrated

https://doi.org/10.5876/9781646422906.c003

community.[1] Though Monte and I had bought a home in a central Denver neighborhood, we had close ties to Park Hill, as it was where he had grown up, his parents still lived, and we attended church. Many people, both Black and white, fervently believed that integration could be achieved, and they believed life would be enriched for all if Blacks and whites lived in a connected community. Through increased home sales, northern Park Hill's Black population was growing, but most of the residents did not want to live in a segregated neighborhood, one that was either all white or all Black.

The Black leaders on integration included Fred Thomas, Senator George Brown, and Rev. Jesse Wagner. White leaders included Martha Radetsky, who often brought large groups of Black and white leaders together in her home. George Bardwell and Paul Klite worked together on statistical information, and Jules Mondschein and Rev. Ramiro Cruz-Ahedo co-chaired Citizens for One Community (COC) along with Thomas. Other important leaders were Helen Petersen and her staff at the city's Commission on Community Relations; Art Branscombe, who later became an education reporter for the *Denver Post*, and his wife, Bea Branscombe; Kay Schomp; Dick and Lorie Young; and Bruce and Ginny Rockwell. Kay Schomp and Ginny Rockwell later became members of the school board. Hundreds of others provided many hours of extraordinary leadership.

Monte was a thirty-four-year-old lawyer when he joined Ed's pro-integration campaign to win two at-large seats on the Denver school board in May. We had recently bought a home in the attendance area of Dora Moore Elementary School; our oldest child, Sarah, was in second grade and our son, Ted, was in kindergarten there. Monte and I were co-presidents of the Denver Cooperative Preschool, and I was on the Dora Moore Lay Advisory Committee. We were also involved in Democratic politics. I had been a committeewoman in our former precinct and continued to volunteer in party activities. Monte was on his way to becoming a Democratic district captain. We were as active in civic affairs as we could be with his new law practice and our young family.

In November 1968 we had our fourth child, Willy. The day after his birth he needed an operation due to meconium ileus, a blockage of the intestines that was by that time recognized as an indication of cystic fibrosis. One of the hardest things I ever had to do was call Monte, who was with a client in Sterling, Colorado, the day after Willy was born to tell him he had to return

FIGURE 3.1. Monte Pascoe. May 7, 1969. Bildnachweis: Millard Smith [photographer]. Editorial number 162096604 DPI_1763775. *Denver Post* via Getty Images.

to Denver to check the baby into Children's Hospital for surgery. There, he occupied the same incubator in which our baby had died a year and a half earlier. Willy, however, did well after the operation, and we were able to bring him home before Christmas, with great joy. Though we had much to learn about caring for a child with cystic fibrosis, including physically performing postural drainage or "patting" twice a day, Monte decided in January that it was important to run for the school board.

Monte entered the race because he had a highly developed sense of justice springing from his genuine concern for every person he met. Having been raised in a family of modest means, he had a natural sympathy for the poor and disadvantaged. He believed government had a responsibility to help people who needed help and to give every child the best education possible. In the 1968 presidential election, Monte coordinated Hubert Humphrey's Colorado presidential campaign. It was probably this activism and the fact that others had turned down the opportunity that led to his being asked to run for the school board.[2] Monte was concerned about the quality of the schools his children and other Denver children attended. In addition, he and

Ed were friends: About this time, they started walking downtown to work together. From their meeting place at Ninth and Lafayette, Monte could see Ed coming across Cheesman Park. If one of them wasn't there at 8 a.m., the other would walk on. Each day they discussed school issues and nearly every other topic in the world. They continued this practice for more than twenty years.

Monte was aware of the evidence that minority schools in Denver failed even the separate but equal requirement for segregated schools the United States Supreme Court had established in 1896 in *Plessy v. Ferguson*.[3] This failure was highlighted by the two citizens' study committees discussed in chapter 1. The 1954 *Brown v. Board of Education* Supreme Court decision declared segregated schools inherently unequal,[4] and there was ample evidence that achievement in majority Black schools lagged woefully behind achievement in majority white schools—as indicated in Denver's school-by-school achievement data, which had just been published for the first time. With the national norm at the 50th percentile, grade 5 students in majority Black and Hispanic schools had an average composite score at the 22nd percentile, while grade 5 students in schools that had over 90 percent white students scored at the 66th percentile. Grade 9 students in minority schools scored at the 30th percentile, while grade 9 students in majority white schools scored at the 73rd percentile. Grade 11 students in minority schools scored at the 28th percentile, while grade 11 students in white schools scored at the 59th percentile.[5]

All of these factors clearly indicated that minority students were not provided with an adequate educational opportunity. At the same time, white students were given a very distorted view of life in our city and country when they were denied the opportunity to work and study with minority students. This broader view of the value of integration was shared by many, though the court would later rule for the integration plans on the legal basis—the need to provide equal protection of the law in the form of equal opportunity for all students in a non-segregated setting. This division between what is required under the law and the dream of a diverse and harmonious society permeates the argument for desegregation. The minimal first step was equal treatment by the government entity—the school board—as required by law, while those who were more idealistic sought the end of racism.

The Issues According to Benton and Pascoe

The Benton-Pascoe campaign was organized as extensively as any race for higher office: the campaign raised considerable money, hired a campaign manager, and had an elaborate staff—including public relations professionals—though most of them were volunteers. A look at the candidates' schedules reveals how deeply involved they were and how much the community was focused on this campaign.

Every morning, from January until the May election, the event scheduler, Ginny Rockwell, appeared at our house at 7:00 a.m. with Monte's schedule for the day. The Sunday before the election, Benton and Pascoe scheduled eleven events that included stops at four Black churches, two white churches, one synagogue, and Manual High School, as well as three coffees in homes. They finished the campaign with two meetings on Monday night, the eve of the election. In contrast, Jim Perrill and Frank Southworth, their major opponents, visited two white churches, one Black church, and one synagogue on the Sunday before the election. On Monday they had one meeting in a home.[6] At the same time, both Monte and Ed were maintaining their law practices, sometimes at night, to support their families.

Sometimes Monte came home from campaigning discouraged. One day he spoke with a group of well-educated women from our church who met in a home near Sixth Avenue Parkway. After Monte talked about the advantages of integration, one woman asked, "Isn't it like the bluebirds and the blackbirds that really don't mix?" Monte told me he didn't know where to start in responding to that view, but he often cited it as an example of how much our community needed to learn.

In his campaign announcement in March 1969, Monte said, "We must also be certain our children have the opportunity to learn with each other, regardless of racial or ethnic background. The divisions in our country result, in part, because we isolate ourselves from one another. In the past public schools provided a way for all citizens to communicate with each other. If they do so again our children will receive quality education . . . For eight years Ed [Benton] has spearheaded the community's struggle for quality education for all children and I would like to join in that effort."[7]

Benton's positions had been developed over his years of distinguished service on the board. They were detailed in an interview with Martin Moran of the *Rocky Mountain News*. Moran quoted him directly and indirectly, saying that in looking toward solutions:

> [Benton] feels "It is imperative the board continue to achieve orderly progress toward integration of the schools." The specific problems, he believes, include improved vocational education programs, improved and expanded special education, improvement in efforts to teach minority history and contributions and development of more effective means of community participation . . .
> The alternative, he believes, is to ignore the negative and destructive conse-quences for children in a racially and ethnically segregated school system. He says the consequence of a segregated school system with its deficient achieve-ment, the negative attitudes that are developed by the community and the hostilities that are generated will result in greater costs in crime, delinquency, welfare, and social disorganization. The wrongs of the past, he says, are reflected in minority areas by older buildings, less experienced teachers, [and] deficient instructional materials and programs.[8]

The Benton-Pascoe campaign literature cited the many different issues that needed improvement in the Denver public schools (DPS) and some-times suffered from too many messages, although integrating the schools was always the primary concern. Another piece had profiles of Ed and Monte and a one-page information sheet captioned "Opportunity, Understanding, Achievement," which appeared to be themes for the campaign. The sheet offered facts for voters to think about, such as that about half of the elemen-tary schools had achievement scores at grade 5 that were 10 points below the national norm; dropout rates in several high schools were at 50 percent or more; and true racial balance in Denver would mean 70 percent white, 13 percent Black, and 17 percent Hispanic students. In addition, it suggested that property values would go up following school integration.[9]

An internal campaign document showed how many complex issues the campaign could address (though eventually, opponents managed to reduce everything to simply being for or against busing for racial integration):

Overall theme: a better educational opportunity for all
Issues to be dealt with: integration, racial balance, busing, property stabilization
Educational innovation and improvements: technology and vocational training,
    shift funding off property taxes, improve teaching and assistance to teachers

List of ideas for advertising

Free publicity opportunities

Pascoe can stress old expectations and practices not good any more

Benton can stress efforts to improve overall system, each of you can help us go
forward in a way that would astound you.[10]

A major exposition of Benton's and Monte's beliefs came in their second
position paper:

Denver is in the unique position of being one of the few major American
cities left where the potential for solving fundamental urban problems still
exists.

For too long a time Denver has ignored the educational problems of many
of our children who attend schools with a substantial minority population—a
condition created by housing patterns within the community. There is little
question that the educational opportunity afforded by these minority schools
is inferior. We believe that minority children, as well as those from the majority white community, can receive maximum educational opportunity only
in schools which represent a mix of the various racial, social and economic
strata of our community. We reject the concept of separate but equal facilities as not only illegal, but immoral.

Then the position paper reviewed the school board policy adoptions and citizen studies up to that time. The position paper continued:

Thus, by 1967, it was apparent that strict adherence to the neighborhood
school concept would not result in equal educational opportunity.

One year later, May 1968, [the] Noel resolution 1490 was passed directing
the Superintendent to submit to the board "a comprehensive plan for the
integration of the Denver Public Schools . . ."

Resolution 1520 in Jan. 1969 changed attendance boundaries of East High
School and Smiley to begin implementing resolution 1490.[11]

The campaign literature stressed that it might be hard to do the right
thing—that is, to vote for integration—which may not have been the best way
to encourage people to vote for Benton and Pascoe. Here are some quotes:

Ed Benton and Monte Pascoe reject the concept of separate-but-equal facilities as not only illegal, but immoral.

Doing the right thing isn't always easy, but the right thing is always worth doing.

Beliefs strong enough to stand on.[12]

Still another flyer said, "Believe in what's best for all of Denver's children—even if it makes you uneasy. Now." Inside was a picture of a Black child and a white child, both about six years old, working at a table together. The headline read, "Their generation will make enough mistakes on its own. Must they inherit our hang-ups, too?" A box contained the phrase, "Doing the right thing is also practical, logical, and reassuring." The flyer attempted to respond to fears about busing: "The average ride will be less than 20 minutes, under four miles. When we integrate our schools, most children will walk to school." Another slogan appeared at the bottom: "Beginnings are always hard."[13]

Another campaign piece presented a timeline of historical events and then this statement: "Progression toward equal educational opportunity has been a continuing process, with involvement of many segments of the community affected. We believe that the survival of our community depends on the continuation . . . If we halt the progression toward equality, we can look forward only to the creation of separate school systems and therefore a separated community, with all the conflicts, alienations, frustrations and turmoil suffered by older cities."[14]

In the later stages of the campaign, Benton and Pascoe tried to refute some of the extreme claims about busing by stressing the positive results of integration: property values went up in Berkeley, the exodus to the suburbs would stop, every school would be 60–70 percent white, children would play together and learn together without misunderstanding or suspicion, the polarization of our country into separate and hostile societies would stop, achievement of low socioeconomic students would improve while achievement of high socioeconomic students would not be adversely affected.[15]

A fact sheet about the number of students *already being bused* in the metropolitan area was created by Robert Lapp, executive director of Metro Denver Fair Housing. Lapp said a smaller percentage of children in Denver rode buses than in "virtually every other county in the state." The portion was 10 percent in Denver and 80 percent in Cherry Creek. At that time, it was 33 percent at both Hill Junior High and John F. Kennedy Junior High, two white Denver schools.[16]

CANDIDATES FOR THE DENVER SCHOOL BOARD

beliefs
strong
enough
to
stand on

BENTON · PASCOE

DOING THE RIGHT THING ISN'T ALWAYS EASY;
BUT THE RIGHT THING IS ALWAYS WORTH DOING.

Their generation will make enough mistakes on its own. Must they inherit *our* hang-ups, too?

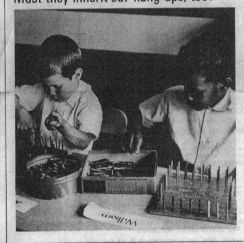

DOING THE RIGHT THING ISN'T ALWAYS EASY; BUT THE RIGHT THING ✳ IS ALWAYS WORTH DOING.

It is also:

✳ **THE PRACTICAL THING**
Fewer of your tax dollars will go for writing welfare checks to support wasted people who drop out of inferior schools.

✳ **THE LOGICAL THING**
Because we have already waited too long, true integration is not possible unless some of our children ride to schools other than those that are closest to their homes.

✳ **THE REASSURING THING**
Integration of Denver public schools does not mean "massive crossbusing from dawn to dark" or "from one side of town to another." The average ride will be less than 20 minutes, under four miles. When we integrate our schools, most children will walk to school.

beginnings
are always
hard.

Believe in what's best for all of Denver's children—
even if it makes you uneasy. Now.

FIGURE 3.2A, B. Benton-Pascoe campaign literature. Pat Pascoe file.

VOTE

MAY 20

DENVER SCHOOL BOARD ELECTION

ELECT   ELECT
JAMES   FRANK
PERRILL   SOUTHWORTH

James C. Perrill, candidate for 6-year term on Denver Board of Education at May 20 election; Colorado state senator 1965-69; mayor's administrative assistant 1960-62; Denver municipal judge 1959-60; assistant U. S. attorney for Colorado 1956-59, Navy veteran of World War II.

Graduate University of Denver Law School and admitted to practice 1953; partner in law firm of Yegge, Hall, Treece and Evans.

Mr. and Mrs. Perrill, who live at 1324 Birch Street, have two daughters. One attends East High School and the other attends Gove Junior High School.

The Perrills are members of the Messiah Lutheran Church.

Frank K. Southworth, candidate for 6-year term on Denver Board of Education at May 20 election; served as manager of revenue from 1960 to 1963. He also was ex-officio treasurer and assessor; was in charge of the city budget; Motor Vehicle Division and Data Processing Division of the Revenue Department. He is now vice president of Frisbie & Company, Denver real estate firm.

He is an Air Force veteran of World War II, and was graduated from the University of Kentucky in 1950. Mr. and Mrs. Southworth, who lives at 1945 South Kearney Way, have two children, both attend Ash Grove Elementary School. The Southworths are members of University Park Methodist Church.

OUR STAND IS:

FOR: NEIGHBORHOOD SCHOOLS Schools should be built in neighborhoods where they are needed. There is also a crying need to upgrade existing schools both in facilities and curriculum.

AGAINST: FORCED BUSING Forced busing deprives children of participation in extracurricular activities. This massive program is wasteful of huge sums of money. We feel that the money could be better used for direct education.

FOR: QUALITY EDUCATION Special program emphasis must be concentrated on the disadvantaged children so that they will have equal opportunities to succeed and benefit from our educational system and share in the American dream. These programs can best be administered and targeted through the neighborhood schools.

YOUR VOTE FOR PERRILL AND SOUTHWORTH INSURES THESE FUNDAMENTAL RIGHTS.

You Must Be Registered, But Need Not Be A Property Owner To Vote In The Election May 20th
Sponsored by Denver Better Schools Committee —Chairman J. W. ASPINWALL

FIGURE 3.2C. Perrill and Southworth campaign literature. Pat Pascoe file.

In an effort to assuage the fears of those opposed to integration, a coalition of Denver organizations—including the Denver Religious Council on Human Relations, the Denver Catholic Archdiocese, the Rabbinical Alliance, the Latin American Research and Service Agency, the Colorado Council of Churches, the Urban League, the Urban Coalition, the University of Denver, and the League of Women Voters—brought a white family and a Black family from Berkeley, California, to talk about the recent integration of their schools. Though they had initially been opposed to integration, they told Denverites that busing works. The families were Ralph and Velma Bradley (Black) and Ruth and Berndt Scharlach (white), and their children "and all of them—from the youngest up—are completely convinced that school integration is a vital necessity in the United States today." Rinaldo, age twelve, asked, "How else will people learn to live together?"[17]

The Issues According to Perrill and Southworth

There were eight other candidates for the two seats up for election on May 20, but the strongest opponents were James Perrill—a lawyer, former municipal judge and state senator, and father of two children in the Denver Public Schools—and his running mate, Frank Southworth, a Denver businessman, vice president of Frisbie and Co., a realtor, and a member of the first board of directors of the Denver Metro Sanitation District. Southworth had two children in elementary school. By design, they were the only two Republicans running. County chairman John P. Wogan said, "An informal group of party officials and others decided to back only two candidates."[18] Their linked campaigns were quickly reduced to touting neighborhood schools, which by definition would stop "massive crosstown busing." This came with a not-too-subtle message against racial integration, though Perrill and Southworth sometimes professed to be for integration but not here, not now, not this way.

On the address side, a Southworth campaign postcard said simply, "Neighborhood Schools! Vote for Frank K. Southworth." The message side presented five points: "opposed to mandatory busing" and "for neighborhood schools" were two of them. The third called for "improvement of existing schools and construction of new schools where children live," which was a reversion to the separate but equal facilities the United States Supreme Court had found unconstitutional in 1954. Finally, the card said, "If elected I hope to be able to work toward stabilizing the School Board and the community by making policy decisions which are responsive to the public's desires." The last statement was a response to the frequently heard argument that the school board was not following the will of the voters, never mind the Fourteenth Amendment's requirement of equal protection of the law. Calvin Trillin's *New Yorker* article summed up the campaign argument: "By the end of the campaign, Southworth was talking about 'forced mandatory crosstown busing on a massive scale.'"[19]

Perrill had a similar campaign postcard. It listed in rather small print several of Perrill's occupations, including Colorado state senator for four years, mayor's assistant, Denver municipal judge, assistant US attorney, US Navy World War II veteran, and partner in the law firm Yegge, Hall, Treece and Evans. The text also included his family members: wife, Marilyn, and daughters Pamela, at East High School, and Judith, at Gove Junior High. Under the heading "Want to help?" the third of the brief points was "Help stop forced busing." Half of the card was devoted to "Dear Taxpayer," with the other half focused on five points that included neighborhood schools and the aim to bring better schools to the disadvantaged.[20]

In an interview with the *Rocky Mountain News*, Perrill explained his views essentially as follows: the main issue was not busing but rather developing a plan for attendance areas that had broad community acceptance. The board needed to listen to the community and be responsive to its will. He said the board had to decide if its primary purpose was bringing quality education to the students or integrating them—without acknowledging that quality education required integration, according to the United States Supreme Court. If elected, Perrill pledged, he would vote to rescind the integration steps already taken by the board.[21]

Both Perrill and Southworth called for neighborhood schools, despite the Denver school board's resolution recognizing that in the past, neighborhood school policies had contributed to segregation. Support for neighborhood schools was understood by most citizens to mean a continuation of the current segregation. Like all the other candidates, Perrill and Southworth said they believed in integration, but Perrill said it "would come about when the economic status of the Negroes improved and when some changes were made in men's minds—the kind of change that could not be dictated by laws or resolutions." According to Trillin, both "he [Perrill] and Southworth said that voluntary busing would be fine—another rule being that any time white people are expected to associate with Black people they ought to have a choice in the matter."[22]

The Perrill and Southworth campaign culminated in a series of newspaper ads, ending the day before the election with a shrill, bold-face ad that said: "Stop the buses—vote Tuesday. Your LAST CHANCE to stop the buses and save our schools!" The ad also said, "Tuesday will be your final opportunity. The pro-forced busers, if elected, will put your money into mass transportation, while the two Neighborhood School Candidates will invest in Education." Later in the ad the text repeated: "Phase 1 Busing can be stopped. While the pro-forced busers spread the myth that it is too late—busing is the law, Perrill and Southworth know better. They will stop the buses before they start."[23]

Endorsements

Many community groups weighed in on the campaign with their endorsements. Doctors for Benton and Pascoe and then doctors for Perrill and Southworth placed full-page ads in the newspapers, signed by hundreds of doctors. According to my obstetrician, these lists controlled referral patterns for years because feelings on this issue ran deep.[24] Though the election was nonpartisan, Benton and Pascoe received the endorsement of the Denver Democratic Party Central Committee, which is composed of all of the city's Democratic precinct committeemen and committeewomen. Benton and Pascoe wrote a letter to all the Democratic committee people urging them to get out the vote. Perrill and Southworth wrote letters to the election judges, presumably of both parties. They repeated their usual themes about supporting neighborhood schools and opposing forced busing. They also wrote to Denver policemen and firemen, trying to arouse fears about violence in the schools: "At the present time it is difficult to tell whether the students are running the schools or the schools are running the students, and when this happens, discipline disappears and rioting with all its consequences follows." They asked for the votes of the firemen and policemen.[25]

Though the Denver Chamber of Commerce did not endorse candidates, a comparison of the candidates' responses to a set of chamber questions reveals the distinctions between Benton-Pascoe and Perrill-Southworth:

1. Why are you a candidate for the Denver Board of Education?

MR. BENTON: The Superintendent and the Board, with widespread support from the community, have moved toward the goal of equal educational opportunity for all. I want to see this movement continued and believe that my eight years of experience can be useful toward that goal.

MR. PASCOE: Denver's Board of Education must continue with its plan to provide equal educational opportunity for all; it must assert more leadership and give more direction on educational matters in the community and it must be more adaptable to change than it has been in the past . . .

2. Is the integration of the various racial, ethnic and economic groups within our city an appropriate objective of the Denver Public School System?

MR. BENTON: . . . Yes. As the Chamber of Commerce itself has recognized, through its task force report on school integration, the economic [well-being] and social well-being of our community are directly linked to the integration of all racial, ethnic and economic groups into the fabric of our society. This cannot happen without integration in the schools, where our children must learn to face the future . . .

MR. PASCOE: Yes. If we are to truly educate our children and if we are to be a city of hope, the Board of Education must take steps to encourage integration of all of our people. This includes providing an opportunity for all children to learn together without regard to racial, ethnic, or economic background.

MR. PERRILL: Yes, so long as board policies do not presume to set moral standards for all members of the community, and do not preclude the freedom of choice by making parental involvement mandatory.

MR. SOUTHWORTH: It is an appropriate objective, but the primary objective [is] to provide the finest educational opportunities possible for all of Denver's children within the economic framework Denver citizens are willing to provide.[26]

I went with Benton and Monte to El Centro Cultural, a community center in Hispanic west Denver, to win the support of a large group of Hispanic leaders who wanted to run Bal Chavez, their own candidate. As I recall, Monte and Benton spoke, and then we were escorted into an oversized closet where we waited anxiously for maybe forty minutes until the group decided to support Monte and Benton instead of running their own candidate. We also went to a party at the Crusade for Justice headquarters, a former church, to reach Corky Gonzales's more militant Hispanic organization. Though Benton-Pascoe did not gain a lot of Hispanic votes, the Hispanic leaders were not openly opposed to them.

Black Educators United also endorsed Benton and Pascoe.[27] The candidates spoke at numerous Black churches, and the votes indicated that Black voters knew that integration was important to their children's education. In some Black precincts the vote was nine to one for Benton and Pascoe.

In a parallel move, the Catholic schools announced their own integration plans. The board governing Catholic schools said it intended to develop "racially, ethnically, and socio-economically integrated parochial schools." This would provide "the spiritual, academic and social benefits of quality, integrated education." The board went further, saying that parochial schools "should not admit anyone trying to avoid integration in another school system."[28]

In a sad attempt to perform an election dirty trick just before Election Day, someone, later identified as an unpaid volunteer for the Perrill and Southworth campaign, took eleven bus drivers to the headquarters of the *Rocky Mountain News* to raise fears about safety on school buses. The volunteer shared a scary story of a boy on a bus who had a gun. He was reported and still returned the next day to put a chokehold on the driver. This group of bus drivers complained to the *News* about the lack of discipline on buses and the lack of support from administrators. They claimed to represent all Denver bus drivers. The complaining drivers pointed out that the school board had ordered twenty-eight new buses; and they described students throwing things, hollering, carrying knives, and slashing tires and seats. Drivers were even assaulted on the bus, they claimed. Later, the drivers' union and the school administration agreed that only the union could speak for the drivers.[29] One of the complaining drivers was later identified as a volunteer for the Perrill and Southworth campaign.

Just a month before the election, Superintendent Robert Gilberts added a new issue to the campaign when he presented Resolution 1531 to integrate four minority elementary schools in northeast Denver—Barrett, Hallett, Stedman, and Smith, each with complicated busing plans—and a proposal to form eight planning groups; each one paired one minority school with one or more majority schools. Six other largely minority schools and seventeen majority white schools were involved. These plans were part of the implementation of the earlier, less specific Gilberts Plan. For "immediate implementation," an additional 2,001 pupils would be bused the following fall. This aroused a new group of supporters—and opponents, who had not been too concerned when only junior high and senior high students were affected.[30] The Noel Resolution had called for the staff to present a plan for integrating the schools by December 1968, but the delay in bringing forth specific plans for northeast Denver elementary schools inserted this plan into the middle of the school board campaign. Craig Barnes described the passage of the third resolution: "On May 16, with [James] Voorhees' support, the last of the three integrating resolutions was passed. That night, there was joy amongst a small group of Black and white friends who gathered to sing and dance under the cottonwoods in Park Hill. But there was panic in the rest of town."[31]

On May 11, the eagerly awaited endorsement of the *Denver Post* came out, which clearly supported Benton and Pascoe. The endorsement said, in part:

[This is] perhaps the most important school board election in the city's history.

It is going to be, in effect, a citywide referendum on one key issue: whether most Denverites want their public schools to keep moving, however cautiously, toward school integration, or turn back toward segregation.

These two men [Benton and Pascoe] meet best, in our judgment, the prime qualifications an urban school board member—particularly in Denver—must have these days. Those qualifications include:

An unflinching commitment to seek ever higher quality in the public schools, no matter where that search leads—including toward greater racial and economic integration in the schools.

An open-minded receptivity to both new ideas and methods flowing in from educational research and to the concerns and wishes of Denver parents, teachers and school children.

The ability to explain simply to citizens what's going on in the school system and why.

Finally, the courage to move in whatever direction school professionals persuade him is best for the children, regardless of counter-pressures.

On all these counts Benton has proved himself over the last eight years. No board member has proven more receptive to new ideas in education or more keenly perceptive of their value; no one has spent more time talking with and listening to citizens of all kinds; no one has more often taken the time to explain to people, in cool and clear words, educational issues; no one has shown more courage under pressure.

His Democratic running-mate, Monte Pascoe, is a graduate of the Denver public schools and Dartmouth College and an up-and-coming young lawyer in whom we see many of the same qualities which have made Benton such an excellent board member: keen intelligence, open-mindedness to the facts on school problems, dedication to quality education and courage. He should make a fine addition to the board.

[Perrill and Southworth] are staking their campaign on opposition to "forced" busing, which is politically popular in some quarters but a poor substitute for a real commitment to quality education. Also, they are pledged to try to rescind the present board's racial stabilization programs at East High and Smiley Junior High.

They disclaim any segregationist intent in either stand, but Denver's Hispano and Negro communities see both as attempts not merely to stand pat on integration, but to turn back the clock. In the rescission case, we have to agree.[32]

Later, right before the election, the paper reaffirmed its endorsement:

Issue: The city's continued health and progress depend on [the] outcome of [the] school board election.

Vote your hopes and faith in the basic decency and forward-looking spirit of this city.

We have endorsed two candidates, Edgar Benton and Monte Pascoe, who represent in our judgment the best blend of courageous willingness to try various ways of solving our school racial problems and conscientious concern for the welfare of all the children for whose education they are responsible.

The board's modest programs of racial stabilization and exploratory attempts at school integration should have a chance to work.[33]

The *Rocky Mountain News*, the other major Denver newspaper, endorsed Perrill and Barnhart, in a peculiarly irrational editorial. First, it said that the Gilberts Plan should be given a chance and the integration of East and Smiley and several elementary schools should go forward,[34] despite Perrill's pledge to *rescind* the modest integration programs for Smiley and East High. The endorsement continued with all the reasons why the integration plans should not and must not be rescinded and the confident assertion that those who pledged to rescind it would not actually do so. Barnhart was endorsed on the grounds that he was a professional educator, confusing the policy role of the board with the staffing role of an administrator. The *News* reran its endorsement on May 18, two days before the election. According to Benton, it was rumored that *News* journalist Michael Howard, grandson of the founder of Scripps Howard Company that owned the paper, wanted to endorse Benton and Pascoe; but his father, Jack Howard, the president of the company in Cincinnati, would not allow it.[35]

The *Rocky Mountain News* staff rebelled immediately after the endorsement was printed. They "disagreed strongly" with the paper's endorsement. Thirteen editorial staff members signed a letter printed in the *News*, saying that "a full scale commitment to racial integration in the city's schools must be undertaken as soon as possible if Denver is to remain a city in which people live and work together rather than one of hatred and division." The thirteen staff members endorsed Benton and Pascoe because "they have such a vision."[36]

The *Post* had an especially pro-integration education reporter, Art Branscombe, who was a leader in Park Hill. The *Rocky Mountain News* had not endorsed Benton and Pascoe, yet many on the staff had rebelled and written a letter endorsing them.

Threats and Violence

The heated campaign drew national attention from the media. Calvin Trillin of the *New Yorker* spent a week in Denver following the candidates, some of that time crammed in the back seat of our Volkswagen Bug. Following a very inflammatory school board meeting at South High School that went late into the night and early morning, he amended a Benton-Pascoe radio advertisement in a conversation with Ed Benton. The ad went something like this: "This is Virginia. Virginia lives in Denver. She wonders what kind of people live in Denver." Trillin said he would answer the question with "Denver people are s—." He was also at a late-night meeting at our house when a phone caller shouted an obscenity at Monte and called him a "N— lover." Monte told the group, "I've probably met that guy at some meeting . . . and he's told me he's all for integration, but what about the effect busing will have on after-school activities or parent participation?" It was not acceptable to be openly racist in 1969, but many other issues were used as proxies for racist views. Such calls and even threats were a regular part of the campaign:[37] "Board members on both sides were the target of abusive language and threats; obscene and abusive phone calls, vitriolic letters and postcards, death threats, and epithets shouted at them as they moved about the community. For the most part, the threats started with the introduction of the Noel Resolution."[38] Because of the hostility toward integrationists in southwest Denver, the campaign policy was that Benton and Monte would never be sent into that part of the city alone.

Because we feared a firebomb would be thrown onto our front porch, Monte and I planned for an emergency. We moved Ted's bed away from the front wall, which was over the porch. If someone rang the doorbell when we weren't expecting anyone, I was to gather up our three children and move to the back of the house while Monte, who never knew physical fear, would go to the door and meet whoever was there.

Election Day Results

Finally, May 20, Election Day, arrived. Hopes were high in the Benton-Pascoe campaign, despite the heated opposition the candidates had faced. They were not very surprised to lose, but they were shocked at the margin of the loss. When the tally was in, Perrill and Southworth had beaten Benton and Pascoe by a two-to-one margin. Total votes were Southworth, 75,596; Perrill, 73,932; Benton, 31,098; Pascoe, 28,948. Barnhart received 11,726 votes, and five other candidates received fewer than 5,000 votes apiece. Benton and Pascoe carried predominantly Black areas, but Perrill and Southworth carried fifteen of eighteen election districts.[39]

"I think it shows the board did proceed unilaterally with far-reaching policy changes," said Perrill, "and the community was not willing to accept that kind of action on the part of the board." Southworth said the results meant "the people have recovered their school system." Board president James D. Voorhees Jr., who had endorsed Benton, said the vote "shows a city that maybe thinks it's gone too far too quickly." But he hoped the integration steps wouldn't be rescinded: "The thing that bothers me is that those who discuss rescission offer no alternative," he said.[40]

Dr. John Amesse, a pro-Benton-Pascoe board member, predicted that the board would be sued if the integration steps were undone. "I'm sorry and concerned," he said of the vote. "But we must above everything now work for harmony and goodwill and Denver must never go down the drain." Rachel Noel said, "I think it shows the city to be very racist." When asked if she would remain on the board if the integration steps were rescinded, she said, "I may not." The campaign attracted nearly 110,000 voters of 215,000 who were registered, compared to only about 51,000 voters the last time a school board election was held without a city election.[41]

When Monte and I went with Ed and his wife, Stephanie, to what was supposed to be the Benton-Pascoe "victory" party, the mood was somber. High school students who had worked so hard on the campaign wore black armbands. Indeed, something important had died with that vote, not just because the campaign for justice had been defeated by slogans but because it had been defeated by such a large margin. The students from East High could see their school becoming a minority school rather than a racially integrated one if Perrill and Southworth carried out their promise to reverse the integration plans. For the adults, the election shattered the illusion that Denver, an aspiring cosmopolitan city, was different from cities in the South where hardened racism prevailed. We had to face the fact that racism in many guises was strong in Denver.

Reactions to the Election

After the election, Rev. Jesse Wagner said that busing was highly unlikely in Denver. He added in an article in the *New York Times*, "The dream is over. The white majority is not willing to take on the commitment and make our country one . . . Unfortunately, Denver's whites have also strengthened the city's black separatists."[42] He also wrote a letter to the *Denver Post* addressed to the Bentons and to our children. Someone later framed copies of it for each of our children. It read, in part:

To the families of Edgar Benton and Monte Pascoe . . .

There will be some individuals who will say that your husbands, that your fathers, lost this election. Yes, they lost, but so did we—our city—all of us. We lost. There is no more time for tears—only the sudden awareness of reality that these people in this time and place were unable to overcome and meet the difficult problems that separate us as black, brown and white.

It is a rare privilege to meet in one's lifetime truly great men. It has been my honor to meet three great men. One, the late Dr. Martin Luther King who had a dream that all men, Jew and gentile, Catholic and Protestant, black and white, would sit the table of understanding and peace together. Your father and husband was and is a great man. Not just because he too dared to dream, but because he was willing to stand for his convictions and crusade for an unpopular cause in [the] face of an ocean of opposition. He dared and tried to be a leader, and not just a straw in the winds of public opinion. And really, this is what makes a man great and enables him to change the world . . .

Your fathers were meaningful to me—a ray of hope in a frustrated world.

They are loved and respected by thousands, and you have a right to be proud. I am grateful that my life was touched by theirs, for I would rather be a part of a losing cause that is destined to win, than to be a part of a winning cause that is destined to lose.

The greatest want of the world is for the want of men. Men who cannot be bought or sold. Men who in their innermost souls are true and honest. Men who are not afraid to call sin by its right name. Men who will stand for right, though the heavens fall.

> With great respect and love,
> Jesse Wagner
> Denver[43]

These same words could have been used to describe Wagner, a soldier in the battle for interracial understanding.

Rachel Noel responded to the vote: "I can say now, however, that I am greatly concerned for the future of minority children in this city—especially black children—because of the racist vote and the racist appeal made by the successful candidates for the board. The promise for progress in humanness is at a low ebb in this city."[44]

In summarizing the campaign years later, *Keyes* case attorney Robert T. Connery said the election was "one of the most bitter and vitriolic ever conducted in Denver, bordering on violence . . . We could not have had more qualified, committed, and eloquent candidates than Ed Benton and Monte Pascoe. And they gave their all to the campaign."[45]

The race for racial justice was not without its cost to the proponents. At a seminar on the fortieth anniversary of the *Keyes* case, Craig Barnes called Monte a hero who might have been governor or a senator if he had not supported this cause. It is difficult to know whether Monte's involvement in desegregation affected his losing the race for mayor in 1983. Barnes knew well the cost of involvement in the desegregation battle because the year after the school board race he ran for the US Congress against long-time incumbent Byron Rogers, winning the Democratic primary by thirty-one votes. Two weeks before the general election, the polls showed Craig 15 percentage points ahead until his Republican opponent, Mike McKevitt, repeatedly ran an advertisement showing a facsimile of the *Keyes* complaint form with Craig's signature on it, thus identifying Barnes as a proponent of desegregation. Barnes lost the general election to McKevitt, the first and last Republican to represent Denver in the US Congress in living memory.[46]

When Benton spoke at Monte's memorial service in 2006, he recalled their school board race thirty-seven years earlier, saying, "It was the right thing to do then; it is the right thing to do now." Then he asked our whole family to stand. Sarah, Ted, Will, and I stood and faced the overflowing congregation to thunderous applause, which was a kind of late affirmation. Whatever the cost to his later achievements, Monte never regretted this campaign.

The fervent coalition that backed Benton and Pascoe did not die but rather regrouped. All eyes turned to the new school board, to be installed on May 27. Its first substantive meeting was to be held on June 9, when supporters of desegregation were hopeful that the already adopted desegregation plans for the northeast section of the city would be implemented.

4

The New Board Moves to Resegregate

At its first regular meeting, the new board majority took the steps that courts, including the United States Supreme Court, later labeled *de jure* segregation.

Perrill and Southworth Take Over

James Perrill and Frank Southworth went to their installation as new members of the Denver school board at 2:00 p.m. on May 27, 1969. Technically, this was a meeting of the old board to canvass the votes in the election and issue certificates of election to the winners.[1] Following that procedure, the board president, James Voorhees, stated that this concluded the business of the board and that Edgar Benton, who was retiring from the board, wished to make some remarks. Benton commented:

> The electorate, which must make the final judgment, isn't always to be
> counted on . . . to take into account all things that are pertinent. One thing
> pertinent to this community, he said, is the matter of deep and abiding injus-

https://doi.org/10.5876/9781646422906.c004

tices affecting many of our citizens and children in the school system. For example, adults in this community who are unemployed, disillusioned, psychologically destroyed human beings who, in another era, were in the Denver Public Schools [DPS] and victims of a segregated society and segregated education within that society. He indicated that this election has not eliminated these problems; they are still here . . . He felt the ideals of freedom, equality, justice and human dignity have "taken a beating" because the community has become confused in the use of the terms of integration and equality of opportunity and at the same time taken steps that would result in the absence of these qualities . . . Mr. Benton stated he had acted in a nontraditional way by not congratulating the winners of this School Board election but to do so would be to say there is no injustice in this school system; no black children rotting in the schools; that there wasn't anything wrong in playing on the doubts and fears of a community.[2]

The next special meeting of the board convened a few minutes after the first one for the purpose of swearing in the newly elected board members and selecting officers of the board. The Honorable Robert H. McWilliams, chief justice of the Colorado Supreme Court, administered the oath of office to Perrill and Southworth. After the swearing in, Allegra Saunders and Benton gave up their seats to Perrill and Southworth.

In the election of officers, William Berge, part of the new majority, defeated Voorhees for president, and Stephen Knight defeated Amesse for vice president,[3] solidifying anti-integration control of the board.

The first substantive meeting of the newly constituted board was set for June 9, twenty days after the election. For that meeting, public interest was keen. According to the reporter for the *Denver Post*, 100 people jammed into the meeting room, standing against the walls and sitting on the floor, while another 50 sat in the hall and listened over a loudspeaker.[4]

In the first business of the day, Perrill moved and Southworth seconded a motion to rescind Resolution 1520, concerning the integration of East High School and Smiley Junior High, which had passed in January. Then Perrill explained his intention: if this motion passed, he said, he would also move to rescind Resolutions 1524—concerning the movement of 850 students from Smiley to other junior high schools and the movement of pupils from Hill and Merrill to Hamilton and Thomas Jefferson Junior-Senior Highs—and Resolution 1531, concerning the integration of twenty-three elementary schools in northeast Denver. In rather lengthy comments, Perrill said, among other things, that "it was his opinion that this elected body, as a public entity, must determine where it is; where the community is; where it intends to go and where it intends to lead the community." He felt the school board had to maintain its credibility with the numerical majority. Though the school board was involved, it could not "stand out in front of everyone and direct efforts and devise solutions as far as community involvement in social and ethnic problems by the community at large is concerned." Thus, his comments alternated between the idea that the board should lead and the statement that the board should follow the community. Perrill still saw a role for the school board to "help direct an effective school program designed to promote the best educational opportunities for all children and an effective unified community involved in the solution of its social problems."[5] He proposed that Resolution 1520 be rescinded to "clear the air," start anew, and begin a new involvement on the part of the Denver community. Ironically, he called for "new involvement" by the community after an election that had been the community's major focus for at least five months.

Voorhees argued that the replacement resolution (1533)

> was a terrible thing. He said the recent election is not a mandate to do what this resolution proposes . . . He commented that what the election does say is that the previous board has failed to communicate to the entire community the urgent and desperate need contained in the resolution being considered for rescinding . . . He added that the election does not request a Board of Education with any fortitude at all to do what Resolution Number 1533 [the replacement resolution] and the two to follow consider doing. He stated that it would take a lot of "guts" to say to the people that the Board recognized what they are trying to say in this election, but that the Board does not interpret their vote as a vote to take a step backward. He pointed out that the areas most opposed to forced busing in the election results were areas not involved in forced busing.[6]

He urged a vote not to rescind Resolution 1520.

Another board member newly in the minority, Amesse, pointed out that the area involved in these resolutions was the one where there had been the most votes against Perrill and Southworth. The rescission of these resolutions, he said, would do Denver no good because a lawsuit would be taken against the city and the school district. He predicted that Perrill's plans to organize the city toward unity would be a laughable matter, especially in northeast Denver. Amesse felt that children should not be denied transportation that helped achieve racial balance and that the board should do all it could to bring into effect quality integrated education.[7]

"Rachel Noel stated that a vote . . . to rescind Resolutions 1520, 1524, and 1531 [the resolutions that would have integrated Park Hill], is a vote against minorities—particularly black children. It would also be a vote for segregation which means the Board member believes in separatism and prejudice." She believed the election vote was based on deliberately stirred-up fears. The people who stirred them up, she said, would live to regret it. She called for courage, "to stand for the right and not hide behind the smoke screen of neighborhood schools; to enable children to go to school together, learn together, and be given equality of educational opportunity." Otherwise, a backward step would be taken.[8]

Board president Berge said that after great "soul searching," he was convinced that the resolution to desegregate as it stood was wrong. He believed they needed a majority of support from all sections of the city. Voorhees commented that the way to get integration was to start.[9]

On a roll call vote, Berge, Knight, Perrill, and Southworth voted "yes" on the rescission of Resolution 1520, and Amesse, Noel, and Voorhees voted "no," a vote of 4 to 3. The bloc of segregationists voted against the bloc of integrationists, a pattern that would become very familiar.

Perrill then moved and Southworth seconded the repeal of Resolution 1524. Voorhees noted that this resolution would integrate Smiley Junior High, which had gone from 90 percent white to 75 percent Black in five years. The resolution called for the transfer of 800 or so primarily minority children out of Smiley, to spread them through several junior high schools in east Denver. Some white children already being bused would merely have their bus change direction. He said, "This is not massive, forced integration." Nevertheless, the repeal passed by the same 4 to 3 vote.[10]

Then, again, Perrill moved for the rescission of Resolution 1531, concerning elementary schools in northeast Denver. Again, Amesse and Voorhees spoke against the rescission. They argued for a start in bringing about understanding among children, and they said the citizens had not voted to rescind this resolution, which was a backward step.[11]

Noel agreed with Amesse's remarks, adding, "We who have lived so long and seen so much discrimination had hoped that in 1969, such things as the rescission of Resolution 1531 could not be possible." She said that prejudice was taking over, and a vote to rescind the resolution would be a vote for segregation. The motion to rescind carried on the same 4 to 3 vote.[12]

The Plan of the New Majority

Stephen Knight next moved on Resolution 1533, with a second from Southworth. The resolution reinstated only the voluntary aspects of the rescinded resolutions. The resolution claimed that the three rescinded resolutions had been "hastily prepared," a statement several members objected to. The superintendent was directed to continue planning for elementary schools in Complex 1 and Complex 2 of the Gilberts Plan, with only voluntary compliance. Plans were to go forward only with local parental approval. Busing to relieve overcrowding at Stedman, which had four mobile units, was to proceed. The resolution called for voluntary plans for Hallett, the integration of which was already under way, as was a mentioned preschool program, as Amesse pointed out. Voorhees asked that the views of the audience be heard before votes were taken on the resolution, but this was not done. When asked to comment, Gilberts pointed out that not all schools in northeast Denver were included as they had been originally.[13]

Noel commented that "there are many words in the resolution but there is no substance and nothing will happen." The resolution passed on the same 4 to 3 vote.[14]

Southworth moved that the superintendent develop concentrated and effective plans for voluntary open enrollment between Smiley and East attendance areas, on the one hand, and South High, Thomas Jefferson Junior-Senior High, and George Washington High attendance areas on the other hand. These plans were to take effect in September or, at the latest, in the second semester of the next school year. The motion was passed 4 to 3 by the new majority.[15]

Consequences of the Board's Actions

These rescissions and the return to voluntary programs hammered the lid on the coffin of district-directed integration in Denver. It made it easier to prove that the DPS was guilty of *de jure*, or government-ordered, segregation. The schools could no longer argue that Denver's highly segregated schools were just the result of *de facto* segregation, choices made by citizens about where they wanted to live. Eventually, in the subsequent lawsuit, it was clear that in the past, even what looked like *de facto* segregation had been aided and abetted by actions of the school board as well.

In other board action, Superintendent Gilberts was asked to come back with a report on the district's capital needs. This was in line with the Perrill and Southworth pledge to improve neighborhood schools. Voorhees offered an amendment that called for the building report to consider the earlier report, "Planning Quality Education," which had the goal of integrated education. Amesse observed that the Noel Resolution had not been rescinded, so therefore Gilberts should still consider integration in his suggestions for buildings. The Voorhees amendment was defeated by the same 4 to 3 margin.[16]

Next, Southworth moved for a review of the purchase of twenty-seven buses in light of the other actions of the board. As opponents of busing, he and Perrill wanted to make sure that the new buses were not used. This issue was deferred until staff could research it.[17]

Park Hill Black leader Fred Thomas was one of several disappointed speakers from the audience: "He said he hoped the Board would get the right kind of response to its mandate, but that he and others who had walked the streets to try to keep peace in the community would no longer do this. Public support from the black community, he said, was not the same support the Board would have gotten last year."[18] The closing comment appropriately came from Mrs. Noel: "Mrs. Noel stated that tonight's actions of the Board mark a low level of concern for the children of Denver—especially minority children. She said the Board's majority had listened to stereotyped fear. She remarked to those present to remember who did these dastardly deeds and do not understand the meaning of equality of educational opportunity."[19]

5

The Keyes Case Is Filed

The rescission of three resolutions designed to integrate schools in a small part of Denver, an act that allowed the new board members to carry out an election promise, was a clear case of state action to segregate Black students. A few days after the June 9 board meeting, Monte and I attended a gathering of integration supporters in Martha Radetsky's crowded living room. I remember University of Denver mathematics professor George Bardwell saying, "Well, damn it, if the board won't do it, we'll take them to court."

The Lawyers, the Financial Backers, and the Plaintiffs

Within ten days of the board's rescissions, *Keyes v. School District No. 1* was filed, with the distinction of being the first northern big-city desegregation case. The story behind the initial filing has been carefully told by Holland and Hart attorney Robert Connery in a personal memoir.[1] He recounted that he had been involved in the Park Hill Action Committee's Schools Committee along with Fred Thomas, an avid supporter of integration. Connery had also

https://doi.org/10.5876/9781646422906.c005

studied United States Supreme Court decisions with a small group of law-yers. He thought there were parallels to Denver's situation in the Supreme Court opinion in *Hobson v. Hansen*.[2] *Hobson* was a massive case about the denial of equal educational opportunity in the Washington, DC, school sys-tem, including "optional zones," just like Denver's, and claims of "emotional upset" that were used "for whites to escape predominantly [B]lack neigh-borhood schools." Blacks were kept in the minority on the Washington school board for sixty years, although the schools were 90 percent Black. As in Denver, there were such factors as teacher segregation, resource deficits, and funding differences that disadvantaged minority schools. The district court in *Hobson* found that the neighborhood school policy was responsible for the discrimination against minority and poor children. Whether the test was "separate-but-equal, *de jure* segregation, or de facto segregation," the schools failed to provide equal educational opportunity. The judge in that case required the district to provide that equal educational opportunity.[3]

Edwin S. Kahn and Lawrence W. Treece, two other Holland and Hart attorneys, and Connery had many discussions in late 1968 and early 1969 about what it would take to file a successful lawsuit against the Denver Public Schools (DPS) board. Kahn was an experienced litigator, but Connery was just three years out of law school and Treece had just finished law school. As it became clear that the newly elected board would rescind the plans to inte-grate the schools in Park Hill, the lawyers held a flurry of meetings to try to determine whether a case should be filed. The feeling among the lawyers was that if the integration plans were rescinded, the case should indeed be filed.[4]

Treece wrote the first draft of a complaint and motion for preliminary injunction, that is, an order to prevent the school board from canceling the plans to integrate northeast Denver schools. He was also responsible for observing that the Denver schools were not even providing the separate but equal education that had been required by the Supreme Court since 1896 in *Plessy v. Ferguson*.[5] That ruling had a major effect on the evidence that would be presented. Mathematics professor George Bardwell had a vast amount of data to prove the inequality of minority schools, data he had collected over several years and analyzed extensively with the computers at the University of Denver.[6]

The greatest need of the "young lawyers" was for an experienced litigator to present the case. After being turned down by a number of attorneys, they found that person in Gordon Greiner of Holland and Hart, an experienced litigator of complex cases. A Goldwater Republican, he was in his fourth year at the firm.[7] Greiner recognized that this was a major case, but he probably did not expect that the court oversight of Denver schools and his representation of the plaintiffs would continue for twenty-six years until their last appeal was denied in 1995.

Holland and Hart wanted at least one attorney from another law firm to help Greiner. Connery suggested Craig Barnes, whom he admired for his thoughtfulness and eloquence, but Barnes was a student in international relations at the University of Denver. Nevertheless, Connery tried to recruit him. Barnes described how he became involved in *Keyes*: on the morning after the rescissions, Connery called him and tried to recruit him to work on the case. He wanted Barnes to work "on a draft complaint to sue the school board on behalf of all those children in Denver who were being denied an equal educational opportunity." A short time later, Bardwell called him. He and Paul Klite, a professor at the University of Colorado Medical School, "had been gathering facts for months and probably knew as much about classroom statistics and distribution of students by race as did the school administration itself."[8] They had observed clear discrimination and deliberate segregation. According to Barnes, "As the black population of north Denver had gradually moved east across the northern tier of the city, school boundaries for elementary schools had also regularly shifted eastward. The effect was that black children who had moved across boundary lines into white districts were recaptured by the new lines and brought back into redrawn black districts."[9] After careful consideration and consulting with his wife, Michaela, Barnes volunteered to work at least through the emergency injunction and its appeals. For the next nine months, Greiner, Bardwell, and Barnes were "welded at the hip."[10]

A number of pro-integration individuals had formed the Denver Equal Education Opportunity Fund (DEEOF) to support the effort financially, although the lawyers all worked on a pro bono basis and the national Legal Defense Fund (LDF) of the National Association for the Advancement of Colored People (NAACP) had agreed to pay the out-of-pocket expenses.[11] Members of the DEEOF board were Edgar Benton, Field Benton, Omar Blair, Eugene Bowes, Dr. George H. Curfman Jr., Anne C. Gibson, William Grant, Monte Pascoe, Martha Radetsky, Donard Roe, Nina Salazar, and Richard E. Young. Doug Hoyt was treasurer and Fred Thomas was chair.[12]

The plaintiffs in the case were racially and ethnically diverse. There were Black plaintiffs, including Wilfred Keyes, Christine A. Colley, Irma J. Jennings, Roberta R. Wade, and Edward J. Starks Jr.; a Hispanic plaintiff, Josephine Perez; and two white plaintiffs, Maxine N. Becker and Eugene R. Weiner, all filing on behalf of their children. The lead plaintiff was Wilfred Keyes, a podiatrist, whose wife was a special education teacher in the DPS. The plaintiffs were carefully chosen so that each child would be seriously and negatively affected in the schools they would attend if the rescissions were allowed to stand, with the exception of the Perez family, whose children attended segregated schools not immediately affected by the resolutions. All together there were five Black, one Hispanic, and two white parents acting in a class action on behalf of their children.[13]

The plaintiffs were joined on January 1, 1974, by the Congress of Hispano Educators et al., intervenors, represented by attorneys from the Mexican American Legal Defense and Educational Fund (MALDEF). They complained of unequal educational opportunity and the absence of Chicano teachers and bilingual, bicultural programs. Their greatest success was Judge Doyle's inclusion of the Cardenas Plan for bilingual education in the 1974 court order, but the appeals court rejected it (see chapter 16).[14]

On June 12, 1969, just three days after the rescissions, the entire legal team along with Gail Oppenneer of Fairfield and Woods, Bardwell, and Klite (the two men who prepared the statistical evidence and the graphs and charts to illustrate it) met to go over their draft complaint to make sure the facts were "consonant" with their legal strategy.[15]

Barnes described what happened after the suit was filed:

> Controversy exploded. At home, my family started getting our first hate calls, callers in the middle of the night. Our lives, all of us, and those of the plaintiffs, especially the Keyes family, had become suddenly public. Two-thirds of the voters of Denver had voted against the candidates who supported the integration resolutions, and a small minority were about to try to reinstate the integration option. It was not right, said the majority. It was what the Constitution required, said the plaintiffs. It was not what the Constitution required, and elections should not be upset by the courts, said the majority. All this debate raged in the offices, on the streets, and on the editorial pages of Denver's newspapers.[16]

The Brief for the Plaintiffs

On June 19, the plaintiffs' lawyers filed two motions, one for a preliminary injunction and another for a permanent injunction and a declaratory judgment. The purpose of the preliminary injunction was to prevent the district from destroying the plans for integration under the integration resolutions; such actions would have prevented their implementation in September of that year. The lawyers asked the judge to grant a preliminary injunction to prevent the school district from canceling the order to buy twenty-seven buses and prevent the district from changing the plans for or destroying any documents relating to the planned implementation of Resolutions 1520, 1524, and 1531. It also would have prohibited the district from communicating to teachers and parents in any way that would make implementation of those resolutions more difficult, though the district would have been allowed to prepare alternative plans as it desired.[17]

The body of the argument for desegregation was in the "Complaint for Permanent Injunction and Declaratory Judgment," which was also written by Barnes and Greiner with the assistance of LDF attorneys Jack Greenberg, James M. Nabrit III, and Conrad K. Harper. In addition to the children affected adversely by the rescissions, the class of children affected included those children "who by virtue of the actions or omissions of the Board . . . will be and have been attending segregated schools or substantially segregated schools, and who will be and have been receiving an unequal educational opportunity."[18] Among the questions of fact were whether the board action increased segregation and whether that violated the Fourteenth Amendment, which was the first cause of action, and whether students had been attending segregated and substantially segregated schools and receiving an unequal educational opportunity in violation of the US Constitution, which was the second cause of action.

The plaintiffs sued the school board, naming all of its members, as well as the superintendent, Robert D. Gilberts.

First Cause of Action [Violation of the Fourteenth Amendment]

This cause of action related very specifically to the resegregation caused by the rescissions of the three integration resolutions. The brief explained what the rescissions meant to specific plaintiffs and the schools they would have attended under the plan. In each case, under the resolutions the racial balance would have been improved at both the sending and receiving schools, although some of the plaintiffs attended highly segregated schools and there was no plan to change their situation.

Then the authors reviewed the campaign and election of new members of the school board, who promised to and did, in fact, rescind the three integration resolutions applying to East High, Smiley Junior High, and elementary schools in northeast Denver. Plaintiffs argued that the board should not be allowed to destroy the means of transportation until the court decided the case; nor should the district destroy the means of implementing the resolutions.[19]

The first cause of action was divided into six counts, as follows.

First Count:

The rescissions encouraged minor acts of discrimination.[20]

Second Count:

The defendant board members were motivated by racial and ethnic considerations in rescinding the resolutions, and Black and Hispanic plaintiffs viewed the actions as a significant defeat in their attempt to obtain equal educational opportunity.[21]

Third Count:

The board in acting to rescind was motivated by a desire to maintain racial and ethnic separation, which would have been alleviated by the resolutions.[22]

Fourth Count:

Through the rescissions, the board reassigned children who would have been in integrated schools to segregated schools.[23]

Fifth Count:

Before the passage of the resolutions, the pupils in the affected separate minority schools were receiving unequal education: they had higher dropout rates, they had disproportionately large numbers of Black and Hispanic faculty, they had a disproportionately large number of mobile units, and they had pupil memberships with generally lower economic status. The implementation of the resolutions would have significantly eliminated these inequalities.[24]

Sixth Count:

The resolutions would have desegregated the subject schools. The rescissions resegregated those students. "Defendants have acted to deny plaintiffs an equal educational opportunity by implementing and effectuating a policy the effect of which is to confine plaintiffs to schools which because of the rescission will be actually segregated on the basis of race or ethnicity."[25]

Prayer for the First Cause of Action

The plaintiffs said they wanted the school district to be prevented from destroying the plans for integration or canceling the purchase of buses until the case was settled and permanently thereafter.[26] Any motions of the board to cancel the resolutions, they argued, should be declared null and void as a denial of the Fourteenth Amendment of the Constitution of the United States. Defendants should be required to implement Resolutions 1521, 1524, and 1531 beginning in September 1969 and be forever enjoined from acting to nullify, modify, delay, or deny to plaintiffs or others similarly situated the equal educational opportunity guaranteed to them by the Fourteenth Amendment.[27]

They asked that the court adjudge that the board's rescissions of the resolutions constituted a denial to Black or Hispanic children of equal protection of the laws and a denial to white children of "the advantages, educational benefits, intellectual stimulation and practical preparation for a multiracial world afforded and available to those Anglo children attending racially balanced and integrated schools within the School District . . . depriving said plaintiffs of equal protection of the laws."[28]

Second Cause of Action [Children Receiving Separate and Unequal Education]

What the district claimed as *de facto* segregation—merely created by housing patterns—was actually aided and abetted by board and district decisions, thus making it *de jure* segregation or, at the very least, blurring the distinction between the two.

First Count:

"Defendants . . . have over the years and are at present deliberately and purposefully attempting to create, foster and maintain racial and ethnic segregation within the School District." This was the result of the neighborhood school policy and school attendance area boundaries created "with the purpose, intent and effect of creating, fostering and maintaining racial and ethnic segregation within the School District." Certain, mostly white, children were given optional transfers outside established (largely minority) school boundaries. Black and Hispanic faculty and staff were assigned to predominantly Black and Hispanic schools. As some schools made the transition to increasing proportions of minority children, the defendants created optional attendance areas designed to allow the transfer of white pupils to predominantly white schools and to retain minority pupils in schools with predominantly Black and/or Hispanic pupil populations. As a result of such board policies, in September 1968, 59 percent of the white students in the DPS were in schools that were over 85 percent white, 62 percent of Black students were in schools that were over 85 percent Black and/or Hispanic, and 50.2 percent of Hispanics were in schools that were over 50 percent Black and/or Hispanic.[29]

Second Count:

Minority schools were allocated resources substantially inferior to those allocated to schools with predominantly white pupil populations. This included inferior materials, supplies, and curricula. A disproportionately large number of less experienced faculty were assigned to minority schools, and more experienced faculty were assigned to white schools. Sarah S. Weiner, the white child of a plaintiff, who open-enrolled at majority Black Hallett Elementary School, experienced this allocation of inferior resources.[30]

Third Count:

Defendants adopted and continued to maintain a neighborhood school policy, creating a school system segregated on the basis of race and ethnicity.[31]

Fourth Count:

The track system or ability grouping had the effect of separating students on the basis of race and ethnicity and denying Black and Hispanic plaintiffs educational opportunity available to whites of equal ability.[32]

Prayer for Relief for Second Cause of Action

First Count:

"That defendants . . . be permanently enjoined and restrained from directly or indirectly continuing, maintaining, requiring, promoting or encouraging, through their rules, regulations, resolutions, policies, directives, customs, practices and usages, the segregation and separation by race and ethnicity of the pupils of the schools within the School District."[33] The plaintiffs asked:

That defendants be required to submit to this court, within a time . . . for implementation of such program for the beginning of the school year commencing on or about September 1, 1970, a comprehensive plan for the school district as a whole and for each school therein where such condition exists, which will (i) remove the segregation and separation of schoolchildren by race and ethnicity within and among such schools; and (ii) afford and ensure to every school child, regardless of race or ethnicity and regardless of the school such child attends, an equal educational opportunity.[34]

The district is also to be permanently enjoined and restrained (i) from adjusting boundaries with the intention to discriminate on the basis of race or ethnicity, (ii) from creating or enforcing optional areas intended to discriminate on the basis of race or ethnicity, and (iii) from assigning staff to schools on the basis of race or ethnicity and thereby furthering the racial or ethnic character of the school.[35]

The plaintiffs further requested:

That the court . . . adjudge and decree that the actions of defendants in purposefully and knowingly creating and maintaining the segregation and separation by race and ethnicity of the schoolchildren within the district are unconstitutional and void, as depriving plaintiffs . . . of equal protection of the laws . . .[36]

Second Count:

The plaintiffs asked that the district be ordered to stop the unequal allocation of resources to schools; that it submit a plan by September 1970 to remove any existing disparity in facilities, faculty, and staff and make them equal or as nearly so as would be practical and feasible under the circumstances; and that the defendants be enjoined "from adopting or continuing

any policy which is intended or in fact does result in an unequal allocation of such resources as physical plant, equipment, materials, supplies
and curricula on the basis of race or ethnicity." Also that the district be
prohibited from assigning faculty of less experienced, less qualified staff
to predominantly Black or Hispanic schools. Finally, they asked that the
court find that the actions of defendants in allocating inferior resources to
predominately Black and Hispanic schools were in contravention of the
Fourteenth Amendment.[37]

Third Count:

To whittle down the prayer for relief under the third count, the plaintiffs asked:

That defendants . . . be permanently enjoined . . . from encouraging or
promoting the segregation and separation by race and ethnicity of the pupils of the schools within the school district. That defendants be required
to submit . . . by September 1, 1970, a comprehensive plan for the district
as a whole . . . that will remove segregation and separation of schoolchildren, [and] afford . . . each schoolchild . . . equal educational opportunity;
that the defendants . . . be permanently enjoined . . . from creation . . . of
boundaries . . . intended to discriminate on the basis of race or ethnicity . . . ; that the court . . . adjudge and decree that the actions of defendants which resulted in the actual segregation and separation by race and
ethnicity . . . are unconstitutional and void as depriving said plaintiffs . . .
of equal protection of the laws . . .

[Alternately,] that defendants . . . submit to the court . . . a comprehensive plan to effectively mitigate . . . the segregation and separation of
schoolchildren by race and ethnicity . . . and minimize effects of remaining
segregation.[38]

Fourth Count:

The memorandum asked:

That defendants . . . be permanently enjoined . . . from maintaining . . .
the existing track system . . . which is either intended [to] or does in fact
discriminate between pupils on the basis of race or ethnicity . . . or does
in fact accord Negro and Hispano students an educational opportunity
unequal to that accorded Anglo students of comparable abilities and
qualifications.

The court should find that the "track systems which discriminate
against Negro and Hispano students . . . are unconstitutional and void."[39]
This concludes the summary of the plaintiffs' brief.

Two days after the suit was filed, the plaintiffs' attorneys met to assign the
research and preparation of exhibits—charts and graphs—to prepare for
the trial. Seventeen volunteer men and women, all white and mostly lawyers, were listed at the top of the meeting agenda, in addition to Bardwell
and Klite, who had been analyzing the school district data for years. One or
two people were assigned to research each of these topics: dropouts, curricula, effects of integrated education, number of college-bound students,
discipline, school facilities, residential patterns and boundaries, case studies,
costs per student, allocation of federal funds, accelerated classes, and the
track system (ability grouping). The paper called for volunteers—draftsmen,
chart drawers, artists—and the anticipated expenses of travel, purchase of
publications, and charges under open records law. It also listed the need
for support services such as secretarial and reproduction for this massive
undertaking.[40]

Other Community Reactions to the Rescissions

While lawyers were working on the lawsuit, there were strong reactions
in the community to the rescissions. The East Denver Ministerial Alliance
responded two nights after the school board meeting. It decided to request
that the US Department of Health, Education, and Welfare (HEW) "investigate the actions of the Denver School Board in rescinding plans that would
have given meaningful integration in our schools." The alliance wanted to
ask HEW "to investigate the racial composition of all schools. It is our feeling that their investigation will prove that our schools are segregated and
thus will lead to the cutting off of federal funds to the entire school system."
There was other discussion about neighborhood school control, boycotting
schools in east Denver in September, refusing to support voluntary busing,
and upgrading east Denver schools as to curriculum, facilities, and teachers:
"There [is] an obvious feeling that the Black community definitely is going to
react to actions of the school board. The only question that remains is what
the reaction will actually consist of."[41]

The Colorado Civil Rights Commission responded to the rescissions immediately, applying to yet another federal agency, as reported in the *Denver Post*: "The Colorado Civil Rights Commission Thursday accused the Denver Public Schools of treating minority group students unfairly, and asked for a federal investigation." James A. Reynolds, director of the commission, sent a letter to Leon E. Panetta, director of the federal civil rights office within HEW, asking for an investigation of what he called *de facto* segregation in Denver schools. The commission noted that thirty-five schools in Denver had enrollments with more than 50 percent minority pupils: "In the commission's judgment the Denver Public School system is failing to provide equal educational opportunities in the schools which are attended primarily by minority group children." The commission noted high dropout rates and an "inordinately" large number of inexperienced teachers assigned to such schools. The complaint was made under Title 6 of the Civil Rights Act of 1964, which forbids racial discrimination in federally assisted programs, including education. "The ultimate penalty if discrimination is found would be withdrawal of federal aid to Denver [schools]," the spokesman said. The district that year was receiving about $5.3 million in federal aid.[42]

The Southwest Denver Human Relations Council, a group of several hundred predominantly white people in favor of integration, wrote a letter to the secretary of HEW asking the department to intensify efforts to desegregate the schools.[43] Fred Thomas, the equal employment opportunities officer at the Air Force Finance Center, was the author of another petition of complaint addressed to Panetta at HEW. He petitioned HEW to take action to enjoin the school board from carrying out the rescissions. The petition had approximately 300 signatures. These actions were taken under Title 4 of the Civil Rights Act of 1964, which would put the petition in the hands of the attorney general.[44]

East High seniors rebuked those school board members who opposed integration at their graduation ceremony: "All three senior speakers challenged the school board members sitting in front of them—two considered by the students to be at best lukewarm on school integration—to get with it." Twenty-five or more students handed personal letters to the board members "urging them to act more positively to maintain racial integration at East and in its community."[45]

Denver's new mayor, William McNichols, under pressure to do something about the rescissions, said the city had no right to interfere with the policies of the Board of Education. He declined to comment on the board's action rescinding integration, and he said the city could contribute to integration through dispersed housing and urban renewal and model cities.[46]

As a family, we had our own response to the election and the rescissions of the plans to integrate the northeast Denver schools. We decided to open-enroll our two school-age children in Hallett Elementary, a northeast Denver school with mostly Black children, which would require about a thirty-minute bus ride. After attending kindergarten and first and second grades at Dora Moore, Sarah would be in third grade, and Ted would be in first grade. Hallett had many open-enrolled white children whose parents had been supporters of integration and the Benton-Pascoe campaign. Integration efforts were targeted to that one elementary school.

There were mixed reactions to open enrollment after the rescissions. Gil Cruter, the school community relations director and a Black person, said, "I think there is a feeling of rejection . . . And I think then the crystallization probably took place at the time the board made the decision to rescind. People said, 'They don't want us.'" The parents most active in the voluntary busing for Hallett tended to be disappointed supporters of failed school board candidates Benton and Pascoe. "I have vacillated up and down," said Ruth Weiner, whose elementary children took the bus to Hallett that spring. "We were all involved in the Benton-Pascoe campaign, and you want to say, 'Oh, the hell with it. I'll send my kid to school three blocks down the street.'" Active parent Carolyn Etter said, "Let Southworth and Perrill come up with the volunteers they say they have." She also said she was waiting to see if an expected suit against the school board would restore the compulsory integration steps.[47]

Though some people expected a quick resolution of the *Keyes* case, that was not to be. But there was an immediate trial on the temporary injunction to prevent the rescissions of Resolutions 1520, 1524, and 1531 and to implement the plans to desegregate northeast Denver in the fall. The first court action, a hearing on the injunction, had a major, long-lasting effect on the outcome of the case.

6

The First Court Hearing

The evidence in the *Keyes* case was so extensive and the actions of the school board so flagrantly racially motivated that the lawsuit was in large part won for the plaintiffs at the first hearing. This was the consequence of the great amount of preparation by the plaintiffs' attorneys and the years of research by George Bardwell and Paul Klite.

Judge William E. Doyle

The plaintiffs were fortunate that Judge William E. Doyle was assigned to their case, for a number of reasons: among other things, he eventually became sympathetic to their cause and he was a careful, thoughtful man. Doyle, who had been appointed in 1961 by President John F. Kennedy, came from a humble Denver background. His father, William R. Doyle, was a teamster for the Tivoli Brewing Company, and his mother, Sarah Harrington, was the daughter of a laborer. Doyle was selling newspapers by the time he was eight. While at West High School he was named to the all-city football

https://doi.org/10.5876/9781646422906.c006

team as a tackle. He worked throughout high school and college and then put himself through George Washington University Law School in Washington, DC, working as a guard in the Senate Office Building. While he was in law school, he met his wife, Helen Roberta Sherfey, another law student. He worked briefly for his brother-in-law, John S. Carroll, who was married to his older sister, Dorothy Doyle Carroll, and then served as deputy district attorney. In 1942, Doyle joined the US Army and saw action in the North African Campaign and in Italy, France, and Germany before being commissioned as a second lieutenant while in Germany at the end of the World War II. According to John Carroll's granddaughter, Sheila Macdonald, during the war Carroll arranged for a desk job for her great-uncle Bill in Italy. Carroll was a major because when he saw that war was coming, he had joined the army in the late 1930s to go in as an officer. After the war, Doyle returned to private practice.[1]

In 1952, Doyle ran unsuccessfully for the Colorado Supreme Court, but he was more successful in running John Carroll's race for the US Senate in 1956. Then he ran again for the Colorado Supreme Court in 1958 and won.[2] According to Macdonald, he always felt he was under a cloud because he was appointed to the Federal District Court while his brother-in-law was a US senator. Doyle, she said, was very sweet to Sheila and her siblings but tougher on his own children.

Someone put a bomb on Judge Doyle's porch in 1968. Later, some people mistakenly assumed that the bomb was a response to his role in the *Keyes* case, but the incident occurred before Doyle was assigned the desegregation case and had received criticism for his role in it. During the *Keyes* case, he received many threats. As soon as their daughter was married, Doyle's wife, Helen, a brilliant lawyer, moved to Florida, where Doyle visited her twice a year. They never divorced, for reasons that were "totally religious. Uncle Bill didn't want to admit he failed at that," Sheila said. She saw him often because he came to her grandparents' house every night.[3]

Judge John Kane praised Doyle's writing in his biography of the judge. About the opinions in the *Keyes* case, Kane said, "His numerous opinions in the sisyphean school desegregation case of *Keyes v. School District No. 1, Denver, Colorado* are exemplars of judicial craftsmanship."[4] Doyle earned another degree, a master's in economics, before his death in 1986 at age seventy-five.

FIGURE 6.1. Judge William E. Doyle, judge of the Federal District Court, where he supervised the *Keyes* case, and then of the Tenth Circuit Court of Appeals. Picture courtesy of Sheila Macdonald.

Preparations for the Trial

The preparation for the first court hearing was intense, as described by Craig Barnes: "Two days before trial, Gordy [Gordon Greiner, the lead attorney] and I worked through the whole night preparing arguments, lists of questions for witnesses and cross-examination, copies of exhibits, opening argument, and briefs on the law. Gordy was the primary brief writer; I was his lieutenant."[5] The attorneys benefited from the research George Bardwell had been doing for years. He sometimes knew more about the schools than did the school staff. Some weeks before the trial Bardwell had been in the school superintendent's office asking for certain records concerning teacher assignments. When the superintendent said they didn't keep those records, Bardwell said, "Oh, yes, you do, they are right there on that shelf, in the red book behind you." And they were there.[6]

Bardwell, according to his son Andrew, was committed to a meritocracy and opposed to inheritance of privilege and status. He was deeply committed to work that created value and a higher quality of life for everyone. The court relied on his statistics right up until the district reached unitary status (in 1995).[7]

The Testimony for the Plaintiffs

The hearing on the complaint and temporary injunction started on July 16, 1969, just two months after the end of the Benton-Pascoe campaign. The request for a temporary injunction related to the first cause of action in the suit, which was the rescission of the three resolutions designed to integrate the schools at all levels in northeast Denver. These rescissions were a serious error by the new board majority because they were easily proven to be an egregious act of *de jure* segregation, that is, state action to create and enforce segregation. The plaintiffs also asked the court to prohibit the board from canceling the order for twenty-seven buses or destroying the plans to carry out integration in northeast Denver in the fall. Thus, the argument in this hearing related only to the desegregation of the northeast Denver schools and other schools affected by that plan. The extensive data and exhibits of the plaintiffs were all based on publications of Denver Public Schools (DPS) or US Census data, as the defendants learned every time they unsuccessfully challenged the data. Both the census data and the school attendance zones were critical in demonstrating that as the Black population moved east, the district boundaries were moved east to ensure that Blacks were kept in segregated schools.[8]

Hundreds of hours of preparation were put in by Gordon Greiner, Robert Connery, Craig Barnes, Lawrence Treece, Edwin Kahn, George Bardwell, and Paul Klite. The plaintiffs sent seventy-three exhibits to the defendants' attorneys half a week before the trial and forty-six more exhibits the night before it started. On the day of the trial, the defendants were clearly overwhelmed. In fact, some people believed the key to the whole proceeding was the number and quality of the exhibits. The judge was also surprised by the number of exhibits. At one point he said, "I think, though, we ought to make an inquiry about where we are going here. Have you changed your plans? Have you now decided to throw everything but the kitchen sink into this hearing, or including the sink?"[9]

Barnes described the judge's early reaction to their request: "When Greiner said the plaintiffs wanted the judge to mandate the reinstatement of the three resolutions[,] Judge Doyle sat back, skeptical, but he listened. He dropped his white head in his hands and looked at Gordon cautiously, but he let the argument go forward. After about an hour it became clear he was going to let us go to our evidence."[10]

Greiner's first witness was school board member Rachel Noel, whose daughter had attended the integrated Park Hill Elementary School but was then forced by redrawn boundaries to go to the segregated Barrett School. Connery described her testimony:

> She was spectacular. Her grace, poise, and utter sincerity infused the entire courtroom. She testified on her kids' experience at the integrated Park Hill Elementary School, her daughter's assignment to the new and segregated Barrett Elementary School, and the effect on her daughter's education of doing in fifth grade what she had already done in fourth grade at Park Hill Elementary School. She also spoke with simple eloquence of the isolation of Black students resulting from school board actions over several years, the resulting segregation of Black students at Stedman, Hallett, and Smith Elementary Schools, and the effect that segregation was having on Park Hill and Phillips Elementary Schools, Smiley Junior High School, and East High School . . . Judge Doyle, who had grown up in West Denver, was largely unaware of these developments. He listened with rapt attention in a hushed courtroom.

Rachel also described the Noel Resolution, passed in 1968 after the assassination of Martin Luther King Jr.[11]

Rachel said the advisory council appointed by the board in 1966 "came to the conclusion that no schools should be built in northeast Denver until plans are developed to implement . . . consideration of the ethnic and racial characteristics of the school population." Later she added that "the neighborhood schools had resulted in [racial] concentration" and "reduction of this concentration should be considered in the location of new schools."[12]

Next, Barnes put on former board member Ed Benton, who had helped write the Noel Resolution and had supported the desegregation plans that were rescinded by the new board. Those plans, Ed said, would have changed Barrett from 100 percent Black to 80 percent white and Smiley from 70–75 percent minority to 70–75 percent white and would have improved integration at Park Hill and Phillips Elementary Schools and at East High School.[13] He also said that problems at Smiley Junior High were constantly brought before the board, as well as problems of segregation: "The educational disadvantages of segregated education were always urged by . . . certain members of the Board as a basis for modifying Board policy."[14] Because the three resolutions did not involve all segregated schools in the district, Ed said, they were "not a drastic step forward."[15]

In further testimony, Paul Klite, using maps, overlays, and graphs he had created, showed the segregatory effect of the recent board rescissions. Exhibit 7 showed the effects of Resolution 1520. The overlay, 7A, showed the effect of the resolution on East, South, and George Washington High Schools. Exhibit 8 had the same kind of information for the eleven junior highs affected by the resolutions. 8A was an overlay for the junior highs. Exhibits 9 and 9A were similar maps of elementary schools, showing how Black schools were to be integrated with new white children and white schools were to be integrated with more Black children.[16]

School board member James Voorhees testified about his conversion from an anti-integration position to a pro-integration one (see chapter 2): "I think based upon what I have observed and found out[,] the probabilities of equal opportunity are reduced and may be entirely eliminated in racially or ethnically segregated schools." He also cited the release of single-school test scores that revealed the close correlation between schools for minority children and low achievement on the one hand and schools for white children and high achievement on the other.[17]

George Bardwell testified on the effect of boundary changes in Park Hill and the discriminatory assignment of teachers based on race in the minority schools affected by the rescissions. The exhibits also showed the greater experience of teachers in white schools compared with those in minority schools. In addition, the district assigned Black teachers to majority Black schools, so that Barrett, a predominantly Black school, had 52.6 percent Black teachers and Stedman, another predominantly Black school, had 21.1 percent Black teachers while only 8.5 percent of all Denver teachers were Black. Similarly, sixty of the eighty Hispanic or Black teachers were at largely Black Smiley and Cole Junior High Schools. This information was introduced to show that the school board identified these schools as Black or Hispanic schools. The complex testimony was presented clearly through the many maps and graphs of Bardwell and Klite.[18]

Bardwell testified that when Barrett opened its doors in 1960, it was 89 percent Black, although it was across Colorado Boulevard from Stedman elementary school, which was 18 percent over capacity with a majority white population.[19]

The capstone of Bardwell's testimony was the introduction of his segregation index, which explained the mathematical calculation in two attached pages (see appendix A). Particularly useful throughout the course of this lawsuit, the segregation index was created by Bardwell to gauge whether a particular school was segregated. Another important use was in comparing desegregation plans to see their overall effects on desegregation. It was based on the deviation in white membership of each school from the Denver mean. Schools with a very low percentage of whites and schools with a very high percentage of whites would both be considered segregated. The scores could range from 0, indicating total desegregation, to 100, indicating total segregation.[20]

Bardwell's charts showed the segregation index of each high school, junior high school, and elementary school in two ways: with the implementation of Resolutions 1520, 1524, and 1531 and without those resolutions if the board rescissions were allowed to take effect. If the desegregation resolutions were reinstated, the segregation index for the three high schools would be reduced from 50 to a low 28, for the junior highs it would be reduced from 65 to about 35, and for the elementary schools it would decrease from 60 to 43.[21] Though the formula was not easy to understand, this was a measure the plaintiffs and the court found useful for years to come.

The last witness on the second day of the trial was Dr. Dan Dodson, professor of education at New York University. He noted the damage segregation does to children, a detrimental effect that varied little whether it was caused by *de jure* or *de facto* segregation:[22] "It is a moot question concerning the *de facto* versus *de jur[e]* . . . because all children are assigned by public school bodies to schools they attend unless it's voluntary open enrollment.

You can get the same segregated pattern from both." He added that segregated schools tend to have lower achievement test scores. Minority children in such schools "fall back half a year per year on the standard norms." He also cited the low expectancy of the community, teachers, and children in such schools.[23]

When the plaintiffs finished presenting their case, the defendants moved to dismiss the plaintiffs' motion for an injunction because they had "produced absolutely no evidence of segregation as that term is known in the law of the United States today." The defendants also claimed that the "evidence has shown that up to 1964, they [the district] followed a colorblind policy." The judge denied the motion.[24]

The Testimony for the Defendants

When the trial resumed on Monday, Howard Johnson, the deputy superintendent of Denver Public Schools, agreed that a racial balance in the faculty was desirable in all schools but that such a goal wasn't mentioned in the district principles about teacher assignment. Greiner asked him if district policy required school faculties to be well balanced in terms of experience, to which Johnson replied "yes." Then Greiner asked, "Then why are there so many inexperienced or less experienced teachers in such black schools as Smiley and Cole, Barrett and Stedman?" Johnson blamed that on the teachers' agreement, which gave current teachers the chance to fill all vacancies before jobs were opened to outsiders.[25] (Experienced teachers did not usually request transfers to Black schools.) When Johnson said the district was trying to reduce the number of Black teachers in minority schools, Greiner pointed out that it had not been very successful. In 1965, Hallett had had one Black teacher and in 1968 it had three. Barrett, which was mostly Black, had eight Black teachers in 1965 and now had ten. Smiley, which was increasingly Black, had ten in 1965 and now had twenty-three. Predominantly Black Cole had twenty-seven Black teachers in 1965 and now had thirty-one. Johnson agreed that the numbers were generally correct.[26]

Johnson was asked about voluntary open enrollment and the request of southeast Denver parents that the principals send a letter asking parents to volunteer their children to attend Hallett. If 300 white students volunteered to go to Hallett and 300 Black students volunteered to go out of Hallett to southeast Denver elementary schools, the voluntary transfers would go through. The district refused to encourage the integration effort by sending the letter. Johnson had met with the parents, who included Barnes, one of the attorneys for the plaintiffs.[27]

Greiner established that when Traylor Elementary School opened and the district had about 500 spaces in southeast Denver at University Park, Cory, and Asbury Elementary Schools, it did not relieve crowding at largely Black Smith Elementary by busing those children to southeast Denver. Smith had twelve mobile units and was overpopulated by approximately 350 children.[28]

Greiner showed in many ways that the district's efforts to integrate were feeble even though Policy 1222-C called for creating a heterogeneous school community. At George Washington High, prior to the policy there were nine Black students. After the optional area was eliminated, there were twenty to twenty-five. Greiner pointed out the failure of these efforts in this exchange.

> Q: It went from nine to 20 and this was a boundary change that you be-
> lieve contributed to the heterogeneous school community, is that right?
> A: Yes, sir.
> Q: No further questions.[29]

On the last day of the hearing, July 22, Greiner established that no mobile units were used at several overcrowded white schools; nor were white children at overcrowded schools bused to Black schools. Efforts to promote voluntary open enrollment were feeble, and families had not yet heard whether they were accepted for the coming September.

Robert D. Gilberts read statistics from the DPS *Review* showing that the plan under the rescinded resolutions would have provided integration for 10,102 elementary pupils in twenty-two schools by the reassignment of 2,001 additional pupils. By comparison, the new Gilberts Plan was weak. One complex, Complex 5, was 97 percent minority. Integration under the board's new resolution, Gilberts said, was to be entirely voluntary in the paired schools outside of the complexes.[30]

Dr. Richard Koeppe, the assistant superintendent, was questioned by Greiner about voluntary open enrollment. The questions revealed that the district had made little effort to publicize or recruit volunteers.[31]

The Plaintiffs' Closing Argument

In his closing argument, Greiner clearly laid out his case. He reminded the judge of the salient points in the plaintiffs' testimony: "May it please the Court, counsel, several days ago I stood here and presented plaintiffs' opening statement. In that statement I told the Court that this was a *de jure* case; that this defendant school board and this defendant school district by affirmative acts and by the refusal to act, had isolated and confined the Negro students of Denver in the schools of northeast Denver and had segregated them in those schools."[32] The rescissions would have segregated such schools as Barrett and Smiley and left schools such as Phillips, Park Hill, and East more vulnerable to further segregation, according to Greiner.

Greiner said the district had effected an affirmative segregative act: Barrett was built in 1960, and the boundaries were drawn to serve Black children but to minimize the number of white children. The eastern boundary was the edge of the Barrett school playground on Colorado Boulevard and excluded whites who lived east of Colorado. It opened at 88 percent Black and at the time of the hearing had just one white child.

And, he said, the district demonstrated a refusal to act: in 1962, boundary changes were proposed to relieve overcrowding for every school in northeast Denver except Stedman. In 1966, some busing was proposed, but Stedman was still overcrowded. Immediately after the boundary changes in 1964, Hallett went from 40 percent Black to 40 percent white and became a segregated school. At the time of the hearing it was 85 percent Black.

Greiner cited the discriminatory use of mobile units. By 1966, twenty-seven of the twenty-eight mobile units were in northeast Denver in majority Black schools. As Rachel Noel observed, these mobile units, like new construction, made room for more segregation. While pupils were moved around in southeast Denver to relieve overcrowding, the children at Smith and Stedman stayed in overcrowded schools with mobile units.

The assigning of minority teachers to minority schools, Greiner added, appeared to be worse than it was when studied in 1964. With another segregative action the optional attendance zones, which were used by some whites to escape transitional schools, were quickly replaced by limited open enrollment in 1964. Optional attendance areas were sometimes used as the vehicle of white flight from areas that were becoming Black.

Board policy statements, Greiner added, contrasted with board actions. Concern about *de facto* segregation was expressed at the same meeting at which Hallett was made 60 percent Black. Optional zones were also abandoned then, but they were replaced with limited open enrollment. A policy to use busing to relieve overcrowding was passed in 1964, but when Traylor opened, no relief was given to more than 400 Black students in mobile units in northeast Denver. The presence of concentrations of Black teachers was against board policy, but such concentrations had increased. When parents tried to create a meaningful program between minority Hallett and white University Park Elementary Schools, they were refused assistance by the administration. Under a resolution passed in 1964, boundary changes were to be made to achieve a heterogeneous community, but the change at George Washington High cited by Johnson added only 100 Black students and 200 white students to Washington, which was still 95 percent white.

In closing, Greiner cited the Supreme Court decision in *Brown*:

Under *Brown*, the issue in this case is intent . . .

Now, in the face of all these affirmative acts and in the absence of any valid justification for those acts on educational premises, and the defendants have been silent in that regard here, what other intent can possibly be inferred other than to segregate and confine these children by race? Without this injunction we will have [Resolution] 1533, voluntary busing instead of mandatory busing, segregated Barrett and Smiley rather than integrated schools. Dr. Dodson testified that the harm which children suffer in segregated schools is the same whether by *de facto* or *de jure* segregation. But it is clear now that this was *de jure* segregation controlled by [the] finding in *Brown v. Board of Education*. There the court said, "To separate them from others of similar age and qualifications solely because of their race generates a feeling of inferiority as to their status in the community that may affect their hearts and minds in a way unlikely ever to be undone."[33]

The Defendants' Closing Argument

Benjamin Craig argued for the defendants that the status quo, which the injunction would return to, was not the three resolutions integrating the schools in northeast Denver that had been rescinded on June 9 because the lawsuit wasn't filed until June 19. Therefore, the status quo would be the new resolution on voluntary open enrollment, 1533. Craig said the plaintiffs were really mandating the implementation of 1520, 1524, and 1531, which he said was the ultimate issue in the case. This would be a decision on the merits and not a maintenance of the status quo.

Plaintiffs in their brief admitted that their theory presented a novel question: "They argue that once a segregatory effect of an action is shown, the burden of showing justification shifts to the defendants." The plaintiffs, Craig argued, have shown no evidence that the board intended to cause damage to pupils due to their race.[34] He also argued that the plaintiffs had a remedy in voluntary open enrollment and that the rescinded resolutions were never implemented.

Greiner repeated that the plaintiffs were complaining about reversal of the three resolutions, 1520, 1524, and 1531, and that if the rescissions were unconstitutional, 1533 should not continue in force. This brought a sharp exchange between Greiner and Doyle:

> THE COURT: Then what you want is really a mandatory injunction requiring them to carry out 1520, 1524 and 1531?
>
> MR. GREINER: I believe that's correct, Your Honor.
>
> THE COURT: I haven't got the power to do that.
>
> MR. GREINER: Oh, sure, you do.
>
> THE COURT: No, I don't. I have the power to enjoin. And I suppose they can come up with a new resolution, "1550," and if it were constitutional, why, it would be all right. I can't tell them what kind of a plan that they should adopt . . .
>
> MR. GREINER: We have asked, Your Honor, that the defendants be prevented and restrained from in effect implementing 1533. That's what we asked.
>
> THE COURT: To the extent it voids 1520, 1524, and 1531?
>
> MR. GREINER: That's correct.[35]

Judge Doyle Rules

Judge Doyle's oral ruling came out on July 23. Allowing a ten-day stay for appeal, he ordered the Denver Board of Education to restore the integration plans it had rescinded following the board election. He said the evidence presented "shows a high degree of probability the plaintiffs will succeed" in the full trial. The board could appeal, he stated.

In the written memorandum on July 31, Doyle forced the school board to put into effect plans for integration in the coming fall.[36] He said there was no dispute as to the propriety of this being a class action or whether the court had jurisdiction. The temporary injunction sought by the plaintiffs was to enjoin the school board from "modifying the purchase order for school buses, destroying documents relating or pertaining to the implementation of Resolutions 1520, 1524, and 1531 and, thirdly, from taking any action making any communications to faculty, staff, parents or students during the pendency of the suit which would make it impossible or more difficult to proceed with the implementation of Resolutions 1520, 1524, and 1531."[37] The defendants, he said, maintained that the segregation grew out of the neighborhood character of the schools.

Judge Doyle reviewed the evidence presented in the hearing. He particularly cited the fact that Barrett Elementary School had been built in a location where it would be predominantly segregated when it opened. He also cited two study committees that had recommended efforts to integrate in the placing of schools and determining boundaries. Then he reviewed the Noel Resolution calling for efforts to integrate the school population "so as to achieve equality of educational opportunity"[38] and the three resolutions affecting elementary, junior, and senior high schools in northeast Denver.

In his additional findings, he pointed out that the advice of the two study committees had been ignored. No effective action had been taken to desegregate; in fact, many of the board's actions intensified the segregation. Teachers had been assigned by race, with most Black teachers assigned to predominantly Black schools. Less experienced teachers were entrenched in minority schools. Adding eight classrooms at Hallett had the effect of concentrating Black students there, and twenty-eight of twenty-nine mobile units were at Black schools, further concentrating the Black student population.

The judge referred to Bardwell's segregation index to measure the effect of the rescinded resolutions: the index of the senior high schools in question would have decreased from 50 to 28, that of the junior high schools from 65 to 35, and the index of the elementary schools from 60 to 43. Thus, these schools would have been much less segregated if the resolutions were implemented. In rescinding the resolutions the board "acted officially to reject the integration effort and to restore and perpetuate segregation in the area. Although this was carried out in response to what was called a voter mandate, there can be no gainsaying the purpose and effect of the action as one designed to segregate."[39]

In a section titled "The Applicable Law," Judge Doyle began with the Equal Protection Clause of the Fourteenth Amendment and then reviewed related cases. The Fourteenth Amendment, he pointed out, "forbids state action which results in unreasonable classifications and deprivations. It prohibits arbitrary classifications which bear no rational relation to any valid governmental purpose."

In *Brown v. Board of Education*:

> The Court plainly stated that segregated schools are incapable of providing quality education and also said that the effect of segregation in the school system was to place an indelible stamp of inferiority on these Negro children who were compelled to attend "Negro" schools.[40]
>
> Many cases impose an affirmative duty on the School Board to take positive steps to remove that segregation *which has developed as a result of its prior affirmative acts* [original emphasis]. In response to this duty, the Denver School Board passed Resolutions 1520, 1524, and 1531. In light of *Brown* and *Dowell*, the effort of the Board to renounce this constitutional duty by rescission must be rejected as arbitrary state legislative action.[41]

Doyle responded to the defendants' claim that they were only doing what the majority of the voters wanted: "The constitutional protections afforded by the Bill of Rights and the Fourteenth Amendment were designed to protect fundamental rights, not only of the majority but of minorities as well, even against the will of the majority. The effort to accommodate community sentiment or the wishes of a majority of voters, although usually valid and desirable, cannot justify abandonment of our Constitution." In his conclusion he said the citizens of the United States "have the right to be protected from official action of state officers which deprives them of equal protection of the laws by segregating them because of their race." He called the new board majority' rescission action "precipitate" after ten years of study before the plans were adopted.[42]

The motion for preliminary injunction was granted.[43]

The *Denver Post* reported the practical effects of the injunction: Doyle's decision restored plans to integrate East High School with transfers between East and George Washington and South High Schools, making East 70 percent white; it called for the transfer of about 550 pupils from Hill Junior High to Smiley and busing about 850 Smiley pupils to several white junior highs. The ruling would make Smiley 72 percent white instead of 72 percent Black. Busing and boundary changes would increase white enrollment at Park Hill and Phillips Elementary Schools, and 275 students from predominantly Black Cole Junior High would go to predominantly white schools. This wouldn't integrate Cole, but it would provide room for more educational programs.[44]

The pro-integration forces in the community were overjoyed at the decision. There could not have been a clearer ruling in their favor. Judge Doyle had been persuaded by the voluminous and carefully developed testimony that took years to generate. Bardwell expressed the jubilation in a letter to the United States Commission on Civil Rights: "Five days ago the Court handed down a decision which upheld our position in every detail, so that a somewhat euphoric condition pervades the 'integrationist' camp here in Denver."[45]

The Denver Board of Education immediately asked the federal appeals court for "a stay of execution of the preliminary order to restore integration plans in the fall," promptly filing its request for a stay with the Tenth Circuit Court of Appeals. Arguments were to be heard before a panel of judges the following Monday.[46]

The plaintiffs' victory was short-lived because the court of appeals quickly overturned the temporary injunction and sent the case back to the district court. A three-judge panel in the Tenth Circuit, Chief Judge Alfred P. Murrah, Jean S. Breitenstein, and Joseph J. Hickey, heard the arguments and ruled on August 5, vacating the district court order. The court of appeals wanted Judge Doyle to consider the Civil Rights Act. In a hearing before Judge Doyle on August 7, Greiner argued that the Civil Rights Act provision didn't apply to the Denver case. It only applied to *de facto* segregation, whereas Doyle found the district's legislative acts had resulted in *de jure* segregation. The two federal appellate courts that had previously considered the Civil Rights Act said it did not apply to cases of segregation caused by laws (and thus it didn't apply to *de jure* segregation). Victor Quinn argued for the school board that many schools in the plans were segregated, but not by board action. Doyle reminded him that he was ignoring the rescission of the integration plans.[47]

The attorneys argued over what was the status quo, which the Denver Board of Education said was the situation *after* the rescission. Greiner asserted that it was the plan before the rescission when teachers and students were notified of the schools they would be assigned to and schedules were drawn up for the new schools; these plans were never changed.[48] The court of appeals had granted a crucial motion to return the case to Judge Doyle immediately rather than after a twenty-one-day delay. The time was critical because both sides had said August 15 was the last day the school administration could change plans for that fall for the 3,900 students affected.[49]

Judge Doyle again ordered a temporary injunction on August 14, 1969.

Meanwhile, as the decisions were either for or against the resolutions, the children and the parents of the children who were to be bused but then were not to be bused thought again that they were going to be bused in September. But there was more uncertainty as the defendants again appealed the injunction to the court of appeals, where it was again overturned and immediately appealed to the United States Supreme Court.

During the trial on the injunction, Benton's friends organized a large dinner to recognize his eight years of pro-integration work on the board. A letter circulated that night from the campaign committee thanking all those who had helped support the "principles advanced by Ed Benton and Monte Pascoe." The event was the same night the first man landed on the moon. I recall going behind the draped head table to see one fuzzy black-and-white TV set that showed this remarkable event. The committee members who attended were Mrs. Helen Amter, Gladys Bates, Bea Hall, Ruby Kirk, Rachel Noel, Martha Radetsky, and Ginny Rockwell.[50]

Monte received the Martin Luther King Humanitarian award from the Church of the Black Cross for fighting to make quality integrated education available to all students a short time later.[51]

Denver lost one of its Black integration leaders when Rev. Jesse R. Wagner, co-chairman of Citizens for One Community, was reassigned to Detroit by his church. He held his last service at Park Hill Seventh-day Adventist Church in August 1969. He was going to a Black Detroit, Michigan, neighborhood with a population of 700,000, where he would be "combatting the ghetto merchants who charge high prices for inferior goods. Wagner had moved from the back to the front of the buses in the South; he'd integrated Alabama lunch counters. He lived in an actively integrated neighborhood. And he'd tried to desegregate the schools." Wagner said Denver's Black population had not believed that Denver was a racist city until the school board election and the reversal of integration plans, something no other city had done. He believed that since the school board had done nothing to improve the inner-city schools that had the lowest achievement, Black people now thought they should run their own schools. He commented, "If this city couldn't make the commitment, then what people could? . . . I am no longer needed . . . It is now a legal struggle."[52]

7

The United States Supreme Court

After Judge Doyle again issued an injunction restoring the three integration resolutions, the defendants again appealed to the Tenth Circuit Court of Appeals, and on Wednesday, August 27, the appeals court again stayed the injunction and decided that the integration plans should wait until the full hearing of the case on its merits.[1] The appeals court ruled against the district court injunction except for the part requiring the school board to keep the equipment, documents, writings, and memoranda necessary to implement the integration plans in the future, and it argued that it needed more time to carefully consider the complex and lengthy case. It also declared that *Brown v. Board of Education* had only required desegregation "with all convenient speed," misquoting the United States Supreme Court, which had instead called for "all deliberate speed."[2]

Late that day, Robert Connery received a call from the clerk of the court of appeals, who told him that Judge Doyle's injunction had been overturned by the appeals court for a second time. There was a sense of urgency because the schools were to open the following Tuesday after the Labor

https://doi.org/10.5876/9781646422906.c007

Day holiday. Thirty-nine hundred children were uncertain about where they would be going to school as the rulings changed again and again. According to Connery, the plaintiffs' attorneys had expected the court of appeals' stay, so they were ready to appeal to the United States Supreme Court to ask it to stay the Tenth Circuit's anticipated action and reinstate the injunction. The appeal just needed a little modification to respond to the court of appeals ruling.[3]

Gordon Greiner and Craig Barnes had escaped the tension of waiting for the court of appeals decision by going fishing near Glenwood Springs, Colorado. They learned the news on the car radio and called Connery from a gas station. He had already picked up the opinion; revised their motion; and copied, signed, and delivered it to the defendants' attorneys. He was on his way to the airport to fly to Washington, DC, at 9 p.m.[4]

Early the next morning, Connery waited outside the imposing building for the Supreme Court to open. He met a "courtly gentleman" at the door who asked him for the whole story of his case. Later, Connery found out that he was the clerk of the court, John Davis, the distinguished former assistant solicitor general of the United States.[5] Davis began calling justices. The motion to remove the stay on the injunction was addressed to Justice Byron White, who usually covered Colorado cases, but Justice White thought he might have a conflict of interest because he had once represented the Denver school board. (Benton recalls that Justice White was fishing in Colorado at the time he was called.)[6] Justice Thurgood Marshall's wife said that Marshall could not be disturbed (he was trimming roses in his yard). However, Justice William Brennan was in town and agreed to "consider the matter."

Connery conferred with Greiner and Barnes in Denver and with James Nabrit and Conrad Harper of the National Association for the Advancement of Colored People's (NAACP) Legal Defense and Educational Fund in Washington. He incorporated their ideas and filed the supplement to the motion.

On Friday morning, August 29, Connery and Barnes sat in the Supreme Court lawyers' lounge waiting for the opinion. Craig recalled, "Eventually, the school district's lawyers arrived. They were unhappy. They had had to get up at an ungodly hour, write a response brief within minutes, get on the plane, and bring it to Washington, DC, in a highly irregular and unprecedented procedure. They looked sleepless and disgruntled."[7]

Later that day, Justice Brennan ruled that the Tenth Circuit had "supplied no support in law for its action" in staying Judge Doyle's injunction. He said, "An order of a district court granting or denying a preliminary injunction should not be disturbed by a reviewing court unless it appears that the action taken on the injunction was an abuse of discretion." This is particularly strong when the injunction involves constitutional rights.

The district court had found *de jure* segregation in the schools. "The time for mere 'deliberate speed' has run out," he said, quoting an earlier Supreme Court decision. The appeals court provision for time for "developing public support for a plan" could not be used to justify "delay in implementation of the plan."[8] Justice Brennan ordered the reinstatement of the injunction.

As a last-ditch effort, the next day the school board again appealed the decision to the court of appeals, which, not surprisingly, rejected the appeal.[9]

Over the Labor Day weekend, then, just two days before the first day of school, the desegregation plans for northeast Denver schools were reinstated.

8

Desegregation Begins

Despite the United States Supreme Court's ruling, the winners of the school board election continued to oppose the partial desegregation of Denver schools. The *Denver Post* ran quotes from Frank Southworth warning that "the schools are being taken over by 'theorists and educational tinkerers,'" and "he urged concerned citizens to write their congressmen about it." Southworth also warned that the federal courts and certain "ultra-liberals" had imposed their will over the wishes of the majority in the controversy over busing. He continued to assert, "This great nation was founded on the will of the majority" and to claim that there was no conclusive evidence that the quality of education is inferior in schools that don't have racial balance.[1]

On the other side of the struggle, the Park Hill Action Committee honored attorneys Gordon Greiner, Craig Barnes, and Robert Connery, along with Dr. Paul D. Klite and Dr. George Bardwell, who were the key actors in the trial that led to the limited desegregation in northeast Denver.[2]

At the national level, Daniel P. Moynihan, counselor to President Richard M. Nixon, wrote a memorandum on the status of Black people in which

https://doi.org/10.5876/9781646422906.c008

he famously said, "The time may have come when the is[s]ue of race could benefit from a period of 'benign neglect.' The subject has been too much talked about. The forum has been too much taken over to hysterics, paranoids, and boodlers on all sides. We may need a period in which Negro progress continues and racial rhetoric fades."[3] The phrase *benign neglect* was scorned by those who were fighting for racial equality. Moynihan began this memorandum by citing all the "extraordinary progress" Black people had made. However, in the education arena, he pointed out that only 16 percent of Black high school seniors had verbal scores at or above grade level.

In Denver, volunteers who supported integration rushed to prepare for the changes in the three days between the Supreme Court's ruling and the implementation of the desegregation plan. Bardwell and Kay Schomp organized volunteer aides to ride the buses the first week of the desegregation changes. I was one of the thirty-five to forty volunteers, all women as I recall, who met in Schomp's living room the weekend before the beginning of busing, all determined that desegregation would go smoothly and without the violence seen in Little Rock, Arkansas, and other cities. This meeting was organized at the last minute because of the lateness of the Supreme Court order before the start of school. My assignment was to ride the bus with mostly Black junior high students from northeast Denver to a mostly white southeast Denver school. Very early on Tuesday morning I drove to northeast Denver to board a very overcrowded bus, as the district had apparently undercounted the population in that area. I stood at the front of the aisle, nearly pressed against the door with a boisterous and nervously energetic group of teenagers. When we got to Hamilton, I was pleased to see teachers meeting the buses to welcome the new students to this unfamiliar territory. A Black northeast Denver mother drove me back to pick up my car. We repeated this routine every day for a week. Eventually, the bus overcrowding, which we reported to the school district, eased up.[4]

Our children open-enrolled at Hallett Elementary School, a majority Black school, for the 1969–1970 school year. Sarah remembers a family meeting in our living room when she and Ted decided to volunteer to attend the school, although she was only eight and he was only six. She recalls that this meeting took place after Monte and Ed lost the school board election. Sarah understood that "it was the right thing to do." At least we had the certainty of knowing where our children were going, although we did not know what the racial proportions would be when we volunteered. According to a newspaper report, 216 children, mostly white, had chosen to go to Hallett and 151 children, mostly Black, had chosen to go out of the Hallett attendance area to predominantly white schools. The goal was to have 500 children from Hallett choose to go to other schools and the same number of white children from other schools choose to enroll at Hallett, according to William Berge, the new president of the Denver Board of Education. Superintendent Gilberts supported the volunteer plan. He said: "There is a rapidly growing need to 'bridge' the gap in understanding that has developed between segments of our community. The experiences children can have in an integrated setting will contribute in significant ways toward a better education and an improved society. Your willing participation can make integration a constructive and productive experience for both your children and our city. We urge your support and participation."[5]

A February 1970 Denver Public Schools (DPS) publication put the number of open-enrollees into Hallett that year at 221 and those volunteering out of Hallett at 205, far short of the district's announced goals.[6]

We hoped that an integrated experience would be beneficial for our children, though we had no illusion that the entire district could be integrated by volunteers. Many Benton-Pascoe supporters volunteered their children to go to Hallett as well, and the Parent-Teacher Association was a collection of the strongest liberal activists in Denver.

We felt we were brave and our children, who were very young, were braver still to take a bus to another part of town that was predominantly Black and where we did not know anyone in that neighborhood. We could have been accused of using our children to make a political point, but we wanted to demonstrate that integrated schools would provide equal educational opportunity to all. We also believed our children would be better equipped for a multiracial society if they related to people of other races and ethnic groups.

In interviews with my two oldest children forty-five years later, they shared some of their memories of that year. Ted, who was in first grade in a class that was half Black and half white and had a white teacher, doesn't think he had any Black friends. He particularly remembers the bus rides. Of course, the passengers were all white children going into Hallett.

Sarah, who is now a high school teachers' coach herself, fondly remembers Miss Bradley, her third grade teacher. She still remembers that Miss Bradley's father died and the teacher explained to the class that he had led a good life and that life was valuable, depending on how you lived it. Going to school with Black students didn't feel any different to Sarah, but her best new friends that year were other white girls who had open-enrolled.

Sarah complained that the bus ride was long, particularly because it did not go directly to Hallett, which was about twenty minutes from our house at that time; the return trip was extended because of additional drop-offs.

Sarah also can't remember any negative experience there. The Hallett facility was considerably newer than Moore's, and she can't remember if her class was integrated or how many Black students were in the class. She said they sometimes played on the playground with Black students, but most of the time she played with her white girlfriends.

She did not return to Hallett for a second year. She missed her friends at Moore, and she liked the convenience of walking two blocks to school. We expected integration to become policy in the coming year, so we supported her decision and believed the schools would shift to a more equal structure. The following school year, 1970–1971, Sarah and Ted returned to our neighborhood school, Dora Moore.[7]

Although the resolutions applying to northeast Denver had been implemented, from 1969 to 1974 there was a great deal of uncertainty about the court case as it moved through the many appeals and remands, which, if the plaintiffs won, would effectively expand the area to be integrated to the entire school district. Much of Denver was waiting anxiously to see the final outcome.

In December 1969 the *Denver Post* surveyed parents, teachers, and students to see how the plan to desegregate northeast Denver was working. Then, in a series of articles, the newspaper reviewed the situation at each school level. Most reporters then were white, which may have given them a biased view of the situation. The only Black reporter I knew of was the *Denver Post*'s George Brown (a state senator and later lieutenant governor), but I did not find any articles by him on the desegregation plan.

According to the *Post* survey, many parents were pleased with the changes, though they tended to feel the same way about busing as they had before it started. The survey revealed widespread fear and anger in the wake of the court order: "Integration hasn't been smooth . . . in some junior highs. But tensions appear to be receding . . . Several schools have begun to make a conscious effort to help black and white pupils get along. Some realtors see signs of neighborhood stabilization as predicted by advocates of integration." Racial tensions in elementary schools, the survey found, were muted or non-existent for the most part (which differed from surveys of middle and high schools). The main problems in elementary schools centered around the physical job of transporting children to and from school each day. A small number of parents who were bitterly opposed took their children out of public schools.[8]

At the junior high level, however, the writers found that "a social mix hasn't materialized." Students bused from Smiley stuck to their old friends, especially the ninth graders. The seventh and eighth graders did more mixing. Home meetings of parents were "stilted," partly because some Hamilton Junior High parents had never had a Black person in their homes. Some had never spoken to a Black person. Though some social interaction would have been beneficial, the purpose of desegregation was to provide equal educational opportunity, not necessarily to create social relationships. I found, though, that those ties that did result from desegregation helped bridge the separation between racial groups. Nevertheless, the lack of genuine warmth and "the remembrance of the election last May of anti-busing school board candidates created an awkward situation of real proportions."[9]

Another article, which focused on schools' disciplinary issues with students of color and sometimes revealed teacher bias, reviewed discipline in desegregated schools. The journalists found that teachers had little experience with Black students and some, especially at Hill and Merrill Junior Highs, believed "discipline is 'shot.'" Black students, they said, either "don't give a damn" or "are openly defiant in class." Others said some of their best, most punctual students were Black. On discipline, white students complained early in the year that Black students weren't disciplined because the teachers were afraid of them. According to then-assistant superintendent Dick Koeppe at Place Junior High, one teacher said a Black kid took a full carton of chocolate milk and squashed it on the floor. The teacher related that he was afraid to say anything. A Black parent said, "What do you mean you won't do anything about it?" She wanted her child disciplined just like a white child would have been. The teachers were afraid of Black students because they had little

experience with them.[10] Then, on the other side, many teachers were crack-
ing down on them. Principals admitted that there was a double standard. At
Hill and Merrill, Black students were reportedly most often late to class and
unprepared. Discipline was less of a problem at Grant Junior High due to the
principal's policies—teachers were in the hall during every passing period, a
teacher grapevine reported problems between kids during the day, and the
principal met regularly with an elected representative student committee.

Many of the Black students struggled with the more challenging curriculum, according to the *Denver Post* article, illuminating an issue with the segregated schools themselves: "In the area of curriculum, many Negroes need
tutoring as evidenced in the few on honor rolls. At Thomas Jefferson Junior
High the principal estimated that at least 25 per cent of the Negroes were
having severe academic problems and another 25 per cent were having difficulty. Some schools have altered programs. Merrill did away with 'modified'
[actually, remedial] classes because they were afraid they would be predominantly black."[11]

The DPS central administration offered little help to the schools receiving
new students. Administrator Donald Goe said in an interview, "Administrators
and teachers at the schools were pretty much left to their own resources."[12]
Some administrators were openly racist, including one administration official who told Ed Benton, "We have a serious problem in our schools with the
kinky heads."[13]

During most of the early turmoil over desegregation, Robert Gilberts
was superintendent, but he resigned in March 1970 after being instructed
to prepare a plan to desegregate the schools. William Berge called assistant superintendent Dick Koeppe and asked him to come to his home.
The board had decided to name Howard Johnson superintendent, and he
would do what the board wanted him to do.[14] Koeppe was told he couldn't
be superintendent because he was not political enough. His problem, he
believed, was that he told the truth. He was supportive of the desegregation
efforts, as indicated in the open enrollment of his daughter to Hallett in
1969–1970 and his comment that he felt sorry about Rachel Noel's treatment
by the rest of the board. He wanted to call her, but he knew that if he did,
the administration would find out. In 1972 he became superintendent of the
Cherry Creek School District, though he returned to Denver as superintendent from 1988 to 1990.[15]

Koeppe said there was an atmosphere of "'I'm not sure these black kids can learn.' This was communicated by comments and facial expressions. Discrimination was apparent in underachievement, and in placement of mobile units and inexperienced teachers in minority schools."[16]

He stated that "after the first *Keyes* case court order, Gilberts and I flew to Stanford for a week for ideas for creating another plan to comply with the court order." According to Koeppe: "The message from the board suggested that [we] should not try too hard because the majority of the board didn't really want to do it. It had to be enough of a plan not to be found in contempt of court. It was as if the court and plaintiffs were stepping on the gas and the board was stepping on the brake. You could smell rubber burning. The board wanted a stay of execution. We had to make two plans: one plan for the court, one (less disruptive) plan for the board."[17]

In fall 1970, George Washington High School was integrated under the reinstated resolutions of the court's first ruling, but it did not go smoothly. Fighting broke out among an estimated 150 students after a conflict between two girls in the community room following a "rap session" about problems and grievances, according to the principal, Jack Beardshear.[18] As the rap session ended, a white girl called a fellow student "a Black b—." This exploded into physical violence in the hall, he said. About fifteen students and one teacher were injured and two young men were arrested, one a student and one a non-student.[19]

Just two weeks before school started, 257 students, mostly Black, had been transferred from East High School to George Washington. Washington had had only 126 Black students among 3,000 students the previous year. The principal said, "Two weeks before school started the boundary changes were announced, and here came these kids who didn't want to come here in the first place. They were quite happy where they were and were resentful and hostile when they were told they had to come to George Washington."[20]

An additional problem was transportation, which was not provided by the district. Students could come by private cars or public bus, but they might have to wait some time for a ride both before class and after their classes were over.[21]

To temporarily ease this problem, the district began running a free bus from Monaco Street and 38th Avenue to George Washington before school, returning shortly after school. For a second day, violence broke out when fifteen youths, most non-students, started throwing chairs in the cafeteria.

Several students were injured. School was closed at 12:30 p.m.[22] Koeppe said the teachers were terrified. They had control of the classrooms but not of the lunchroom, the halls, or the parking lot. When the school reopened the following week, the administration put Washington on split session: sophomores in the early half of the day and upper classmen in the afternoon, with no lunch period.[23]

The district held separate meetings for each class and their parents to discuss ways to solve the problems.[24] At a discussion session, Black students told the *Rocky Mountain News* that "at the heart of their discontent is the federal court ruling ordering integration in the Denver Public Schools system." One student said, "The busing plan sounded like a good idea at first . . . but the Denver School Board has shown by fighting it in court they don't want us in these whitey schools. And I don't want to be anywhere I'm not wanted."[25]

In October, the administration was surprised by a third outbreak of violence at George Washington High School when a white off-duty policeman tried to break up a dice game in a stairwell. A Black student allegedly tried to take the policeman's gun from him, at which point he fired two shots in what was reportedly an attempt to summon help. A short time later, a false fire alarm was sounded. A general melee ensued involving many policemen. A *Denver Post* photographer was attacked, and one of his cameras was smashed. He was struck in the ribs with a thrown piece of his smashed camera and sprayed with a chemical. The school nurse treated about forty-five students with injuries, and seven students were arrested, six Black and one white.[26] It is possible that arrests were made with bias. Violence also erupted at West High, and the school was closed for two days. Four firebombs were thrown at the school. There were a few minor injuries, and seven juveniles were arrested. West reopened the following Monday.[27]

At a community meeting at the East Side Action Center in a Black neighborhood, students and parents agreed that the solution at George Washington had to start with removal of the police. Leaders including the Black state senator, George Brown, and the Democratic candidate for the US Congress, Craig Barnes, attended the meeting. The group decided to pressure the school board to remove police from the schools.[28]

Benton recalls the school board meeting that followed these events. Though he was no longer on the board, he proposed that police be removed and that teams of three parents—one Black, one Hispanic, and one white—be placed in each high school. He spoke at the end of the board meeting, and President Berge paid no attention. Benton said, "And I'm going to stay here in this board room until the board adopts this plan." The board adjourned shortly thereafter. A reporter asked him if she had heard him correctly. He repeated, "I'm going to stay in the people's room of the board of the Denver Public Schools." A newspaper picture shows Benton and David Waite, a Denver Community College student; Barry Scoles, vice-head boy at West; and Jules Mondschein still there at 6:30 the next morning.[29]

During the night, when Benton was laying in a hallway trying to get some sleep, someone set off a fire alarm and a fireman tripped over him as he was running down the hall in the dark. Finally, Benton suggested to Brown, a reporter for the *Denver Post* and a state senator, that he call Mayor William McNichols and ask if he would approve the proposal to put teams of parents, as described, in the high schools. Before responding to this request, the mayor got the chief of police, George Seaton, on the phone. The chief approved the plan if he could keep a police car a couple of blocks from the school in case of trouble.[30]

While the first section of the city was experiencing integration under the three reinstated resolutions, the attorneys for both sides prepared for the definitive trial on the merits, which would determine whether the entire school district would be desegregated.

9

The Trial on the Merits

The Plaintiffs' Case

The much anticipated trial on the merits began Monday, February 2, and ran until Friday, February 20, 1970. The plaintiffs described the many ways the Denver school board, by acts of omission and commission, discriminated against and segregated minority children. In response, the defendants claimed that segregation was caused by shifting residential patterns and that the school district, believing Denver had no racial problems, did nothing deliberate either to cause or to avoid segregation.

The Plaintiffs' Opening Argument

Gordon Greiner, lead attorney for the plaintiffs, began his opening statement with a summary of the action related to the temporary injunction. He said the previous summer's cause of action was limited to the school board's rescission of Resolutions 1520, 1524, and 1531 and the schools affected by the rescissions. Those rescissions were found to be evidence of *de jure* segregation, and the three resolutions had been reinstated by the United States Supreme Court.

https://doi.org/10.5876/9781646422906.c009

The current trial, Greiner said, related to the second cause of action concerning all schools in the district. Under this cause of action he laid out two legal arguments. The first was that the district, by affirmative acts or lack of appropriate acts, had maintained racially identifiable, and thus segregated, schools. The second legal argument was based on the existence of unequal educational opportunity in the minority schools, a violation of the Fourteenth Amendment's guarantee of equal protection of the law.[1]

Under the first legal argument about separate schools, he said he would introduce witnesses to testify to the gerrymandering of boundaries, the use of limited open enrollment, and discriminatory use of mobile units—all having the effect of keeping minority students in certain schools and white students in others. The effect of the gerrymandering was to establish boundaries that correlated with racial residential patterns. These changes involved Manual and East High Schools; Smiley, Morey, and Byers Junior High Schools; and Boulevard, Brown, Harrington, Columbine, Stedman, Park Hill, and Barrett Elementary Schools.

Limited open enrollment facilitated the flight of white students from minority schools because in most cases, only white parents and a few middle-class Black parents were able to provide the transportation needed to get their children to schools outside the neighborhood. Students were also overcrowded and attending classes in mobile units in minority schools rather than being moved to nearby white schools where space was available. Of the twenty-nine mobile units in the city, twenty-seven were in minority schools while space existed in southeast and southwest Denver white schools. The concentrating of minority teachers and principals and assistant principals in minority schools made schools even more easily identified by race.[2] Denver Public Schools (DPS) had effectively created a dual system, though Greiner did not use this term, which became more important after the final Supreme Court decision on the case.

To prove his second legal theory, that the minority schools were separate but not equal, Greiner would have witnesses testify to the inferiority of the education provided in minority schools. In those schools, the teachers were less experienced or on probation (in their first three years of teaching), with high turnover. Dropout rates were higher in minority schools, facilities were older or less adequate than those in majority white schools, and there was evidence of lower achievement.[3] The first legal theory related to deliberate systemic segregation of minority students was an effort to prove that Denver had segregated schools, which were prohibited by *Brown v. Board of Education* (1954). The second was based primarily on the much older decision in *Plessy v. Ferguson* (1896), which had allowed separate schools only if they were equal, though that decision was overruled by *Brown*. The second argument was also based on the Fourteenth Amendment guarantee of equal protection of the law.[4]

The relief Greiner sought was "the disestablishment, root and branch, as required by the Supreme Court of segregated racially identifiable schools throughout the schools of this district."[5]

After a question from William Doyle about neighborhood schools, Greiner answered that the case was not about minorities who simply moved into racially separated neighborhoods: "This case will show a series of affirmative acts [by the board] which were designed to and did in fact capture the minority population in these minority schools . . . This is, in the final analysis, still, a *de jure* case."[6]

The Defendants' Opening Argument

William K. Ris, attorney for the school board, said there were two questions in the case: "One, is there an actual denial of equal protection? Secondly, is this denial affirmatively created by the district?" The board only had the duty to make available equal educational opportunity, he said. Judge Doyle said that argument had been rejected by the Fifth Circuit, and the Supreme Court denied cert (that is, refused to take it up).[7]

Ris also complained that much of the data collected by Bardwell and Klite used hindsight, not the conditions at the time. They took census and school board data, "collating it, adding it up and analyzing it and in some instances putting it through computers." Bardwell and Klite's use of computer analysis was indeed dazzling at a time when only academics had access to this powerful tool.[8] When former superintendent Dr. Kenneth Oberholtzer arrived in 1947, he learned that the Colorado Constitution prohibited classification of students by race or color. Some forms still asked principals for the racial composition of their schools, and those data were used by Bardwell, although the board at the time did not have that information. From about 1961–1962 on, the district began to be conscious of race.[9]

Ris said the final finding of the court would be that the minority separation was created by *de facto* segregation. Doyle asked what solutions Ris would offer and he replied "Resolution 1533," which was the resolution adopted at the June 1969 meeting immediately after the three desegregation resolutions were rescinded. Then Doyle said, "In other words, it will be a voluntary open enrollment policy that you suggest will take care of it, eventually?"[10] Judge Doyle and Ris then had this exchange:

> THE COURT: Well, finally, I suppose that everyone can agree that busing is
> a terrible imposition on everybody.
>
> MR. RIS: No question about it.
>
> THE COURT: I don't suppose the minority people like it any better than
> anybody else does. There are parents who worry about what's going
> to happen on the bus, and they are concerned about the time involved
> and everything else . . . And, of course, the record ought to be very
> clear that nobody else does. Sometimes it is put in a context whereby
> I think that the impression gets abroad that busing per se is something
> that everybody wants to achieve. Nothing could be more ridiculous.
> As I say, it's an expedient.
>
> MR. RIS: That's basically the plaintiffs' plan, though; that's their position.
>
> THE COURT: Well, that isn't their philosophy, I don't suppose.[11]

The Plaintiffs' Case

Greiner first had Paul Klite testify, not as an education expert but to intro-duce a number of exhibits he had made that effectively told the story of steps the district took or failed to take to keep Black children in majority Black schools. Klite was a mathematically astute surgeon and a professor at the University of Colorado Medical School. He was a sculptor as well, with an artistic talent that was evident in the many outstanding exhibits he pro-vided. He testified that in 1953, when the new Manual High School opened, it was at 64 percent capacity with 550 empty seats, while neighboring East High School was at 100 percent capacity. The percentage of Black students at Manual was 35 percent and at East, 2 percent.[12] If attendance boundaries had been changed slightly, Manual could easily have been desegregated. The eastern edge of Manual's attendance boundary was only half a block from the school.

There was a parallel situation at the junior high level, Klite testified. In 1951 Cole Junior High School, which was 40 percent Black, was at 70 percent capacity and Smiley, which was 5 percent Black, was at 126 percent capacity. Optional areas were made permanent for Cole, sending the increased Black population to Cole instead of Smiley.[13] Some of the white students overcrowding Smiley could have attended Cole and integrated the school. Instead, a boundary change at the demarcation between Black and white residences sent Black students to Cole and white students to Smiley. The eastern boundary for Cole was just four blocks from the school. (One boundary change was proposed and another actually adopted by the board, as indicated in Exhibit 333, which depicted the change. Exhibits 212 and 212-A showed the boundary changes actually made in 1956.)[14]

When Barrett Elementary School opened, the playground was the eastern boundary of the attendance area; not coincidentally, it was also the eastern boundary of the Black population. Consequently, Barrett was almost entirely Black on the day it opened.

One program the defendants thought of as an effort at desegregation was the Limited Open Enrollment Policy (LOE, Policy 1226-A), but it contained no integration requirement as of September 16, 1966, Klite said. This meant that white students could leave a school with a high Black enrollment to go to another school with a high white enrollment.[15] Greiner carefully established the negligible effect of LOE on integration. Only a total of 267 out of the 50,000 elementary children in DPS participated in it. The maximum number of students who participated in integrating transfers, ones that improved the racial balance in the receiving schools, was 29. Exhibit 89 showed a list of ten schools that were predominantly white, under capacity, which were receiving students by bus but, according to the district, had no spaces for LOE. In fact, these schools had a total of 482 slots to fill before they would reach capacity. At the same time, in contrast, a group of minority elementary schools had announced LOE spaces and did not receive students by bus. They had 203 of the total number of the announced 365 openings in the district. The average white enrollment at those schools was 12 percent.[16]

In another exhibit that indicated that Denver had separate and inferior schools for minority children, Klite compared the achievement of children in the heavily minority Black or Hispanic schools to that of children in the heavily majority white schools.[17] The achievement of students in minority schools was clearly below that of students in white schools.

On Tuesday, February 3, at a meeting in chambers, Doyle asked that neither lawyers nor litigants make comments to the press while the trial was ongoing, which indicated the intense community interest in the case. The lawyers agreed.[18]

In the public testimony that day, Klite continued with extensive material about the disparity in achievement between majority white and majority Black and Hispanic schools. He said that 87 percent of the city's Black students and 78 percent of the city's Hispanic students attended the forty-five schools that scored below the 40th percentile on achievement tests. The twenty-two schools achieving above the 60th percentile were attended by 42 percent of the white children but only 4 percent of the city's Black and Hispanic children. In tests administered at grade level 4.6 (that is, at fourth grade in the sixth month), the average grade-level score in white schools was 5.44, or almost a year above grade level; in minority schools it was 3.58, a year below grade level.[19]

Klite explained the system whereby low expectations were set based on a pretest of the children's IQs. Then, after a composite score at such schools as Cole came in at the 21st percentile, the community was told, "The general situation here is good and the median and Q-3 at expectancy and Q-1 only slightly below it" in the 1956 report. Thus, the achievement test, not surprisingly, merely confirmed the IQ test.[20]

Klite introduced Exhibits 242 to 308, which were computer printouts rating the faculty in each facility by experience to make the case for the inequities between white and minority schools.[21]

The fact that the district did not furnish transportation was an important factor in LOE, Klite asserted. There also had to be space available in the receiving school. There were 266 students on LOE in junior high and 332 in senior high, for a total, including elementary school, of 874. LOE was changed to voluntary open enrollment (VOE) in the second semester of 1968–1969, though as late as 1969 those who had started LOE earlier were allowed to continue. The system was changed in important ways. First, the district provided transportation, and, critically, a student's move had to improve integration at both the sending and receiving schools.[22]

Next, Lorenzo Traylor, an employee of the Urban League, was questioned by Barnes. In late 1955, Traylor learned that the optional areas near

Manual High School were going to become part of the mandatory Manual District and that Cole Junior High School boundaries were affected, and he started investigating. He saw on a map at the DPS office that Manual, with a capacity of 1,600, was under-enrolled, at 1,066; East High, with a capacity of 2,462, was over-enrolled, at 2,558. Gove Junior High, with a capacity of 936, had an enrollment of 883, while Smiley Junior High, with a capacity of 1,446, was over-enrolled, at 1,688. Morey Junior High, with a capacity of 1,478, was grossly over-enrolled, at 2,082. And Cole, with a capacity of 1,900, had an enrollment of only 1,582. He also checked mileage to various schools and found that the changes put students farther away from their schools in some cases. In several community meetings he rebutted the Denver schools' administrators presenting the proposed boundary changes because they made schools more segregated.[23] He believed the changes were discriminatory. Over-crowdedness was not relieved; schools with empty seats still had empty seats. Cole's boundary moved four blocks east, corresponding to the movement of the Black population; both Cole and Smiley became more segregated. Though Morey already had empty seats, the changes were creating more empty seats there. East was over capacity by 96 students and Manual had 534 empty seats, but the movement of the line between the two schools relieved the overcrowding at East by fewer than 50 students. Traylor suggested that students living north of Twenty-ninth Avenue were closer to Manual than to East. Why didn't they bring a large number of white students to Manual and fill the empty seats there, creating integration in Manual and relieving overcrowding at East, he asked. They could take all three junior highs and create empty seats and integration in all three.[24]

Traylor also met with Superintendent Dr. Oberholtzer and others about hiring more Black teachers. At that time, fewer than 30 Black teachers had been hired by DPS. As part of Traylor's job at the Urban League, he referred more than 150 Black teachers to the district. In four years (1952–1956) the number of Black teachers doubled, to 59 or 60.[25]

An attorney for one of the intervenors asked a question that suggests the considerable impact represented by the duo of Bardwell and Klite. He was trying to challenge Klite's expertise as a mathematician. In one of the lighter moments of the trial, Charles F. Brega asked Klite where he had received his training in computers, leading to this exchange:

Q: Did you receive that [training] working with Dr. Klite?

A: I am Dr. Klite.

Q: I mean Dr. Bardwell.[26]

Barnes called Mrs. Ethel G. Rollins to the stand. She was a social worker who, she said, was told by Sydney M. Rhea, the director of social workers, that she would have to leave Barnum School because the faculty, all white, did not want to work with a Black teacher and had not had a chance to vote on her joining the faculty. Nevertheless, she stayed for two years (1965–1967) and then worked for one year at Morey.[27]

A clear contrast between white schools and minority schools was evident in Exhibit 82, titled "The Denver Public Schools Look at Themselves" (1968), which the plaintiffs presented on Wednesday, February 4 (see appendix A for the text of this exhibit [Exhibit A.2]). Gerald P. Cavanaugh, supervisor of testing services for DPS, testified about it. Prior to 1968, the annual publication contained no individual school data, he said. The "level of expectancy" was explained to parents after each of the triennial tests in 1950, 1953, 1956, and 1960. It considered the group's IQ and the time of year the test was given. The parents were told that "the general ability of the group being tested was used to set the expectancy. This is why our expectancy of this school may appear different than the citywide expectancy." (Thus, low expectations were a self-fulfilling prophecy.) As a teacher, Cavanaugh "received no comparative test results with respect to other individual schools." Further, he did not receive such comparative data as a principal at Lincoln Elementary School. He had no citywide average as a guideline.[28]

In 1968, for the first time, the decision was made to publish comparative data—test results from each school in alphabetical order for the grades tested. Before that, comparative results were not published or given to the Denver Board of Education. Asked about the reasons for not publishing them, Cavanaugh said, "It was the philosophy of the administration at the time that this would be detrimental to the *esprit de corps*." They changed the process due to the Colorado Open Records law, passed by the Colorado legislature in 1968.[29] (When they campaigned for the school board in 1969, Ed and Monte had used these school-by-school test scores printed on flip cards as evidence of the unequal education of minority children.)

Regarding another district subterfuge that concealed achievement deficits, Cavanaugh testified that the expectancy level for the 1965 fifth grade tests was "standardized," which had the effect of lowering scores for the highest-achieving schools and raising scores for the lowest-achieving schools. Cavanaugh reported a meeting at Stedman at which he tried to explain the reasons for doing this. As expected, the court had questions about it. Cavanaugh said, "The low-achieving school[s] would have grade points added to their actual scores. The high-achieving school[s] would have grade points subtracted from their actual scores." The test publisher provided tables for this adjustment that made Cavanaugh uncomfortable and that were used for only one year. The factor for each school used to make the adjustments in the fifth grade tests was the students' median IQ.[30] The effect of this "standardization" was that real comparison between schools was impossible.

Greiner called Marlene Chambers, who testified about the lack of district support for a plan of parents from six southeast and southwest Denver schools to focus voluntary open enrollment on Hallett, a majority Black school, and from Hallett to their own neighborhood white schools. They met on December 30, 1968, with Lloyd Jones of DPS and the next day with administrators Howard Johnson and Richard Koeppe. The administrators refused to send a letter to recruit parents for their plan, and they refused to allow parents to volunteer their children for voluntary open enrollment on the condition that Hallett would become a majority white school. The administrators did extend the application deadline a few days beyond January 6, 1969.[31] If 300 white children had volunteered into Hallett and 300 Black children had volunteered out, Hallett would have become 50 percent white. Chambers said the reason the administrators gave for not sending the notice was that "the administration would be promoting voluntary open enrollment for integration, not merely informing the parents that there was such a plan."[32] This evidence of lack of administrative support cast doubt on district claims that it would integrate the schools through voluntary open enrollment.

Palecia Lewis, who is Black, testified about her children's schools and her work promoting open enrollment. She said her son wasn't allowed to transfer from Smiley to Hamilton Junior High School under voluntary busing, even though he was eligible.[33] She was employed in Gil Cruter's office, and there were 170 volunteers helping in the effort. The Smith Elementary School parents voted for mobile units rather than busing children out, she said. She agreed that in 1968, Hallett was about 10 percent white. In September 1969 the white percentage (which included two of our children, in first and third grades) was about 38 percent.[34] This testimony illustrated how difficult it was to recruit volunteers for the program. This was suggested in Judge Doyle's comment to Lewis: "And I think what you're expressing is that there was a hazard that, even if there were non-core-city schools, that your children might be sent to these—the core schools that you mentioned? And [you] were not given any choice about where children went."[35]

Judge Doyle would not allow plaintiffs to extend their case to special education, although Greiner argued that minorities were disproportionately moved into classes for the "educable mentally retarded," where they stayed.[36]

Kay Schomp testified that in September 1962, the junior high boundaries for an area from Sixth to Eighth Avenues, including her home, were changed from Morey to Byers Junior High, with the effect of making Morey more segregated. (Eventually, that change included our children, and Sarah started junior high at Byers.[37] Schomp later became a member of the school board.)

The transcript for Thursday, February 5, the fourth day of the trial, is missing, if it was ever transcribed.[38] According to a newspaper report, the trial that day was devoted to the plaintiffs presenting a massive array of computer printouts, statistical studies, and mathematical probability charts to demonstrate that minority pupils were victims of discrimination and segregation. Bardwell spent six hours on the stand, focused largely on the inferior education provided in minority schools. He showed the concentration of less experienced teachers and the higher dropout rate in minority schools compared to that of white schools, as well as the inadequacy of minority school facilities.[39]

Bardwell also presented census data about the gerrymandering of Morey and Byers Junior Highs, which made Morey more segregated. The area transferred to Morey was 52 percent non-white, while the area transferred out of Morey was 1 percent non-white. In 1961, Morey was estimated to be between 65 and 80 percent white, which after the change in 1962 fell to 45–49 percent white.

Bardwell said the exhibits reflected that there was higher teacher turnover at minority schools because of the frequent assignment of new teachers to replace more experienced teachers transferring out. The plaintiffs showed that minority teachers were consistently assigned to minority schools, which added to their identification as "minority" schools.[40]

The *Denver Post* recognized the tremendous impact of the exhibits prepared by Bardwell and Klite when it noted, "The main actors in the drama thus far, however, aren't the human witnesses but the silent testimony of some 200 maps, charts, overlays, printouts and other material introduced as exhibits in the case."[41]

Thursday night, February 5, while the trial was still under way, the city was shocked by the dynamiting of school buses and a subsequent fire at the DPS bus lot. About 30 percent of Denver's bus fleet was destroyed or extensively damaged in a fire ignited by two explosions that destroyed twenty-four buses and four trucks. The authorities thought sticks of dynamite might have been placed under every bus or every other bus. Fireman fought the fire for about thirty minutes to put it out. Witnesses saw three men jump over the fence immediately after the explosions.[42] Robert Gilberts estimated the damage at $200,000 and replacement costs at $400,000. No one was ever arrested or charged with the arson. However, there was little doubt about the connection between the trial taking place that week and the destruction of the buses. Craig Barnes described the anxiety of that time:

> [After the buses were dynamited] I began to receive hate calls in the middle of the night, a practice that continued for nine years. Usually at about 2:00 a.m., some angry man would call up and say "Get up! Time to put your little blond daughter on a bus and send her to school with all those n——" and then hang up. One evening during the trial, I looked out my bedroom window and saw a black car slowly pausing in front of my house as if casing the place. Lead plaintiff Wilfred Keyes's house [which was later bombed] was made of brick and did not burn up when he was bombed. My house was of wood and would certainly burn up if we too were bombed. I had four young children and a wife inside. After that, we were nervous, and friends from the COC [Citizens for One Community] ordered police protection of our home. Such was the nature of these times.[43]

On Friday, February 6, the fifth day of the trial, though the plaintiffs still had another witness to introduce later, the defendants presented a witness out of order. William Jeffs, principal of Barnum School from 1965 through 1968, testified that Black social worker Ethel Rollins was assigned to his

FIGURE 9.1. Buses burned. "Cluster of firemen fights flames in a row of Denver public school buses Thursday night. Blasting caps, fuses and lighters were found among buses and witnesses said they saw three persons jump [a] fence around bus parking shortly after explosions set off flames. About a third of the bus fleet was involved." February 5, February 8, 1970. *Denver Post* via Getty Images, editorial number 161906279.

school. He said there was no discussion or complaint about the fact that Rollins was Black. In addition, Sydney Rhea, supervisor of school social work, said he informed the principal that Rollins was Black, but he denied having told Rollins that she would have to go to two other schools. In the trial transcripts, Rollins said of Rhea's explanation of a district policy, "He explained it that principals were permitted to have their staff and faculty vote as to whether they wanted a Negro on their staff before they received one." Rhea denied that he had said that and denied that there was any such district policy.[44]

Another witness called by the defendants, Robert Hedley from DPS Planning Services, testified that in 1936, all junior highs had two or even three optional areas, and junior high attendance areas were based on elementary school boundaries. Attendance areas for high schools, he said, included junior highs and their optional areas.[45] Judge Doyle interjected that the defendants were trying to show that these boundaries were long-standing and that the changes had "no diabolical significance at all." The defendants agreed with him.[46]

In 1964, optional areas were done away with. Hedley testified that changing elementary school boundaries required no board action and that junior high boundaries in most cases followed elementary school boundaries. To the contrary, Greiner pointed out instances when junior high boundaries for Cole did not follow elementary school boundaries. Greiner concluded, "I believe the witness has also testified that the elementary and junior high school boundaries are not always co-extensive, Your Honor."[47]

Testifying on Monday, February 9, George Brown (Black journalist, state senator, and later lieutenant governor of Colorado) was the plaintiffs' last witness. He said, "The primary concern throughout my whole political career and also during the time that I was writing for the *Denver Post*, in the Black community was the availability and opportunities for an equal education experience for Black youngsters."[48]

He talked about the hopefulness in the Black community when the new Manual High School was built (it opened in 1953). In his discussions with members of the Black community, Brown found that they had pride in the new building and the feeling that it would encourage faculty from throughout the majority community to want to teach there. It would give the school administration an opportunity to better provide a quality curricula.

On January 10, 1956, Brown had met with state representatives who were concerned that the school administration–planned boundary lines for Manual and East High Schools and Smiley and Cole Junior Highs would segregate the Black students at Cole and Manual and the white students at East and Smiley. They wrote a letter to the school board objecting to the boundaries.[49] In comparing Manuel to East, Brown said:

> Yes, we have looked at the fact that Manual had not received the more
> experienced teachers as had been hoped. The quality of the curricula had not
> improved in comparison with other high schools. The dropout rate was still
> high and declining. Even the name had its negative connotations, and there
> was a strong feeling in the black community that Manual was being regarded
> by the Administration as a substandard secondary type school, that the quality
> schools were in the other parts of the city, and that comparison seemed to
> stand out very markedly when you looked at Manual and East.[50]

The boundary between East and the new Manual was about a block east of the new school, even though Manual was not filled to capacity and East was at 100 percent capacity. This was true when Manual opened in 1953 and again when new boundaries were drawn in 1956, moving Manuel's boundary only a few blocks to the east to York Street as the new north-south boundary. Not coincidentally, York was the eastern edge of most of the city's Black population, and there were very few Black families east of York. Some Black families proposed moving that boundary ten more blocks, as far east as Colorado Boulevard. They also pointed out that there was better public transportation to Manual than to East. Board member Frank Traylor had indicated that the lines were drawn to relieve overcrowding and because of room in some schools.[51]

In many community meetings, Brown testified, Black families realized that the school board had no interest in integrating the schools. Greiner asked, "Why did you equate the presence of white youngsters with quality education?" Brown replied, "I felt that if black youngsters were to get a full opportunity for an equal educational experience, that the only way they would get it would be that there would be white youngsters there who would be taken care of and as a result of them being taken care of the black youngsters would also have the same opportunity of being taken care of."[52]

Brown testified that the elimination of an optional area made Manual more segregated. A little optional square was left among Twenty-first Avenue, York Street, and Franklin Street, where white families still lived and where the only two Black elected officials in the city lived. Outside of that small area, students who formerly could have gone to East now had to go to Manual.

Brown's daughter chose to go to Park Hill Elementary, which was predominantly white until the Brown family's block became a mandatory attendance area for Columbine Elementary. Then, his daughter was assigned to Barrett when it was built in 1960. The size and boundaries of Barrett indicated that it would be predominantly Black from the day it opened. The eastern boundary at Colorado Boulevard was the school's eastern property line. Black members of the community questioned whether Barrett should be built there at all, and if it was, "then you should draw the boundary lines of the school on purpose to make it an integrated school on opening day." This was not done. They felt the administration should have included some area east of Colorado Boulevard, Brown said.[53] When comparative data about achievement tests were published, they showed that "black schools were not of the same quality as the white schools, that the teaching, the facilities, the whole ball of wax just wasn't up to par when compared with what was happening in other parts of the city."[54] Brown's testimony continued: "Still remaining a member of the black community in 1964 and still an elected official, at that stage still a writer for the *Denver Post*, I saw that many white people were using limited open enrollment as a vehicle of escape. They may then have lived in a district or a neighborhood where there was a predominantly minority school but they [whites and middle-class Blacks] could use limited open enrollment to transport their youngster to a school far removed from that locality."[55]

Brown pointed out that because the family of the student had to furnish transportation, LOE was really only available to middle-class families. Thus, students were separated by economic class, which often resulted in separation by race as well.[56]

Brown gave this evaluation of the 1969 school board election: "The election results showed overwhelmingly that the Black community wanted integration because those two candidates [Benton and Pascoe] carried very heavily in Northeast Denver." Brown said the Black community responded to the campaign more as a unit than ever before, but after the election there were different plans for responding to the results. "First, there were black citizens who felt that they had to do something to demonstrate to the rest of Denver what they could have had had they voted for integration and transportation . . . and [they] started putting together hopefully plans for what they called a free school [that had] the advantages of an integrated situation . . . but then there were those who felt that this took care of only some of the youngsters, that the bulk of the black youngsters were going to be put into the neighborhood school situation."

They wanted to improve those schools in every way: facilities, principals, teachers. A third response came from a group that wanted community control of schools outside the system, with locally elected school boards and more parental control. The fourth type of response was to create Black pride storefront schools: "Integration was not the outstanding factor anymore in the black community." A very small part of the Black community still favored integration: "Those who doubted the existence in Denver of white racism no longer had such doubts."[57]

Ris asked Brown if during the planning and just before the construction of Barrett he had predicted that the Stedman area would be predominantly Black within a very few years. Brown's answer described the process whereby seemingly innocent neighborhood segregation easily becomes school segregation:

> We used the same kind of reasoning that we had used back in 1956 and recognized that the schools had become a very good element in the determination as to what happens in the pattern of residential area, that . . . if the residential area becomes predominantly black and then the schools become predominantly black, school administrations seem somehow to lose the interest that they had before and the availability of funds and services and the like become[s] less, and as a result, you move—you have just expanded the ghetto and the schools have been a sponsor in aiding that expansion, when had the schools gone the other way and done some positive things, the schools could have been a factor in maintaining the status quo in more communities.

He said he would have also predicted that Stedman would become predominantly Black.[58]

Brega, an attorney for the intervenors, had this exchange with Senator Brown:

Q: So, it is your opinion, Senator, that all the schools in Denver should be made up in such a way that each racial or ethnic group is represented in each school in the same percentage as the total of the city's breakdown?

A: I introduced a bill on racial balance a couple of years ago, and I believe that if you want to get the most out of an educational system that this is the route that you would go.[59]

The Hispanic population at Manual was at about 35 percent in 1949, Brown said. If the Hispanic and Black populations were combined as minority, Manual was a majority minority school. In contrast to Manual, East was mostly white and overcrowded. A school district publication showed building capacity of 2,462 at East, with an enrollment of 2,468 in March 1955. The projections of enrollment for September 1955 were 2,636; for September 1960, 3,112; and for September 1965, 4,215, well over the building's capacity. These were projections at the time the boundary was changed that eliminated most of the LOE area.[60] At Manual the capacity was 1,600; in March

1955, enrollment was 994; for September 1955 it was projected to be 1,155; for September 1960, 1,280; and for September 1965, 1,605—finally reaching building capacity after ten years. It was obvious that some of the students at East could have attended Manual during those years.[61]

After the conclusion of Brown's testimony, Greiner announced "the plaintiffs rest their case."[62] The defendants immediately moved for the dismissal of the plaintiffs' complaint, a motion the judge rejected.[63] Next, the defendants would present their case.

10

The Trial on the Merits

The Defendants' Case

The defendants presented the next portion of the trial in the *Keyes* case. William Ris, the lead attorney for the defendants, said he wouldn't take any time to argue about the first cause of action—the rescission of the three resolutions, which the US Supreme Court had found to be *de jure* segregation the previous summer.[1]

The second cause of action contained four counts, Ris continued. First was that the district purposely caused racial imbalance throughout the district in violation of the constitutional rights of the plaintiffs and the class they represented. "We submit that all the evidence submitted to the court fails to sustain those particular allegations," Ris said.[2]

The second count was "predicated upon the alleged fact that the school district allocated inferior resources to minority schools [including] . . . the physical plant . . . equipment . . . curriculum and materials . . . [and] less experienced teachers but there has been no evidence that these teachers as such are rendering an inferior education or giving these children an unequal education."[3]

https://doi.org/10.5876/9781646422906.c010

The third count was "based upon a theory that regardless of intent that the school district has maintained a neighborhood school policy resulting in racial imbalance [which] denies equal educational opportunities." Ris cited an issue of law, namely, whether "very rapid trends in the northeast area [were] causing a change in the neighborhood, a change in racial proportions which the board had to contend with and whether that under the circumstances constitutes as a matter of law the type of segregation which this Court would have jurisdiction over. And, we contend that it did not."[4]

The fourth count, as Gordon Greiner pointed out, was abandoned on November 24 the previous year.

The court said of the third count, "He [Greiner] might not be pressing that as hard." Greiner replied: "We are pressing it. The Court will recall we stated that we had two primary theories underlying our theories of relief; two legal theories. One was *Brown*, namely intentional segregation. The other was *Plussey* [*Plessy*]; that regardless of intent, if there was in fact inequality of educational opportunity which could not be justified on educational grounds, that that would also constitute a violation of these plaintiffs' constitutional rights."[5] Greiner then reviewed Fourteenth Amendment decisions in non-school cases: "The first type of case are [*sic*] the jury cases where it has been found that on the basis of probability analysis, that the fact that a jury panel in the South, for example, contained no Negroes on it, that fact was improbable as having arisen merely by chance, that it in fact changed the burden of proof and it made the defendants have to come forward to explain why, for example, in a county that had 17 percent Black population, there had not been a Negro on the panel for some ten years."[6]

Another line of cases concerned "whether or not the facts of the particular case reflect state action . . . If the board has done what the plaintiffs contend it has done in this case, we have no problem about finding state actions." Greiner added, "The constant and rather blinded adherence to the neighborhood school policy in the face of knowing exactly what the racial requirements of that policy are and will continue to be—"

> THE COURT: What you're saying is that state action results from state inaction, is that right?
>
> MR. GREINER: That's correct, Your Honor. And of course there is no magic in the term "neighborhood school."[7]

Greiner pointed out that many children were assigned to schools farther away than their neighborhood school. Many children were bused from annexed areas past the closest school to schools with room for them. So the neighborhood school policy had not always been *the* policy. The judge asked which schools Greiner was claiming had an inequality of educational opportunity. Greiner listed fourteen elementary schools: Barrett, Boulevard, Bryant-Webster, Columbine, Crofton, Ebert, Elmwood, Fairmont, Fairview, Garden Place, Gilpin, Greenlee, Hallett, and Harrington.[8]

The court and Greiner agreed that the United States Supreme Court had never held this,[9] apparently referring to the affirmative duty of a school board to prevent schools from becoming segregated, even in a northern school district where there was never the overt creation by law of a dual school system. Greiner admitted he was asking the judge to consider a new kind of ruling:

> THE COURT: Well, as I say, nevertheless, you're asking that I innovate here?
>
> MR. GREINER: Yes.[10]

Greiner then cited a Pasadena case decided about "ten days ago" in which US District Court Judge Real said: "I think that the problems that are faced by Pasadena as a community and as a school district are unusual in today's world. I think that certainly if a majority of the community is dedicated to the proposition that *Brown against Board of Education* is the law of the land, that it applies not only to those situations in which there are recognizable dual systems of education, but it applies to all systems of education at which there is a minority community which was segregated into its own schools."[11]

As his first witness Ris called Lois Heath Johnson, who had joined the Denver school board in 1951 and served for twelve years. When she was on the board, she said, they never received statistics about school racial makeup or neighborhood racial composition. The board attorney even told the board that the *Brown* decision did not apply to Denver's situation. Asked if she had desegregation in mind in setting Manual's boundary, Heath said "no." This testimony was an attempt to prove that there was no intent to segregate Blacks because the board members did not know the racial composition of schools or neighborhoods.[12]

Johnson said the Voorhees committee was the result of community meetings in which attendees objected to a junior high school at Thirty-second

Avenue and Colorado Boulevard, which the board decided not to build. Proposed changes to the Stedman District were not made, but Johnson said there was no intent to segregate Blacks in Stedman and permit whites to get out of the Stedman District.[13]

Johnson began to pursue racial and ethnic studies after Mildred Biddick in the Denver Public Schools (DPS) office of community relations was given a special assignment in 1962. Also, because the board was eager to hire more minority teachers, recruitment was expanded to southern schools.[14]

Plaintiffs' attorney Craig Barnes demonstrated to Johnson that both Manual High School and Cole Junior High were under-capacity in 1955 and that over-crowding at East High School and Smiley Junior High would have been relieved by moving the boundary between Manual and Cole further east.[15] Barnes also established that Johnson wanted to do whatever the majority wanted.[16]

The court asked Johnson if arguments were made against Barrett Elementary School and changing the boundaries, and she said yes.

> THE COURT: Was it a fact that this matter was not really considered in depth in those days?
>
> THE WITNESS: Well, up until the time of the *Brown* case, it wasn't considered at all. And for some time after that, we felt that we had—that we really didn't have this problem in our community. And it wasn't until shortly before Miss Biddick was appointed and the Voorhees Commission was established that we had a feeling that the school board had certain responsibilities.[17]

Johnson admitted that the board realized that the quality of education in minority schools might be affected negatively.[18]

On Tuesday, February 10, Barnes continued his cross-examination of Johnson. She agreed that by the time of the proposal in 1962 to build the junior high at Thirty-second and Colorado, there was more awareness of race than there had been in 1959 when Barrett was built, and the area west of Colorado Boulevard had become nearly entirely Black. She added that the projections they had looked at the previous day did not show the building proposed at Smiley in the late 1950s.[19]

> Q. [BARNES] The only thing I can't understand is how, if there were these serious financial problems, it was possible for the district to avoid the

use of space in Cole and Manual. If these financial problems were really serious, why wasn't that space used?

A. [JOHNSON] Again, as I told you, we were not planning for just today . . . Some of the buildings were not fully occupied when we completed them, in the southwest, I think also in the southeast area, but we knew that within two or three years they would be, and it is far more expensive to go ahead and build a small building and then have to add to it.[20]

The court established that in 1952 the new Manual became a general high school, including college preparation just like all the other high schools. Johnson said, "Everything was offered in each school in the same way." Then, under questioning by the court, she seemed to contradict that statement when she said that a person who wanted to do well on the college boards should attend East or George Washington because college board preparation was emphasized there, and the schools' level of scholarship was higher.[21]

The next witness for the defendants was Palmer Burch, who was in the Colorado House of Representatives for most of a twenty-four-year period and was still a representative. In 1959, he was elected to a six-year term on the school board. He said that in 1965, the superintendent had recommended building an addition at Stedman with a capacity of 90 and an addition at Hallett for 180 students while the excess children from Stedman would be bused to four or five white schools, thereby eliminating the double sessions at Stedman. The parents at Smith, which was also overcrowded, voted to accept mobile units rather than transport students out of the neighborhood.[22]

The 1962 boundary changes for Cole, Morey, and Byers Junior Highs came as a package, Burch said. The board moved the boundaries of Morey northward so that some of the enrollment at Cole could go to Morey, moved the border for Byers northward so that children attending Morey could attend Byers, and moved the boundaries of Byers so that children attending Byers could attend Grant and Merrill. None of the studies the board considered gave the racial or ethnic composition of various neighborhoods.[23]

The proposal for a junior high school at Thirty-second and Colorado was first released in 1962, which Burch said was the first time he became aware of the opposition of civil rights organizations such as the Congress of Racial Equality (CORE), the National Association for the Advancement of Colored

People (NAACP), and B'Nai B'Rith, among which there was unanimity that the school would be *de facto* segregated and the quality of education would not be the same. This opposition led to the creation of the Voorhees Committee and to Policy 5100 in 1964 calling for "racial and ethnic consideration" in setting boundaries. The policy also observed that the neighborhood school policy had led to concentrations of minority children in some schools and that reductions of such concentrations were necessary to provide equal educational opportunity.[24]

Next, Burch was asked about the 1964 Gove Junior High boundary changes. Board member Jackson Fuller, elected in 1961, thought the board should abolish all optional areas, Burch said. Following the Voorhees Report, sixty-four changes were made "to achieve a degree of racial balance." The board abolished the optional areas between East and Manual and between Cole and Smiley and put the boundary somewhere around Fillmore Street. Students west of that boundary went to Cole; those east of the boundary went to Smiley. Gove's boundaries moved north to Thirty-second and Harrison or Garfield: "Again, the change in the boundaries at Gove was the result of the Voorhees report, to achieve a degree of racial balance." Burch said that following the Voorhees Report, for the first time, reports gave the racial and ethnic percentages in various schools. He left the board in May 1967.[25]

Under questioning from Greiner, Burch said that in the spring of 1962 Johnson, then superintendent, told Burch there were 256 minority (Black, Hispanic, and Asian) teachers in the Denver schools. From the Voorhees Report in 1964, Burch learned for the first time that minority teachers were assigned to minority schools and that roughly 5 percent of the teachers were minority. Board members had no discretion in teacher hiring decisions, he said.[26]

Burch said there was public protest against building a junior high at Thirty-second and Colorado because of the Voorhees recommendation "that school boundaries [will] be hereafter fixed with respect to racial and ethnic considerations." The junior high admittedly would have been majority Black when it opened.[27]

Then, Greiner asked Burch about achievement in minority schools. Burch said that between 1959 and 1967, he received the results of the triennial tests (achievement tests given every three years) for the district as a whole, but he never received school-by-school results. Cole, Baker, and Smiley had compensatory education programs. The Baker and Smiley programs were the result of the Voorhees Report, so the district was aware that students at these schools weren't doing as well as students at other schools.[28]

With the help of an exhibit (Exhibit 416), Greiner had Burch establish that Byers was overcrowded in 1955, with an enrollment of 1,971 when its capacity was 1,355. Projected enrollment for the next fall was 1,096. Enrollment was projected to increase until 1961–1962. Meanwhile, Cole appeared to be under-enrolled, but Burch said that was due to special education programs there that required more space. Morey had a capacity of 1,170 and an enrollment of 894, so there was little reason to remove students from that school. Burch said he had received a lot of objections from people who had formerly gone to Morey and were changed to Byers. He said, "The racial question was never raised, sir."[29]

The intervenors' attorney, Charles F. Brega, asked Burch about a report from a special subcommittee of the Voorhees committee about a confidential poll of public attitudes toward busing.[30] The publication was called "The Equality of Educational Opportunity in Denver, Colorado," and it was developed and authorized by the Voorhees committee under the auspices of Research Services, Incorporated. Part of it appears in the Voorhees Report as appendix 38, "Excerpts from an Opinion Study." One question was, "Would you approve or disapprove [of] a plan whereby elementary school children would be taken to different schools by bus so that no one school would ever have mostly minority group students?" Forty-three percent of Black parents and 61 percent of Hispanic parents disapproved of moving students by bus to another school. Seventy-one percent of Black parents and 79 percent of Hispanic parents voted in favor of the neighborhood school plan.[31] This information was not made public during the Benton-Pascoe campaign, though it would not have changed the candidates' advocacy of school desegregation. The defendants were trying to show that busing was not the will of the majority, never mind a violation of equal protection of the law.

Smith parents voted for more mobile units rather than busing, Burch said, and Benton and Noel—supporters of integration—voted for the mobile units. Also, there was a unanimous vote to bus students out of Stedman. Greiner had Burch read that between 1956 and 1962, there was an increase in special education students at Cole of thirty-seven students, from 44 to 71. That doesn't account for the difference in rated capacity, which changed from 1,908 students in 1956 to 1,525 students in 1962.[32]

Next, the defendants called William Berge, the forty-six-year-old president of the Denver school board. He had attended Moore and Park Hill
Elementary Schools, Gove Junior High, East High School, and Dartmouth
College. He graduated from Denver University Law School in 1950. He had
three sons, two at Thomas Jefferson and one at Hamilton. Berge became a
member of the school board in May 1967 after chairing the Advisory Council
on Equality of Education Opportunity in 1966. The council included people
from all parts of town and representatives from groups such as the Park Hill
Action Committee, CORE, NAACP, and LARASO (La Raza). Their charge
was "to determine whether or not the school policy No. 1222-C, which dealt
primarily with neighborhood schools, should be kept in effect so far as the
construction of new buildings was concerned in northeast Denver."[33] The
preliminary findings were that "*de facto* segregation did exist in certain districts in the city. But, to the best of our knowledge, neither the Board of
Education nor the administration had taken any active part either directly or
indirectly in promoting *de facto* segregation."[34]

The council basically endorsed the neighborhood school concept, Berge
said. It recommended a cultural arts center for sixth grade students drawing from Hispanics, Blacks, and whites who were given the option to
attend. The council recommended a "superior school program for Smiley
and Baker" and an educational center with a variety of programs, including vocational education. It also recommended a further school capacity
study. The council held that no more schools should be built in northeast
Denver until the racial concentration could be alleviated. Berge continued,
"[Its] basic recommendation was that a voluntary open enrollment plan be
established and that this be submitted and explained and advanced with the
idea being that you could explain it to members of the community . . . you
would be able to accomplish some realistic integration."[35] The cultural arts
center plan was accomplished, as was part of the superior school program.
The council could not establish the education center, he said, because there
was no site for it.[36]

After Traylor Elementary School opened, Berge proposed moving students from Smith and Fallis and possibly Phillips to University Park under
the Limited Open Enrollment Policy (LOE). The district didn't provide
transportation, but during Berge's term in office it shifted from LOE to voluntary open enrollment (VOE)—he believed in November 1968—effective

in January 1969. Under the new system, transportation was provided, and a student's move had to improve racial composition at the receiving school.[37]

After referring to the three resolutions (1520, 1524, 1531), Berge said most of the busing at that time was temporary until schools could be built in annexed areas. After the three resolutions were rescinded, they were replaced with Resolution 1533. Basically, the important change in Resolution 1533 was that "participation by individual families shall be optional." Resolution 1533 kept the complexes described in Resolution 1531. The court said that when Gilberts testified at the preliminary injunction, he did not consider the complexes to be optional. Berge agreed that that had been Gilberts's original plan, but Berge wanted them to operate on a voluntary basis:[38] "The majority of the board feels that until you can get a plan which the majority of the people involved will accept and back, then, regardless of any plan which the board adopts, you are not going to be able to make it work."[39]

Barnes read a section of the Berge advisory council study on the subject of racial concentrations in certain schools, which admitted that such a concentration "usually adversely affects the quality of educational achievement." Berge responded, "Yes, there are some results exactly as stated in that paragraph, but that doesn't mean all the results are that."[40]

Barnes pointed out times when the district did not follow the neighborhood school policy, such as when children were bused from the Montbello neighborhood and when Barrett Elementary School was built right up against its boundary.

Barnes asked:

Q: Why if the policy can be modified or compromised in some instances, it was not and has not been modified or compromised in order to promote—in order to overcome the disadvantages which you noted on the page[s] 135 and 103 of the advisory council report?

A: Because the advantages which are noted in the pages which you suggested cannot be accomplished without community acceptance and participation. And until you can get a plan which the majority of the community will get behind and make work, it's just not going to be feasible to put it in operation.[41]

When Barnes asked Berge whether some of the children in mobile units at Smith could have been moved to University Park, he said, "Yes, they could, if they could [*sic*]." He understood that the children who went from Phillips to University Park were volunteers.[42]

Berge said he had opposed Resolutions 1520, 1524, and 1531. In 1520, for the first time in DPS history, an area was designated primarily for its racial composition—an area taken from East High School to go to South High School, with transportation provided. Resolutions 1524 and 1531 had similar plans. In Gilberts's cluster plan, approximately 2,000 children would have been integrated out of the 96,000 children in the district.[43]

Charles Brega, counsel for the intervenors, asked Berge to read from the council report: "Underlying the council's thinking in regard to such transportation was the working premise of the council that forced busing of pupils for the sole purpose of achieving integration should not be involved in any suggested solution." Berge said a majority of the council definitely agreed with that.[44]

Barnes, in questioning Berge, established that VOE was instituted in the middle of the 1968–1969 school year. He had Berge read a quote from Gilberts from Exhibit 11: "A major consideration in formulating these recommendations to provide quality integrated education is the welfare of Denver's children. I have been guided by these well established and accepted principles, sound fiscal management, availability of personnel and staff resources, and the extent of potential community acceptance."[45] At this point the judge interjected questions of his own:

> THE COURT: Does the board have any long-term plans for Manual, Cole; these other schools in the near east side so as to bring them into equality from the standpoint of—I mean, for furnishing quality education? That isn't even a separate but equal system from what I have heard.
> THE WITNESS [BERGE]: Well, I would disagree with that statement as far as Manual is concerned and partially as far as Cole is concerned. The board . . . does not have any specific plan other than 1533, which we feel we have not had an opportunity to really put into effect the way we would like to do it . . .
>
> Well, I think the eventual answer is basically this: that you're only going to get some meaningful realistic integration in this city when you can adopt a plan which the majority of all segments—and by that I mean the majority of the Hispano community, the majority of the Negro community, and the majority of the Anglo community—will

get behind and sponsor. To me, it's totally unrealistic to say to members of a minority community that you are . . .

THE COURT: But then I take it that you're going to wait until the public
accepts the necessity for integrating these schools, or the housing
patterns change, is that right?

THE WITNESS: Well, that would certainly enter into it, yes.

THE COURT: Meanwhile, there is just not going to be any basic change
except what you might work out on a voluntary open enrollment basis,
is that right?[46]

On Wednesday, February 11, the defendants called board member James
Perrill, who testified for most of the day. Perrill had a daughter who was a
senior at East and another who was an eighth grader at Gove. He served in
the Colorado State Senate from 1965 to January 1969. Also, he was a Denver
municipal judge in 1959 and 1960. He voted in the senate for the amendment to the open housing bill (broadening it) in 1965.[47] He had been elected
to the school board in the highly controversial election of May 1969, when
he teamed with Frank Southworth to oppose mandatory "forced" busing.
Perrill spoke at the April 1968 board meeting against the Noel Resolution,
which called for the integration of the Denver schools. He was the only person in opposition, although he said there were other people scheduled to
oppose "but something happened to them."[48]

After a question from Greiner, Perrill and Judge Doyle had a colloquy
about the place of public opinion in setting public policy when it conflicts
with the US Constitution:

THE COURT: Now, you made repeated reference to community acceptance. What is the significance of that in your thinking, Mr. Perrill?

THE WITNESS [PERRILL]: Well, I think it means something special in this
community; where people have control over their public institutions,
the leadership of which is selected by the election process. If you don't
have community acceptance for the policies and thrust of your elected
officials, then they are going to be replaced, and this is rather a basic
part of our political structure.

THE COURT: There is no problem on that score. Everybody understands
and appreciates this. It's only, I suppose[,] when a problem gets in a
constitutional area that this matter changes, so long as it's a political

question—and the Supreme Court made this very clear prior to and
subsequent to the Brown against School Board [case]. And before
Brown it was always a political question. It was always subject to [a]
vote of the people. Isn't that right, Mr. Perrill?

THE WITNESS: I don't know.[49]

Perrill admitted that mostly minority children from the Barrett area were
moved from mostly minority Smiley Junior High to mostly white Gove and
that this plan worked. Greiner zeroed in on the integrating effect of the mandatory busing from Smiley to Gove:

Q [GREINER]: Well, my point, of course, Mr. Perrill, and I think you recognize it, is that that's the same kind of activity contemplated by 1520,
24 and 31, was it not mandatory busing? A change in attendance area,
and integration?

A: Yes.

Q: And it worked, according to your testimony, is that right?

A: I think so. I think it worked pretty well.[50]

By questioning the vagueness of the Gilberts Plan, Greiner illustrated the
ephemeral nature of the school board's plans for integration:

Q [GREINER]: You would agree with me that it is pretty difficult to read
Exhibit D [the Gilberts Plan] and come up with an exact number of
students who might be integrated as I defined that term to you, is that
right? There aren't any numbers?

A: I don't think there are. I don't think there are any numbers in that
regard at all.[51]

Under close questioning from Greiner, it became clear that Perrill did not
believe the school board had the responsibility to integrate the schools:

A [PERRILL]: The reason for my campaign was to be elected to the school
board. Part of my campaign was that, if elected, I would vote to rescind these resolutions.[52]

Greiner pointed out that Perrill campaigned on building schools in neighborhoods where the children were living:

Q: Now, I take it that when you build schools where the children are in
Northeast Denver, those become black schools, do they not, for example? [Perrill agreed, rather circuitously.]

Q: Right. Now, I take it that you haven't abandoned hope, Mr. Perrill, of eliminating all-black schools, is that right? You think voluntary open enrollment would achieve that purpose, is that correct?

A: I don't know that all-black schools ever will be or should be abandoned. I don't have quite that much insight because I don't think we have the same definition of that term integration.

Q: Well you understand what an all-black school is? That's pretty clear, isn't it? You don't look upon VOE then as a device which might in fact change a minority school to one which is predominantly Anglo?

A: I can answer your question. You don't promote understanding by mixing people. This in itself doesn't do it. Integration—the definition of integration—or integration exists when, through resources, equal ability to generate resources and through a complete destruction of resistive-type attitudes, people are able to live wherever they really and truthfully want to live. Then you've got integration in the community. It's up here. It's a community attitude . . . If people then still want to live in somewhat . . . in a cluster situation, then, I'm not going to be for telling them they have to. It's what the atmosphere, the community attitudes reveal. Now, when you send school kids to another school for the purpose of helping improve that attitude, that's what you're doing. You're not sending them to that school so that you're going to break down and diffuse minority school kids throughout the community, because that won't do it. They're going to go back home after they get out of school.

Q: Well, I take it then that the answer to my question is that you don't think—you do not think that voluntary open enrollment will change a predominantly minority school to a predominantly Anglo school?

A: I don't know. I don't know. I am just saying that that isn't necessarily the objective to be achieved.[53]

Greiner asked Perrill about the effectiveness of compensatory education:

Q: Do you know whether the compensatory programs employed by the District in the past have been successful in raising the achievement levels in minority schools?

A: As a matter of statistics, apparently there has been minimal increase in the statistical achievement improvement.[54]

Then, Perrill suggested that compensatory education didn't work as well as it should have for political reasons and that the administrators, students, and parents weren't really behind it. When Greiner asked if "in the future there is any way to insulate future programs from these very same factors," Perrill replied, "well, I wouldn't try to insulate them. I hope somewhere along the line that we can all start moving in one direction with our effort in public school education in this town to the interests of better education, to the promotion of better understanding so that we don't continually fight each other on political issues to the end that the effectiveness of the program is diluted and the community is divided."[55] Greiner then took Perrill through questions establishing what the three resolutions would have done and how that compared with Resolution 1533, which the new majority passed after rescinding the original three.[56]

Through a series of questions, Greiner demonstrated how difficult it was to achieve desegregation through volunteers. Perrill said there were 290 whites at Hallett in the spring semester of 1970 after extensive efforts to recruit volunteer whites to go to Hallett and to recruit the same number of Blacks to enroll outside of Hallett. Prior to these efforts there were 71 whites, according to Greiner. White composition at Hallett grew to only 38.2 percent of the student population. Greiner established that even after great efforts were made to increase white enrollment there, especially during the summer of 1969 under Palecia Lewis, these efforts were not successful:[57]

Q: Well, as of today, Mr. Perrill, is Hallett predominantly Anglo?

A: Not according to those statistics.[58]

Perrill said he had discussed with Gilberts the idea of using students to persuade their parents to favor VOE. Under Brega's questioning he said:

Well, I referred to this I think earlier in my testimony, but the idea of getting students involved in generating interest and participation in voluntary open enrollment, particularly at the high school level, he [Gilberts] thought was a good idea, and he had thoughts on this technique himself using student councils, using officers of classes at the pertinent high schools, and getting the children interested in helping to change community attitudes, not in opposition to their parents, but each of them being responsible for convincing their parents that participation in VOE was a useful thing and a useful part of their education.

He added that they proceeded on this idea until the filing of the lawsuit "preempted many things."[59]

Defendants' attorney Tom Creighton called John Temple, former teacher of mathematics at South High School and at that time head of the Office of Planning, Research and Budgeting (formerly the Department of Budgetary Services), who testified about the number of students in the Denver schools and the racial makeup of that enrollment. The absolute number of white students in DPS decreased from 41,000 in May 1962 to 32,500 in September 1969, Temple said. In that same time, the number of Hispanic students grew from about 9,000 to 13,000 and that of Blacks from 6,000 to 8,000. Brega said total school population was 96,438 in 1962 and 96,534 in September 1969. From 1965 through 1968, 970 pupils participated in open enrollment, of which approximately 470 were Blacks, he said.[60]

The court apparently recessed until the following Monday, February 16, day nine of the trial. At that time Temple continued his testimony about sending Black children to Barrett when it opened:

> THE COURT: Your point is that this was the necessity, the crowding of the situation produced this decision, is that right?
>
> MR. CREIGHTON: Yes, Your Honor, we think the last two exhibits show that all the schools having a relationship to the Barrett site were overcrowded, that the planning of Barrett achieved exactly what it was designed to do, namely to equalize the capacity utilization of the related schools, and further to show that Stedman in the year after the change actually increased in its capacity utilization.[61]

Greiner asked Temple:

> Q: Now is it fair to say, Mr. Temple, that the original Plaintiffs' Exhibit 210 showed that throughout this period, at least up until 1958 that Manual was underutilized while East was either at or over capacity; is that correct?
>
> A: Yes.[62]

Greiner carefully went through almost all of the exhibits the defendants had produced and revealed that most of the numbers, except for minor differences in what was counted, were the same as those in the original plaintiffs' charts and graphs. Temple didn't count kindergarten or special education in calculating teacher-student ratios, and there were other variations. For example, plaintiffs used average daily attendance while the district used the count in the fourth week of September for a school's enrollment.[63]

Greiner led Temple through questions showing that opening Barrett still left several neighborhood schools over capacity and that Barrett's border could have been extended considerably to the east without exceeding the mile beyond which the district would have had to bus students. The defendants' next witness, Jean McLaughlin, who was the principal of Barrett when it opened in 1960, said Colorado Boulevard was "very dangerous" at the time because of heavy traffic. Barnes countered that some pupils at two elementary schools farther south—Teller and Steck—had to cross Colorado to go to and from school.[64]

McLaughlin had been a DPS employee since 1945 and principal at many schools. At the time of the trial, she was the principal at Cory Elementary School. Her testimony suggested that the district had made efforts to reduce the overcrowding of some schools. She knew that Hallett, Smith, and Park Hill were overcrowded in 1962 while Phillips was not overcrowded in 1964. She said fifty of the seventy children bused into Phillips in 1964–1965 were Black. She also said there was the same amount of money for materials and supplies for each child in the district no matter what school they attended.[65]

Under Barnes's questioning, McLaughlin agreed that Hallett was at 120 percent capacity before and after the boundary changes in 1964, and Phillips was at about 100 percent capacity before the change and 125 percent after.[66]

Then, Creighton called Dr. Harold A. Stetzler, director of elementary education for the Denver Public Schools, to testify about the distribution of minority teachers in the district. In 1964 he was asked to reduce concentrations of minority teachers and to assign them throughout the district. Between 1962 and 1968, approximately 40 percent of the teachers hired had previous experience, and about 19 percent had three or more years of teaching experience. Between 4 percent and 10 percent had master's degrees. Said Stetzler, "We have a negotiated agreement concerning the transfer policy, yes [which contributed to the concentration of minority teachers in minority schools]." This was a reference to the system whereby teachers within the district had first call when a vacancy arose. From 1964 to the current year [1970], the number of schools with a minority teacher has changed from fifteen to about seventy, and they are located all over the city, according to Stetzler.[67]

On the tenth day of the trial, Tuesday, February 17, defendants' attorney Michael Jackson continued to question Stetzler, who said that in 1964, Barrett had approximately 39 percent Black teachers. That number rose to a high of about 58 percent in 1967 and dropped back to about 52 percent in 1968 and to 50 percent at the time of the trial. Stetzler described how the transfer system worked (and how it resulted in the segregation of faculty). First, a list of vacancies was published, and teachers could apply for transfer. They were placed on the basis of seniority, which favored the large number of white teachers historically hired by DPS. Jackson said, "In the twenty minority schools, the median experience would be just under four years, and at Traylor, a majority Anglo school, about eleven years."[68]

Until the time of the busing from Stedman and Phillips, whether pupils were minority was not considered. At that time, Stetzler said, "The transportation from these two schools, the primary consideration was to transport youngsters to schools of primarily Anglo attendance areas." The majority of pupils bused from Smith and Stedman were Black.

Barnes asked:

Q: You recall . . . that in 1964 the percent of minority teachers in the elementary schools was nine percent . . . and in 1968 it was still nine percent?

A: I would agree that this is about right.[69]

Stetzler also agreed that in a majority of cases, the interviewer of teacher candidates knew the applicant's race. Teachers used to be required to remain in their first assignment for three years, but that was no longer true. Stetzler seemed to indicate that the district was aware of the segregation of teachers when he said the district was considering a teacher exchange that would help move minority teachers out of minority areas.[70]

Barnes asked, "Do you recall whether any Anglo children were ever moved into minority schools where there was space?" Stetzler answered, "I don't." Stetzler said youngsters had to be moved when "a school becomes so crowded that [a] decision has to be taken to remove youngsters to relieve the crowding, then there has to be communication of the parents involved."[71]

Barnes asked if the teacher applicant could be asked whether he or she would like to be assigned to a minority school. Stetzler said, "Yes, we get his feeling about this kind of an assignment," and that DPS probably would not hire the applicant if he or she preferred not to teach in a minority school. When DPS recruited, it had no list of vacancies. It "may be true" that there are a larger numbers of vacancies in minority schools, he said.[72]

Under Barnes's questioning, Stetzler referred to his memo, Exhibit 426, which referred to Gil Cruter's suggestion that to begin with, only three or four (presumably Black) students should be put in any class at Beech Court or Stevens if students from Stedman were bused in.[73]

Next for the defendants, Jackson called Lidell Thomas, assistant executive director of secondary education, who gave graduation rates for each high school in Denver the preceding year: Abraham Lincoln, 48 percent; East, 59 percent; George Washington, 73 percent; John F. Kennedy, 74 percent; Manual, 58 percent; North, 41 percent; South, 51 percent; Thomas Jefferson, 78 percent; and West, 44 percent. The schools with lower rates than Manual—North, South, West, and Abraham Lincoln—were all majority white except West, which was closely divided between white and Hispanic. Manual was right at the citywide average.[74]

Thomas described special remedial courses at Cole Junior High in reading, math, social studies, and science. After he described some special programs at Manual, Greiner questioned him: "These pre-med, pre-law, pre-engineering programs which you have described [at Manual], when were these instituted?" Thomas responded, "The 1970 school year—this year." In other words, the programs were created after the lawsuit was filed. Thomas agreed with Greiner that by the time a student entered Manual in the ninth grade, he might be reading at the seventh grade level. Even by the time students entered Cole in seventh grade, they might be two grade levels behind where they were supposed to be. To defend the system Thomas said, "[It's] the same in every junior and senior high school in Denver."

Q: Oh, is it in terms of proportion, Mr. Thomas?
A: Not in proportion, but there are students.
Q: There are more of them in the minority schools, are there not?
A: I will agree with that, yes.[75]

Thomas didn't know the dropout rate at Manual, but Greiner supplied it: more than 50 percent. Greiner established that each high school had regular, modified (remedial), and advanced courses in English, science, social studies, and mathematics; but there would be more of the modified courses at Manual than at Thomas Jefferson.[76]

Greiner observed that in recent years, LOE of whites to Manual was two or three students. The previous fall it was between twenty-five and forty students, who could volunteer for a half day.[77]

Ris next put on Dr. Charles Armstrong, assistant superintendent for planning and engineering. He gave Armstrong the chance to deny that buildings were sited to "contain" minorities:

> Q: With respect to the site planning, Dr. Armstrong, in the years that you
> have been involved since 1948 has there ever been a site planned by you
> or by the administration for the purpose of containing minority students,
> meaning either Negro, Hispano, or both, in certain schools so as to keep
> them separate from Anglos?
>
> A: No.

Armstrong said that until the Voorhees Report in 1964, racial makeup was not taken into consideration in establishing boundaries because the data weren't available. It had been taken into consideration since that time.[78]

The transcripts for February 18, 19, and 20 are missing or were perhaps never transcribed, but we can glean some idea of what happened in the trial from newspaper accounts. Armstrong continued to testify for the defendants, and they called Dr. Kenneth Oberholtzer, the DPS superintendent from 1947 through 1967. The intervenors called a number of witnesses, and on the last day, February 20, the plaintiffs called Dr. Dan Dodson as an expert witness.

On Wednesday, February 18 (day 11 of the trial), Oberholtzer said the actions under attack by the plaintiffs were not designed to segregate. He said the changes at Smiley, Manual, and East were prompted by the opening of a new junior high with extra capacity. Barrett was built to accommodate a rapid rise in enrollment in northeast Denver, and the eastern boundary was set at Colorado Boulevard because of concerns about traffic. He said optional attendance areas were used all over Denver when he came to the city, and they weren't devices to segregate pupils by race. Parents at Smith were consulted before the use of mobile units.

Minority teachers, he said, were sent to minority schools as role models. Other board witnesses testified that Oberholtzer set out to reduce the concentration of minority teachers in minority schools. On the subject of low achievement in minority schools, Oberholtzer said a number of factors influenced it. Most important was natural ability, he said, followed by "home environment," including socioeconomic indicators such as the educational level of parents, income, and the father's occupation.[79]

On February 19, Oberholtzer testified that the district spent substantial sums to improve lighting, furnishings, and other physical aspects of the old schools. The same basic academic offerings were made in all schools, but low-achieving schools got special help in the form of lower pupil-to-teacher ratios. Many recommendations of a special study committee on educational equality that made a report in 1964 (the Voorhees committee) were carried out, including instituting an open enrollment policy, using racial makeup as one of the criteria in boundary setting, and making improvements at Smiley and Baker Junior Highs.

Oberholtzer testified that the district took note of race or ethnicity only after 1964. He believed that in the 1950s the Colorado Constitution prohibited any steps to alleviate segregation because classification by race was forbidden, just as it prohibited steps to segregate pupils by race. He said East was a high-achieving school and could do well with larger classes while Manual was low achieving and needed fewer pupils per class, so one couldn't just multiply the number of classrooms by thirty to obtain capacity. He also said he didn't have any specific knowledge of the edge of the Black population movement when Barrett was built.

Dr. Gerald Elledge of the DPS research office reported on a study conducted the preceding school year of pupils bused to other schools for integration. The study didn't show any significant differences in achievement for a majority of groups compared with matched groups in both sending and receiving schools. Elledge agreed with Doyle that the study was inconclusive.[80]

Examination of witnesses and offering of evidence was completed on Friday, February 20, at midday. Doyle heard twenty-eight witnesses and received hundreds of maps, charts, graphs, reports, and school records during the trial. He complimented all sides for their preparations. Closing arguments were due on Tuesday, February 24.

The plaintiffs asked Doyle to do two things: order full desegregation of Denver schools and order that alleged inequalities in teaching minority children be corrected. The school board denied it segregated children by its actions and denied it treated minority pupils worse than white children. There was extensive testimony on the curriculum, which the district's witnesses said was equal throughout the city. School officials repeatedly testified that racial and ethnic segregation wasn't a goal in any of their actions. Oberholtzer defended various actions taken when he was superintendent.[81]

Before the closing arguments could take place, there was another violent incident, this time against the leading anti-busing member of the school board: James Perrill. No one was hurt when at about 3:00 a.m. on Saturday, February 21, a firebomb was thrown through a window at Perrill's home.[82] The perpetrator was never found.

In the closing arguments presented on Tuesday morning, February 24, according to the *Denver Post*, Greiner reviewed the evidence, "which he maintained shows that the Denver Board of Education has created and perpetuated school segregation and provided unequal education to Negro and Hispano pupils." The board's segregating actions, he argued, included use of optional zones around Columbine Elementary School, boundary changes that made Boulevard Elementary School predominantly Hispanic, the building of the new Manual High School in 1953 and a subsequent extension of the attendance area to follow the movement of the Black population eastward, the building in 1960 of Barrett Elementary School at the eastern edge of the area in which most of the Black population lived, and the 1969 rescissions of integration plans after a school board election. Also, he cited the admitted assignment of minority teachers to minority schools. Greiner said the plaintiffs maintained that even segregation not created by the school board must be eliminated because the board perpetuated it through affirmative actions.[83]

The defendants also made their closing arguments, as reported in the *Rocky Mountain News*. Ris, the school board's attorney, contended that the plaintiffs were attempting to use hindsight to establish their allegations and that the court must take into consideration the context within which the board and the administration acted. The cases cited by plaintiffs aren't applicable to the fact situation in Denver, he said. There was no evidence that any action was racially motivated. The optional zones, for example, were citywide. The open enrollment plan was an attempt to meet Denver's problems, and when it was found deficient the board approved a voluntary open enrollment plan. Regarding the allegation of unequal educational opportunity, Ris contended that the same course offerings were available in every school, as was the additional assistance that was made available to disadvantaged students. Test scores in every school, he argued, ranged from very high to very low. Teacher assignments were largely dictated by the agreement with the Denver Classroom Teachers Association requiring assignment on the basis of seniority. The board's position was that segregation existed as a result of housing patterns. The rescinding of the three integration plans by the new board majority the previous June, he said, was simply an educational policy matter and an attempt to reach the same end through a different method.[84]

That night, the city was shocked by another home bombing, this time at the home of Wilfred Keyes, the lead plaintiff in the case, where an explosive device blasted the front door and porch and shattered a picture window. There were no injuries, though the Keyes's nine-year-old daughter, Christi, was sitting at the dining room table, which was near the picture window, doing her homework. She could be seen by the person who threw the bomb. Keyes thought it was a firebomb on their porch, so he first tried to put it out with a pan of water. Then he ran to get a hose from the back of the house, but the bomb exploded before he got back to the front porch. Police arson investigators said it might have been two pipe bombs or one large one. It contained bearings like shotgun pellets, apparently placed in the bomb in an attempt to cause injury as well as damage.[85]

On approximately February 25, Berge, an anti-busing member of the Denver Board of Education, received a news clipping about this event and a note saying "you're next." I don't believe this threat was ever carried out.[86]

Denver citizens could not expect any leadership from Washington on the issue of desegregation. The *New York Times* commented that "current statements of both conservatives and moderates within the Administration, as well as those of the President himself, add up to this: Integration will be pursued as a goal insofar as it will achieve an educational purpose and will not disrupt the neighborhood school concept or require considerable additional busing of students." President Richard Nixon had spoken against busing to achieve racial balance in his 1968 presidential campaign, and he was in favor of the neighborhood school concept. As part of his "Southern strategy" to win that election, Senator Strom Thurmond and other Nixon supporters traveled through the South telling voters that Nixon could be expected to soften the guidelines.[87]

After the trial ended, parents and children again anxiously awaited the decision by Judge Doyle.

11

Judge Doyle's Decision and the Remedy Plans

Before Judge Doyle had a chance to rule on the issues of the trial, the defendants appealed to the Tenth Circuit Court of Appeals. In addition, the school board lawyers asked Doyle to throw out the integration suit. They said the board agreed with a statement of the issues in the August 27, 1969, opinion of the Tenth Circuit that said the issue was "whether the neighborhood school concept shall yield to compulsory integration which will be achieved by transportation of students to and from contiguous and noncontiguous attendance districts . . . This statement of the issue," the board's brief said, "would seem to be accurate and, we submit, this [requirement] is not the current law." They said the plaintiffs had an adequate remedy in the voluntary open enrollment policy. The attorneys for the board asked that the earlier injunction be dissolved and that judgment be granted to the defendants. The document was accompanied by a seventy-page finding of fact that repeated arguments the defendants had made in court.[1] The motion to dismiss was unsuccessful.

https://doi.org/10.5876/9781646422906.c011

Judge Doyle's Order

Judge Doyle issued his major "Memorandum Opinion and Order" on March 21, 1970. It was seen as a victory for the plaintiffs. Although he rejected some of their causes of action, he accepted others and ordered desegregation of many schools. He said the case was fully heard except "submission by the parties of tangible plans," which "was deferred pending decision on the issues involving alleged discrimination."[2]

The first cause of action dealt with the rescission of the three desegregation resolutions the previous June that had resulted in the preliminary injunction against the district. The second cause alleged that the district maintained segregated schools, effectively creating *de jure* segregation; the third cause was that the district provided inferior education in minority schools and thus did not even meet the separate but equal standard. Several schools, the plaintiffs contended, were created or maintained as segregated schools.[3]

Section I

Doyle began with the first cause, which was the subject of the preliminary hearing. The site selected for Barrett Elementary School ensured that it would be a segregated school when it opened. This was part of a pattern leading to the concentration of minority students in certain schools, which the three resolutions began to remedy: "From these and other facts, we concluded at the preliminary hearing, and we now affirm that holding, that the School Board intended to create Barrett as a segregated school and prevent Negro children from attending the predominantly Anglo schools east of Colorado Boulevard."[4]

Doyle rejected the defendants' arguments about it being a long-held site (there were others further east) and about the eastern boundary being set out of concern for the safety of children crossing Colorado Boulevard. He cited the failure to relieve crowding at white schools east of Colorado Boulevard and the objections of the Black community at the time that made it clear that the school would be segregated: "From this uniform pattern we concluded that the School Board knew the consequences and intended or at least approved of the resultant racial concentrations."[5]

He reviewed the two Denver Public Schools (DPS) study committees that called for consideration of race in drawing boundaries and building schools. Doyle quoted the Noel Resolution's direction to the superintendent to submit a comprehensive plan for the integration of Denver's public schools. After Superintendent Robert D. Gilberts submitted his plan, the board passed the three resolutions. These resolutions were "to eliminate segregation in the Negro schools in Park Hill while stabilizing the racial composition of schools in transition."[6]

After the school board election changed the position of the majority of the board, the rescission of the three resolutions was "a legislative act and one of *de jure* segregation . . . It was unconstitutional and void." Doyle added, "We now hold that the rescission as it applied to East and Cole was also unconstitutional." Thus, the resolution applying to Cole also had to be implemented:[7] "The Board specifically repudiated measures which had been adopted for the purpose of providing a measure of equal opportunity to plaintiffs and others."[8]

Section II

The first count of plaintiffs' second claim for relief alleged that *de jure* segregation existed at Manual High School, Cole Junior High School, Morey Junior High School, and two elementary schools as a result of school board action through boundary changes and other acts such as the creation of optional areas. In their calculations, Doyle noted, the plaintiffs placed Black and Hispanic people in one combined category.[9] The judge was not convinced that these acts constituted *de jure* segregation.

The judge reviewed the boundary changes for Manual High School and East High School and the boundary changes between Cole and Smiley Junior Highs. Resolution 1524 reduced the population at Cole, while the Morey boundary changes made Morey predominantly minority. The defendants had said that these changes were made to better utilize capacity of Hill, Byers, and Baker Junior Highs.[10] The judge did not find intentional racial discrimination at the elementary level, though he did observe that the board did not take steps to integrate schools: "In examining the boundary changes and removal of optional zones in connection with the several [elementary] schools . . . we do not find any willful or malicious actions on the part of the Board or the administration . . . The substantial factor in this condition is twofold: First, a failure on the part of the Board or the administration to take any action having an integrating effect, and secondly, deeply established housing patterns which have existed for a long period of time and which have been taken for granted."[11]

The board had claimed that it "just found the consensus and followed it." That is, it did what the majority wanted. This was not *de jure* segregation, "which calls for an all-out effort to desegregate. It is more like *de facto* segregation, with respect to which the rule is that the court cannot order desegregation in order to provide a better balance."[12]

Doyle offered the following principles of the essentials of *de jure* segregation:

1. The State, or more specifically, the school administration, must have taken some action with a purpose to segregate;
2. this action must have in fact created or aggravated segregation at the school or schools in question;
3. a current condition of segregation must exist; and
4. there must be a causal connection between the acts of the school administration complained of and the current condition of segregation.

Later, he added that "the important distinguishing factor between *de facto* and *de jure* segregation is purpose to segregate."[13]

Thus, the plaintiffs lost the first count of the second cause of action alleging that the board was guilty of *de jure* segregation permeating the district:

Once you have a predominantly minority school population, other factors come into consideration. For example, the racial and ethnic composition of faculty and staff . . . the equality of educational opportunity offered at the school; and the community and administration attitudes toward the school.[14]

The complained of acts are remote in time and do not loom large when assessing fault or cause. The impact of the housing patterns and neighborhood population movement stand out as the actual culprits.[15]

Of the construction of the new Manual High School in 1953 and the Manual and Cole boundary changes and the Smiley addition, the judge added, "it cannot be said that the acts were clearly racially motivated." It is not *de jure* segregation. The only contribution the board made was inaction:

An essential requisite of a violation of the equal protection clause of the [US] Constitution in the present context is positive legislative or administrative state action which discriminates on account of race, and which produces the condition complained of. The instant situation then cannot be placed at the administration doorstep; if cause or fault has to be ascertained it is that of the community as a whole in imposing, in various ways, housing restraints.[16]

Similarly, it is doubtful whether the 1952 boundary change at Columbine can now be classified as a *de jure* act . . . This act appears in retrospect to have had little to do with the present minority population at Columbine.[17]

The Boulevard School boundary change was not shown to be motivated by an intent to segregate Hispanic students. The Morey changes relieved the concentration of Black students at Cole: "It would strain both the facts and law to say that the administration acted with an unlawful purpose or design in this instance." To call Morey segregated at present, the plaintiffs had to lump together Black and Hispanic people, Doyle said. There was no apparent comprehensive policy other than the negative approach that could be considered in this context. That is, the "Board's eye-closing and head-burying is not the kind of conduct which the Circuit Court had in mind in *Dowell* and *Downs*."[18] In our circuit, "A neighborhood school policy, even if it produces concentration, is not *per se* unlawful if 'carried out in good faith and is not used as a mask to further and perpetuate racial discrimination.'"[19] The Supreme Court has not yet ruled on this question."

He concluded by ruling against the plaintiffs on this count: "In summary then, we must reject the plaintiffs' contentions that they are entitled to affirmative relief because of the above mentioned boundary changes and elimination of optional zones. We hold that the evidence is insufficient to establish *de jure* segregation."[20]

Doyle also rejected the plaintiffs' claim for relief and their urging him to adopt a rule of law that a neighborhood school policy may in and of itself create or maintain unconstitutional segregation.[21] In this manner, Judge Doyle ruled against the plaintiffs' attempt to show *de jure* segregation throughout the school district.

Section III

The plaintiffs' success at the district court level, in addition to the permanent reversal of the rescission of the three resolutions the previous summer, arose from Judge Doyle's ruling on the next count, which contended that the district maintained separate but unequal schools for minority students: "The third count of plaintiffs' second claim for relief alleges that defendants are maintaining certain schools within the district which provide an unequal educational opportunity for the students attending them; that these are seg-regated schools; and that, therefore, the students at these schools are being denied the equal protection of the law."[22]

The plaintiffs maintained that racial concentration produced the inferior schools. Doyle listed twenty elementary schools; Baker, Cole, Morey, and Smiley Junior High Schools; and East, Manual, and West High Schools. Plaintiffs said that all these schools had "(1) low average scholastic achievement; (2) less experienced teachers; (3) higher rates of teacher turnover; (4) higher dropout rates; and (5) older buildings and similar sites."[23]

Judge Doyle decided that any school with 70–75 percent either Black or Hispanic students was likely to produce the kind of inferiority he was con-cerned about. The plaintiffs considered more schools minority and segre-gated than the judge did because they added Hispanic and Black students together for the minority count while Judge Doyle considered each racial group separately. (Racial makeup, achievement, teacher experience, and dropout rates were enumerated in charts in appendices I, II, III, and IV of the order.)

Doyle contrasted test scores for children in majority white schools with those in majority minority schools. Achievement at the elementary level was judged using Stanford Achievement Tests. Third grade scores should have been 3.8 for tests administered in the third grade at the eighth month, and fifth grade scores should have been 5.8. Minority segregated schools achieved approximately 2.96 at the third grade level, almost a grade behind the standard, while the district-wide average was 3.57. The average grade-level score for fifth grade in the twelve minority elementary schools was 4.30; the district average was 5.22, almost a full year above the average scores in minority schools.

As for junior high scores on Stanford Achievement Tests for which the national median score is the 50th percentile, the median score for the district was 53.8; minority Cole and Baker scored only 28.2, meaning that more that 70 percent of students in the country at that grade level scored above the students at those schools.

The median score for district high schools in eleventh grade was 52. At highly minority Manual the median score was 30, which means that 70 percent of students nationally performed better than the Manual students.[24]

In appendix II of the order, teachers at white schools and minority schools were compared on the basis of the number of years of DPS experience. There were columns for the number on probationary status (one to three years), those with three years' experience, and those with ten or more years' experience. The judge used only the elementary schools he found to be segregated by his definition (having 70 percent or 75 percent of students of one minority group) and compared the teacher experience in that group with the teacher experience in the twenty white schools selected by the plaintiffs. There were large contrasts in the amount of experience teachers had. Doyle found similar results when comparing scores of students in minority junior and senior high schools with scores of students in white schools at the same levels. (Manual, by his definition, was the only segregated high school.)[25]

Judge Doyle observed that the union agreement transfer policy based on seniority allowed experienced teachers to leave minority schools, creating vacancies that were then filled by inexperienced teachers. This had a depressing effect on the minority schools and resulted in less experienced faculties in these schools.[26] In a comparison of student dropout rates in the two groups of schools, appendix III of the order showed higher dropout rates at Baker, Cole, and Manual—all minority schools. The judge did not think the age of the building was a substantial factor in the quality of education.[27]

Next, Judge Doyle reviewed the evidence presented at the trial about the negative impacts of segregation on students. He said that Dr. Dan Dodson, a professor of education at New York University, "testified that a segregated school adversely affects a Negro child's ability to achieve . . . He indicated that studies show that by the time a school becomes segregated, it is looked upon by the whole community as being inferior." Dodson said students are not motivated to learn, and the parents then don't try to motivate their children. Teachers in such schools have low expectations and "do little to stimulate higher performance."[28]

The judge came out strongly on the damage done by segregated education: "The defendants do not acknowledge that segregated schools per se produce lower achievement and an inferior educational opportunity. They point to other factors [home and community environment, socioeconomic status of the family, parents' educational background] . . . We cannot ignore the overwhelming evidence to the effect that isolation or segregation per se is a substantial factor in producing unequal educational opportunity." Doyle cited the Voorhees Report and referred to the Berge Report on the inferior education provided in segregated schools:[29]

> When we consider the evidence in this case in light of the statements in *Brown v. Board of Education* that segregated schools are inherently unequal, we must conclude that segregation, regardless of its cause, is a major factor in producing inferior schools and unequal educational opportunity.
>
> The equal protection clause of the Fourteenth Amendment prohibits any state from denying to any person the equal protection of the laws. Simply stated, a state may not treat persons differently without a legitimate reason for doing so. In the area of economic regulation the courts grant broad leeway to the states in creating classes of individuals and treating them differently. All that need be shown is a minimal justification in terms of a legitimate state interest for the inequality of treatment.
>
> The courts, however, have jealously guarded the rights of disadvantaged groups such as the poor or minorities, and have held that where state action, even if nondiscriminatory on its face, results in the unequal treatment of the poor or [a] minority group as a class, the action is unconstitutional unless the state provides a substantial justification in terms of legitimate state interest.[30]

Facilities may be separate, Judge Doyle added, "but a fundamental and absolute requisite is that these shall be equal." He developed that idea:

> Today, a school board is not constitutionally required to integrate schools which have become segregated because of the effect of racial housing patterns on the neighborhood school system. However, if the school board chooses not to take positive steps to alleviate de facto segregation, it must at a minimum ensure that its schools offer an equal educational opportunity.
>
> The evidence in the case at bar establishes, and we do find and conclude, that an equal educational opportunity is not being provided at the subject segregated schools within the District. The evidence establishes this beyond any doubt. Many factors contribute to the inferior status of these schools, but the predominant one appears to be the enforced isolation imposed in the name of neighborhood schools and housing patterns.[31]

Section IV

In Section IV, titled "Discussion of Remedies," in "A. The Northeast Denver Schools," Doyle referred to the preliminary injunction related to schools in Park Hill, which he made permanent, adding the East and Cole resolutions to the order. The preliminary order, he said, would remain in effect for the remainder of the school year, and the present judgment would take effect in September 1970.[32]

In "B. A Program of Improvement," Doyle said he had concluded that "there is a denial of equal opportunity for education in these schools." He cited lower achievement levels, higher dropout rates, and a concentration of minority and inexperienced teachers. Minority schools "are entitled to at least their fair share of the most competent teachers."[33] Remedial education had not had any significant effect. In Superintendent Gilberts and his staff, Doyle said, the board had access to experts who were capable of formulating such a program: "The Court anticipates hearing from experts, including the Board staff."[34]

Doyle approached the touchy subject of busing in the next section under remedies, "C. Compulsory Transportation." First, he acknowledged that no one really likes busing schoolchildren. But he added, "It is, however, conceded to be a necessity where integration is ordered, and it would appear to be the only way to implement the Resolutions . . . For equalizing the educational opportunity, it is not so clear that compulsory transportation is the answer . . . The plaintiffs' evidence establishing the inferiority of minority schools raises a serious equitable question about subjecting minority or majority children to those schools."[35]

Under the last section on remedies, "D. Voluntary Transfer Policy," Doyle suggested that the district make transfer a matter of right without the need for securing a reciprocal transfer from a white school. It should provide transportation based on present distance policy. About the current voluntary open enrollment program, he said, "It seems highly unlikely that students would elect to go to these schools from white neighborhoods and so it is questionable whether any integration would be achieved in a substantial way from this program."[36]

The order finished with this proclamation: "Any decree which is finally promulgated here will not be effective until next fall . . . This opinion does not purport to be a judgment for the purpose of appeal. Final judgment will be entered after a meeting with counsel which hopefully can be carried out within the next 30 days."[37]

Clearly, the plaintiffs had won a tremendous victory. The next step in the suit would be the submission of remedies by plaintiffs and defendants. The story of the decision was front-page news. "Judge Rules Denver Busing to Continue" was the *Denver Post* headline.[38]

Shortly after the judge's opinion was issued, President Richard Nixon commented on desegregation in ways that were less than helpful. He said the neighborhood school was preferred and that busing wasn't necessary. In fact, he quoted a prohibition on busing in the 1964 Civil Rights Act: "Nothing herein shall empower any official or court of the United States to issue any order seeking to achieve a racial balance in any school by requiring the transportation of pupils or students from one school to another or one school district to another in order to achieve such racial balance, or otherwise enlarge the existing power of the court to insure compliance with constitutional standards."[39]

The Remedy Plans

The order had settled many of the issues of law, but the remedy, the specific plans for every school in Denver, still had to be determined after a hearing. The *Denver Post* reported on April 17 on a meeting between the judge and the parties to the suit. Criticizing the board for appealing rather than acting, Doyle scheduled a hearing for May 11 on detailed plans to improve education for many Black and Hispanic children. He rejected a board proposal that would have cleared the way for it to appeal before a final judgment in the case. The judge was surprised and angry when he learned that the board had not been developing a plan for upgrading education in the fifteen minority schools.[40]

Doyle issued a final ruling that the board's June 9, 1969, rescissions were unconstitutional. The parts of those plans that had been under a temporary injunction were from then on under a permanent order, clearing the way for an appeal of that part of the case. The ruling on the fifteen minority schools could not be appealed until Doyle decided on a remedy, however.

William Ris wanted the board to be able to choose among plans, but Doyle made it clear that he would choose the plan while he said he didn't think integration would have some magical effect. In their memorandum, the plaintiffs asked Doyle to expand his original list of fifteen "target schools" to those with combined Black and Hispanic enrollments of 70 percent or more because they were just as segregated as those with 70 percent or 75 percent enrollments of either group alone.[41]

At a meeting on April 22, Doyle approved the DPS program of voluntary open enrollment (VOE) until the court plans were fully executed. He said desegregation would fulfill the constitutional requirement if the white population of each school was over 50 percent. He thought it was desirable to apportion the minority population in each school equally between Hispanic and Black students.[42]

The Plaintiffs' Remedy

The outline from Gordon Greiner and Craig Barnes of the plaintiffs' remedy to be presented at the May 11 hearing was extensive, more than fifty pages long. It demonstrated how careful and thoughtful the plaintiffs were in their proposals. Following are extensive excerpts from the plaintiffs' memorandum found in Janet Bardwell's file, cited in note 43.

[I.] Plaintiffs' approach to remedies encompass [sic] three interdependent concepts as follows:

1. Desegregation; i.e., the elimination of racial and ethnic isolation in the subject schools through the cross-transportation of students and reassignment of teachers;

2. Integration; i.e., the promotion of mutual respect and understanding and the elimination of unwarranted fears and tensions among and between the racial and ethnic communities of Denver;

3. Compensation; i.e., the reduction and elimination of the achievement gap between Anglo and minority students through programs designed to raise the achievement levels of minority children in an integrated school environment.

[II.] Witnesses will include:

Dr. James Coleman would testify on racial isolation which deprives children "of the most effective educational resource contained in the schools; those brought by other children as a result of their better home environment."

Compensatory education in [racially] isolated schools does not over-come this hurdle. Most studies show positive effects on performance of the minority child in integration.

Dr. Neil Sullivan, Commissioner of Education in Massachusetts and former superintendent of Berkeley schools. He will testify on the lack of adverse effect of integration on the Anglo students.

Dr. George Bardwell, Denver University, will testify on the plans, their cost, number of schools effected [*sic*], number of children transported, length of routes, effect on teacher assignments, utilization of school capacities and other details.

William Smith, Principal of Barrett, will testify regarding the implementation of the court's preliminary injunction as it related to Barrett. It will be his general position that compensatory programs in segregated schools have been wholly ineffective in raising the achieve-ment levels of the minority students and that such plans hold no realistic promise of reaching the objective of equality of educational opportunity.

[III.] Plaintiffs' Other Target Schools Should Be Included in the Plan for Relief.

They argue that the results are the same whether a school is 70% or more Negro, 70% or more Hispano, or 70% or more Negro and Hispano combined.

Exhibit 509 shows the court designated minority schools with an average median percentile achievement of 21 and Exhibit 510 shows the plaintiffs['] added target schools with an average median percentile achievement of 20. In the court designated schools median teacher expe-rience was 3.5 years and in the plaintiffs['] target schools it was 3.7 years. [So in these important factors the two groups were very similar—see Exhibits A.6 and A.7, respectively, in the appendix A for Exhibits 509 and 510 data.]

Both the plaintiffs and the defendants were told to develop plans for the fifteen deficient schools, to be presented to Judge Doyle at the May 11 hear-ing. The plaintiffs offered four plans for integrating the elementary schools. The costs for transportation ranged from $623,600 for Plan 1 to $1,292,770 for Plan 4. The current cost of transportation was $382,740. (See Exhibit A.7 in appendix A for a tabular representation of plaintiffs' Exhibit 510, which set forth the comparison of the court schools and the "target schools" the plaintiffs wanted to add.)

In Plan 1, the program minimized the total distance traveled by students. The racial and ethnic composition of these schools ranged from a low of 54 percent white to a high of 60 percent white. In 1969–1970, it ranged from 0.6 percent to 97.7 percent white. This plan gave the smallest possible total student miles of transportation. Plaintiffs' Exhibit 501-A (see Exhibit A.3 in appendix A) gave the average achievement *after* transportation for each of the court schools. Five schools—Hallett, Berkeley, Bryant, Fairmont, and Greenlee—were at the 40th percentile or below while the highest were Fallis, which was still 60 percent white, at the 65th percentile and McMeen, still 59 percent white, at the 63rd percentile.

In Plan 2, court schools were paired with white schools. Grades K–3 would attend one school while grades 4–6 would go to the other school. These schools ranged from 51.4 percent to 67.5 percent white.

In Plan 3, which was similar to Plan 1, ten more schools were added that had a combination of minorities totaling 70 percent. Twenty-two elementary schools were desegregated with children from twenty-eight other elementary schools. (See Exhibit A.4 [503-A] in appendix A.)

Plan 4 was a pairing plan like Plan 2, except that ten target schools were added, resulting in a plan for fifty-three schools and 16,845 students. The minimum enrollment of whites in any school was 50.4 percent. Estimated cost was $1,293,000.

For junior highs, Alternative I discussed reassignment of students then being bused and more realistic utilization of unused capacities. There was the expectation that when Place Junior High opened in 1971, Denver would have unused space for 2,221 students. The plaintiffs' plan would have assigned to Cole 1,038 of the mostly white students then being transported to Thomas Jefferson and John F. Kennedy and assigned to these two white schools those mostly Black students then being transported to Cole.

Alternative II discussed relieving overcrowding at Jefferson and Kennedy Junior Highs by reassigning some of their students to Cole, Horace Mann, Lake, Morey, and Baker, resulting in a 70 percent white student body and a 30 percent minority population at every school. (In appendix A, see Exhibit A.5 [Plaintiffs' Exhibit 505-A], with all junior highs ranked by Iowa Score. Generally, as the percentage of white students declines, the average

percentile score on the Iowa Test also declines. The percentage of white students ranged from 97.2 percent to 1.4 percent. The percentile ranks ranged
from 80 down to 20. Junior high schools Lake, Smiley, Horace Mann, Morey,
Baker, and Cole were all under the 50th percentile on the Iowa Test for ninth
grade in 1967.)

Manual High School could be desegregated by changing boundaries, just
as East was, according to the plaintiffs' memorandum.

In summary, Black and Hispanic students presently attending Manual
High would be redistricted into North and East High Schools; white
students attending East and South would be redistricted into Manual.
Secondary schools redistricting of the populations of East and other high
schools would guarantee against resegregation at East: "If Manual is to
become a school with special programs, they should be open to everyone
in the city. If it can not attract students from all over the city, it will not
alter the isolation of the students and the image of Manual as a segregated,
inferior institution."

According to Section V, "Integration Plans," in the plaintiffs' outline:

> In-service training should be mandatory for teachers placed in schools that
> are integrated. The purpose is to instruct faculty and staff in teaching tech-
> niques, cultural understanding and to improve the attitudes and expectancies
> of teachers teaching minority children. It should be scheduled prior to the
> opening of school in September, 1970. Students and parents should be advised
> as soon as possible what schools they will attend. Teacher assignments should
> also be made quickly. Parents should be advised during the summer what
> programs are being prepared for them in their new schools. There should be
> an opportunity for open houses at the school. [The district needs] volunteer
> and paid aides in the community. The Office of School Community Relations
> should establish a clearing house for the receipt and evaluation of all reports
> of problems so that rumors can be dispelled and problems identified and
> solutions implemented.

In Section VI, "Compensatory Programs," the memorandum used the
example of Barrett Elementary, which had part-time pull-out programs for
those who were behind and those who were more advanced. Plaintiffs said
special learning centers could be created for remedial and advanced learning
on a part-time basis, avoiding isolation and stigmatization of slow learners.

"An integrated environment is essential to the success of compensatory programs," according to the memorandum.

Section VII was an analysis of the school district budget and suggestions on what could be given up to fund desegregation.

Section VIII set out procedures to evaluate the desegregation program:

1. The racial and ethnic composition of any school affected by the court's order shall not be allowed to depart from the city average by more than one standard deviation.

2. Performance of students on standardized tests shall be measured no less frequently than at the beginning of each school year, at mid-year and at the end of the school year.

3. When appropriate, test performance comparisons will be made with control groups of students chosen using probability sampling and [will be] evaluated according to commonly accepted statistical procedures for experimental designs.

4. Data shall be collected by the District showing the number of teachers by race and ethnicity classified according to the number of years of teaching experience.

5. Transportation schedules shall be determined using systems analysis techniques, including linear programming.

6. At least three times a year, area meetings shall be conducted by the Board for receiving complaints and suggestions for modifying the proposed desegregation plans.

7. Modern accounting procedures shall be established for each school to determine the cost of various programs.

8. At least every 6 months the BOE [board of education] shall prepare and publish a report for distribution to the community detailing the operation of the desegregation program and the compensatory educational plans. When appropriate this report will evaluate the effectiveness of such plans and contain recommendations for improvements.

In conclusion, the memorandum rejected the effectiveness of compensatory education alone in overcoming the destructive effects of segregation:

Over a decade's worth of well-meaning compensatory programs in the minority schools, costing millions of dollars, have utterly failed to equalize educational opportunity . . .

No amount of campaigning behind the facades of "neighborhood schools" and "forced busing" can hide neither the failure of these schools to meet their responsibilities, nor the tragic human and economic waste which has resulted . . .

If segregation is not eliminated, that deprivation will continue. The time is come to stop treating the symptoms of this illness and to eliminate its cause.[43]

The Defendants' Remedy

The school board had instructed Gilberts on April 20 to prepare a plan to improve inferior schools. But Gilberts announced his resignation on May 1, effective September 1, 1970. The board's plans for improving education at fifteen Denver minority schools were adopted late on May 7 by the school board. What was conspicuously lacking in the plans was the assurance of any extensive integration that could only be brought about by busing some children. It was just enough of a plan to prevent Judge Doyle from finding the defendants in contempt of court for the failure to adopt anything at all. The plan was built around the concept of open enrollment and voluntary busing to schools outside the home neighborhoods. Voting for the plan were members of the anti-busing majority: William G. Berge, Stephen J. Knight Jr., James C. Perrill, and Frank K. Southworth. Opposing it were James D. Voorhees and Rachel B. Noel, members of the pro-desegregation minority. Board member Dr. John H. Amesse was on vacation.[44]

Also in the district's plan: hiring teacher aides and recruiting volunteers to assist teachers; reduction of teacher turnover in these schools by reducing class size and furnishing better materials; improved in-service training for teachers; establishment of three major complexes involving some of the fifteen minority schools; expansion of early childhood education through intensified study for those from disadvantaged neighborhoods; continuation and expansion of special programs at Manual and Cole; implementation at Fairview Elementary School and Baker and Cole Junior High Schools of special programs with funding through the Educational Achievement Act of Colorado; development of innovative, integrative instructional programs involving cultural arts, as well as student and teacher exchanges; and summer, after-school, and vocational-technical education programs.[45]

Incentives for teachers to teach in minority schools included a month-long extended work year with $1,000 more pay and providing para-professional help for instructors. Model-school complexes maintained the neighborhood schools, but special programs could be provided in the complex. Experimental early childhood programs would be added "to determine the value of expanding such programs."[46]

In another article about these plans to improve education, the various factions on the board were reported as having expressed opposing opinions, depending on whether they supported the plaintiffs or the defendants in the *Keyes* case. Perrill called the plan "a good one, a sound one that has good educational ideas in it." Noel found the plan to be "only a smokescreen with business continuing as usual. It's not a specific plan. It's just a string of words, a collection of promises. It doesn't even specify definitely what will be done. And, the entire question of cost is left with just a question mark."[47]

Voorhees questioned the VOE proposal. "If all the children attending these 15 schools applied for transfers, it wouldn't even be possible to transport them," Voorhees said. "And we would be left with 15 empty buildings . . . The plan is merely a sop to the conscience of the board."[48]

On the other side of the desegregation battle, Berge found the plan "realistic. We have made an honest, conscientious effort to fulfill the order of the court. And I feel that, if given the proper opportunity, this board can go a long way in eliminating the shortcomings of these 15 schools."[49]

The Hearing on the Remedy

At the May 11 hearing, Gilberts said, "There is no evidence to support the theory that school desegregation is the absolute truth in solving the educational problems of the minority child . . . I'm also not aware of any single answer to these complex problems that's been accepted in the education field."[50]

He presented the board's plan for improving the educational programs at the fifteen schools. In questioning the proposal for the educational complex, Judge Doyle said, "These plans are very vague as far as I'm concerned. I can't tell from the proposal how much time would be required or how many new buildings would have to be constructed before they could be opened."[51]

Gilberts said the Denver schools "at this point have no recommendation for desegregation . . . I feel integration must occur but that it will take place on a psychological basis, involving social attitudes. There will be changes of states of mind in which individuals will learn to accept each other." Gilberts described the plaintiffs' integration proposal as "a mathematical solution to a problem that involves real human beings. These people have feelings. And the human factor can't be ignored." The only busing outside of the home school in his plan would be conducted on a voluntary basis. The district would be divided into complexes, with children transported from their home school for special programs. Under the plaintiffs' plan, between 8,380 and 16,845 Denver elementary pupils would be bused, depending on the method employed. Baker and Cole would be integrated through a busing program with other junior highs. Manual would have boundary changes or become a special school.[52]

As the plaintiffs had planned, Dr. Neil V. Sullivan, Massachusetts commissioner of education and former superintendent of the Berkeley, California, schools, testified that the integration of Berkeley schools resulted in the "upgrading of the educational achievement of the Negro child. This was accomplished without the higher learning level of the Anglo child, placed in an integrated school, being changed." He said association with white classmates provided Black children with intellectual stimulation. The grades of some of the Black children dropped, but they began studying. Berkeley had tried earlier, without success, to improve achievement in Black schools with large amounts of money to reduce class size, obtain better instructional materials, and hire teacher aides. They instituted the busing program only after extensive community preparation.[53]

Dr. James S. Coleman, author of the report *Equality in Educational Opportunity*, testifying for the plaintiffs, said: "Performance of pupils from low-income levels was primarily influenced by the characteristics and resources of the other students. We found that these educational resources of children, as brought to school from the home environment, are more important to their classmates than the characteristics of teachers or the input in the school in the form of such things as curriculum."[54] Coleman said his massive study was based on the performances of 60,000 teachers and 600,000 students in 4,000 schools in the United States.

Bardwell, a University of Denver professor, detailed the plaintiffs' plan for upgrading the quality of education at fifteen minority schools. For the twelve minority elementary schools, two of the plans would involve the transfer of pupils or of complete sections of the school between the minority schools and seventeen to nineteen white elementary schools. The transferred sections would involve several grades. The other two plans called for similar transfers involving twenty-two minority elementary schools and twenty-eight to thirty-one white schools. The latter plans combined the twelve minority schools that had Black *or* Hispanic enrollment of at least 70 percent with the ten other minority schools that had a minority enroll-ment of at least 70 percent when Black and Hispanic students were added together. Doyle questioned the addition of these ten schools, which were not on his March 21 list. In any event, he did not include them in his order to desegregate the schools.

At the secondary level, busing would be used to transfer students from Baker to Cole, a school Judge Doyle found to be inferior. Manuel would be integrated through boundary changes or by becoming a special school.

Doyle's Decision on the Remedy

Judge Doyle's decision on the remedy was published on May 21, 1970.[55] He found that the quality of education in minority schools could only be achieved by ending segregation and then providing compensatory educa-tion: "The only hope for raising the level of these students and for provid-ing them the equal education which the Constitution guarantees is to bring them into contact with classroom associates who can contribute to the learn-ing process."[56]

He ordered that in the fifteen schools designated in the March 21, 1970, order plus Elyria and Smedley Elementary Schools, inequality must be remedied through desegregation and a massive program of compensatory education.[57]

Doyle determined that certain schools in the core city were segregated as the result of housing patterns and the neighborhood school system; that constituted *de facto* segregation and was not unconstitutional per se. A cor-ollary finding and conclusion was that the segregated core city schools in question were providing an unequal educational opportunity to minority groups as evidenced by low achievement and morale. The causes of this infe-riority were held to be the segregated condition, together with a concentra-tion of minority teachers, low levels of teacher experience, and high teacher turnover in each of the schools: "We thus concluded that the School District had violated the Equal Protection Clause of the Fourteenth Amendment by maintaining and operating schools which deprived the recipients of an equal educational opportunity. Both plaintiffs and defendants were asked to submit plans to remedy the inequality found to exist."[58]

The judge reviewed the proposed secondary plans. In addition to the features described above, he mentioned compensatory education, faculty, and staff; in-service training and orientation programs for community involvement; tutorial systems; individualized instruction; and increased preschool training and other features similar to the school board's suggestions.[59]

The defendants' program was basically one of compensatory education. Students could transfer to schools of their choice on a space-guaranteed basis with transportation provided by the district. The defendants' plan described programs under way or already proposed for Cole and Manual.

A crucial factual question, the judge said, was whether compensatory education alone in a segregated setting had enough of an equalizing effect: "Dr. James Coleman . . . testified that isolation of children from low socioeconomic families creates an atmosphere which inevitably results in an inferior educational opportunity."[60] Some of education stimulation, Doyle said, must come from other children in the school. Doyle cited Dr. Neil Sullivan and Dr. Robert O'Reilly of the New York Department of Education, who also testified at the May 11 hearing, on the importance of desegregation and the inability of compensatory education alone to provide equal educational opportunity.[61]

The main witness for the defendants was Robert Gilberts, superintendent of the Denver district: "He stated that low achievement among children in the Court designated schools was the result of a number of factors, including home situation, lack of discipline, absence of stimulation by parents, and verbal deficiencies resulting from the families' limited vocabulary . . . He maintained that there is no affirmative evidence that desegregation would aid in providing an equal educational opportunity for minority children. Furthermore, Dr. Gilberts expressed doubt that desegregation could be successful without broad community support."[62]

Gilberts explained that the defendants' plan was designed to reconstruct the educational climate through differential staffing, in-service training for teachers and staff, special innovative programs of vocational and pre-professional training at Manual and Cole, and increased numbers of experienced teachers at the court-designated schools. VOE, when it improved racial balance at both the sending and receiving schools, with guaranteed acceptance and transportation, was the only means of providing some desegregation.

The judge discussed several issues of law. First was the question of whether *de facto* segregation was to be remedied in the same manner as a condition of *de jure* segregation. The schools became segregated "as a result of neighborhood housing patterns." Segregation was not caused "by positive law or as a result of official action." [Thus, he believed it was *de facto* segregation.]

> The second question is one of both law and fact: whether in a setting of grossly inferior minority schools, compensatory education improvement of the minority schools, together with a free transfer policy such as that suggested in the March 21, 1970 opinion constitutes a constitutionally acceptable remedy or whether in order to in truth improve the schools and to thus satisfy the requirements of the Constitution, it is necessary to prescribe and implement also a program of desegregation and integration. We have concluded after hearing the evidence that the only feasible and constitutionally acceptable program, the only program which furnishes anything approaching substantial equality is a system of desegregation and integration which provides compensatory education in an integrated environment.[63]

Then, the judge made these findings and guidelines:

1. The overwhelming evidence in this case supports the finding and determination which we now make that improvement in the quality of education in the minority school can only be brought about by a program of desegregation and integration. This is the positive conclusion of Doctors Coleman, Sullivan and O'Reilly, all of whom are authorities in the field. Their opinions are supported by extensive, comprehensive, in depth studies and, in some instances, actual experience in the field.

2. The evidence clearly establishes that the segregated setting stifles and frustrates the learning process . . . It is now clear that the quality and effectiveness of the education process is dependent on the presence within the classroom of knowledgeable fellow students.

3. The ideal approach, and that which offers maximum promise of success, is a program of desegregation and integration coupled with compensa-

174 JUDGE DOYLE'S DECISION AND THE REMEDY PLANS

> tory education. Desegregation . . . must be carried out in an atmosphere
> of comprehensive education and preparation of teachers, pupils, parents
> and the community. It also must be coupled with an intense and massive
> compensatory education program for the students if it is to be successful.
> 4. [A system of free transfer to designated Anglo schools is] a minimal,
> but . . . insufficient, fulfillment of the constitutional rights of the persons
> involved. It should be used as an interim measure.
> 5. As a prelude to the program of integration, minority schools must be
> vastly improved before sending majority students to them.[64]

Then, Doyle rejected the plans of both sides and specified the provisions of the plan: "Neither the plans submitted by plaintiffs nor those of defendants are wholly satisfactory, we, therefore, now delineate the guidelines of the plan which, based on the evidence and the law satisfies the Constitution and, at the same time, holds some promise of acceptance and success."

The DPS was ordered to desegregate the court-designated schools plus Smedley and Elyria—half before September 1, 1971, and the remainder not later than September 1, 1972. A detailed plan was not adopted at that point. Baker and Cole were to be desegregated. Manual would become a specialized city high school in arts and trades. The board's compensatory education and free transfer programs were also part of the plan.[65]

Elementary Schools

Schools are desegregated when the white population reaches 50 percent or more. It was desirable to distribute Black and Hispanic children equally in each school. Judge Doyle expected the plaintiffs and the school board to work out the details of the plans: "The final details will be subject to review by the Court. We have, of course, been reluctant to decree mandatory transportation, and it should be avoided to the extent possible."[66]

Junior High Schools

Doyle asked that substantial progress be made in desegregating Baker by fall 1971, with complete desegregation by fall 1972. He ordered that Cole achieve complete desegregation in two stages or be used for special education and other special programs.[67]

Manual High School

Doyle directed that the district implement the plans set forth by the defendants and plaintiffs for establishing Manual as an open school for the continuation and expansion of the vocational and pre-professional training programs that had been instituted by the principal, faculty, and staff. He ordered that these programs be capable of attracting students from throughout the city:[68] "Between now and the beginning of school in fall 1971, and continuing through fall of 1972, an intensive program of education must be carried out within the community and the school system in preparation for desegregation and integration. This should include at least a program for orienting teachers in the field of minority cultures and problems and how to effectively deal with minority children in an integrated environment."[69]

Doyle also noted that there should be a similar program for staff and administrators and the community. He added the requirement that there be free transfer with guaranteed space and transportation and a ten-point program for compensatory education as well.[70]

"A final judgment can be entered," he declared. "The remaining detail [the actual plan] is a matter requiring the closest scrutiny and study which will require many months . . . The entire matter can now be appealed."[71]

12

The Court of Appeals

Although Denver still did not have a detailed plan for desegregating the schools and students and their parents were uncertain about what school the students would attend in the fall, the school board immediately appealed Judge Doyle's decision.

According to William Berge, president of the board of education, Denver Public Schools (DPS) would wait until fall to make plans for the desegregation because by then the appeal would probably have been decided.[1] Obviously, Berge was counting on the decision being overruled by the Tenth Circuit Court of Appeals. The board's delay was typical of the district's usual response to the judge's orders.

Superintendent Robert Gilberts, who had never expressed his position on the court order, announced his resignation as of September 1, 1970. Howard Johnson was named to replace him.[2]

Meanwhile, the plaintiffs wanted to get started on the plans. In a letter from plaintiffs' attorney Gordon Greiner to defendants' attorney Michael Jackson, Greiner announced the outstanding volunteer lawyers who would work on the

https://doi.org/10.5876/9781646422906.c012

joint plans required by the court order. The plaintiffs had recruited very capable people, many of them community leaders, including school-community relations: Jim Culhane, David Ebel, and Ron Butz; transportation: Gail Oppenneer; school-teacher relations: Dick Young and Ed Flitton; school-student relations: Bruce Sattler and Craig Lewis; and school finances and federal funding: John Ratigan. Robert Connery was coordinator of the committees. Greiner wrote, "I suggest that you [Jackson] discuss a timetable with him [Connery] for the committee-administration meeting. We would appreciate hearing from you as to what the school administration is doing with regard to the development of supporting programs at the resolution schools."[3]

The desegregation planned in the three rescinded resolutions that had already been in place under the temporary injunction for the 1969–1970 school year continued under the judge's now permanent injunction. Meanwhile, the parties worked on specific plans for the entire district under the rest of the order. The city waited to learn the fate of the appeal.

On June 11, 1971, more than a year after Judge Doyle's decision, the Tenth Circuit Court of Appeals upheld the integration orders for northeast Denver while it rejected the plans to desegregate the inner-city "core" schools, which are referred to as the "court" schools.[4]

First in the opinion, Judge Delmas Carl Hill reviewed the case, starting in 1969 and continuing to the decision on the merits and the decision on the remedies. The original complaint set forth two separate causes of action. The first cause had six counts that all pertained to the rescission of Resolutions 1520, 1524, and 1531, which plaintiffs alleged were an attempt to resegregate what the previous board had tried to desegregate.

The second cause of action had three counts the court said "are pertinent here." The first count was that the defendants had purposely maintained racially and ethnically segregated core area schools. The second count alleged that the school board had maintained inferior minority schools, thus denying these children equal protection of the laws in violation of the Fourteenth Amendment. The third count attacked the neighborhood school policy because, the plaintiffs claimed, it resulted in inferior schools.

In the first cause, the trial court had found that rescinding the three resolutions was an act of *de jure* segregation, or segregation by state action.

On the second cause in the first claim, the trial court had found that the acts complained of in the core city schools did not constitute *de jure* segregation. On the second count in the second cause, though, the trial court had found that core city schools were offering unequal educational opportunity and thus violating the Equal Protection Clause of the Fourteenth Amendment and that fifteen schools should be offered relief. The district court found the neighborhood school policy, the third count, to be constitutional.

On appeal, the appellants (defendants) attacked the findings and conclusions as to the first claim (the rescissions of the three resolutions), the second count of the second claim (the provision of unequal education in minority schools), and the requirement of desegregating the fifteen court schools. The *Keyes* plaintiffs argued for error in the second claim in the first count (*de jure* segregation maintained in part of the city) and the third count (the segregating effect of the neighborhood school policy).[5] In short, each side maintained its original positions on all counts.

Judge Hill, who wrote the opinion, reviewed the Voorhees committee conclusions but found they "were apparently ignored." The Berge committee recommendations were equally ignored, he said.[6]

In his summary, Judge Hill said the Noel Resolution called on the administration to create a desegregation plan for the entire district. The three resolutions established a plan only for northeast Denver schools, but before they were implemented a school board election brought two new members to the board and a new majority, which rescinded the resolutions. In its place was Resolution 1533, providing for a voluntary exchange program. Shortly after that, the *Keyes* suit was filed.

In his discussion of the rescissions, the judge described the eastward movement and expansion of the Black population, the construction of Barrett Elementary as an all-Black school, the movement of white children out of the Stedman attendance area, and the use of mobile units, apparently to keep more Black children in Black schools. White children having been moved from the Hallett area to Phillips left Hallett more segregated.[7]

The opinion said that neighborhood school plans when impartially maintained do not violate constitutional rights. It added: "However, when a board of education embarks on a course of conduct which is motivated by purposeful desire to perpetuate and maintain a racially segregated school, the constitutional rights of those students confined with that segregated establishment have been violated."

In discussing Barrett, Judge Hill said, "Here there is sufficient evidence to support segregative intent . . . We are likewise compelled to support the findings of the trial court regarding the manipulation of boundaries and the use of mobile classroom units within the Park Hill area."[8] These acts, the trial court had found, "tended to isolate and concentrate Negro students into those schools which had become segregated in the wake of Negro population influx into Park Hill while maintaining for as long as possible the Anglo status of those Park Hill schools which still remained predominantly white."[9] Continuing the discussion of northeast Denver schools, the opinion said the failure to adopt transfers in relation to Stedman was not a segregative act.

There was no evidence to rebut or justify the Hallett to Phillips transfer that made Hallett less white. Other transfers made Stedman, Park Hill, Hallett, and Phillips more segregated. Evidence indicated that these were segregative acts taken with knowledge of the effect they would have.[10] At the same time, white students were allowed to transfer out of Smiley, which had a growing Negro population:

> The facts as outlined above simply do not mirror the kind of impartiality imposed upon a board which adheres to a neighborhood school plan . . . In sum, there is ample evidence in the record to sustain the trial court's findings that race was made the basis for school districting with the purpose and effect of producing substantially segregated schools in the Park Hill area. This conduct clearly violates the Fourteenth Amendment and the rules we have heretofore laid down in the *Downs* and *Dowell* cases.
>
> Since we have sustained the findings regarding state imposed segregation in the Park Hill area schools, it is unnecessary to further decide whether the rescission of Resolution 1520, 1524, and 1531 was also an act of *de jure* segregation. It is sufficient to say that the Board's adoption of those resolutions was responsive to its constitutional duty to desegregate the named schools and the trial court was within its powers in designating those Resolutions as the best solution to a difficult situation.[11]

Resolution 1533 called for voluntary desegregation. However, "a realistic appraisal of voluntary transfer plans has shown that they simply do not fulfill the constitutional mandate of dismantling segregated schools . . . Once state imposed segregation is found, trial courts are to employ their broad equitable powers to insure full and immediate desegregation."[12]

Then, the opinion moved from the issue of the rescissions to the second count of the second cause of action, in which the trial court had found the district was providing minority children with an unequal education and in doing so was violating their right to equal protection of the laws. The judge reviewed the trial court findings about the twelve designated elementary schools and Elyria and Smedley Elementary Schools plus Baker and Cole Junior Highs and Manual High, which the trial court had concluded were receiving an inferior education.[13]

Brown v. Board of Education said, "Such an opportunity [of education] where the state has undertaken to provide it, is a right which must be made available to all on equal terms." The appeals court opinion continued: "For the moment we perceive no valid reason why the constitutional rights of school children would not be violated by an education which is substandard when compared to other schools within that same district, provided the state has acted to cause the harm without substantial justification in terms of legitimate state interest . . . Thus it is not the proffered objective indicia of inferiority which causes the sub-standard academic performance of these children, but a curriculum which is allegedly not tailored to their educational and social needs."[14] The appeals court could not find the neighborhood schools system unconstitutional because that would have conflicted with its earlier decisions: "The trial court rejected the notion that a neighborhood school system is unconstitutional if it produces segregation in fact. However, then, in the final analysis, the finding that an unequal educational opportunity exists in the designated core schools must rest squarely on the premise that Denver's neighborhood school policy is violative of the Fourteenth Amendment because it permits segregation in fact. This undermines our holdings in the Tulsa, *Downs* and *Dowell* cases and cannot be accepted under the existing law of this Circuit."[15]

The court had "a firm conviction that we are without power to do so" (embark on a course of correcting the system). Before the court can be involved in such a course, "a constitutional deprivation must be shown": "Unable to locate a firm foundation upon which to build a constitutional deprivation, we are compelled to abstain from enforcing the trial judge's plan to desegregate and integrate the court designated core area schools. Although the Board is no longer required by court order to correct the situation in the core area schools, we are reassured by the Board's passage of Resolution 1562."[16] Resolution 1562 was a plan to improve the quality of education in the core city schools.

The court could order busing as a remedy in the case of the Park Hill schools, but it agreed with the district court's refusal to label the core city schools segregated by state action. It said that Denver had never had a state-ordered dual system and that the burden of proof was on the plaintiffs to prove by a preponderance of evidence that racial imbalance was caused by intentional state action.[17]

Then, Judge Hill reviewed the evidence on this issue: Manual boundaries and Cole Junior High and nearby junior high boundaries: "Thus, although on the surface the alterations appear to be racially inspired, there is evidence to sustain the trial court's finding that the changes were not carried out with the design and for the purpose of causing Morey to become a minority school."[18]

The opinion concluded:

> The Final Judgment and Decree of the trial court is affirmed in all respects except that part pertaining to the core area or court designated schools and particularly the legal determination by the court that such schools were maintained in violation of the Fourteenth Amendment because of the unequal educational opportunity afforded, this issue having been presented by the Second Count of the Second Cause of Action contained in the complaint. In that respect only, the judgment is reversed. The case is accordingly remanded for the implementation of the plan in accordance with this opinion. The trial court is directed to retain jurisdiction of the case for the purpose of supervising the implementation of the plan, with full power to change, alter or amend the plan in the interest of justice and to carry out the objective of the litigation as reflected by this opinion.[19]

The plan Hill is referring to is the one related to the three northeast Denver resolutions, which had been reinstated and been implemented in the fall of 1969 under the temporary injunction. The appeals court upheld Doyle's ruling to make that injunction permanent and thus enable the three rescinded resolutions. With this decision it appeared that only the schools in northeast Denver would be desegregated. Undaunted, the plaintiffs appealed to the United States Supreme Court.

When George Washington High was integrated in September as part of the three northeast Denver resolutions, there were near riots at the school.[20]

The old polarization over busing appeared again in the November 1970 election, which pitted Craig Barnes against longtime congressman Byron

Rogers. Barnes won the Democratic primary by thirty-one votes, as determined by the US House of Representatives in early October. Two weeks before the election, polls showed him 15 percent ahead of his Republican opponent, Mike McKevitt. At that point, Barnes's support for desegregation was used against him. He described the campaign in a later memoir:

> The McKevitt campaign now began running full-page advertisements in the *Denver Post* and the *Rocky Mountain News* featuring a facsimile of my signature on the complaint in *Keyes v. School District No. 1*. Over the next two weeks . . . my fifteen-point lead evaporated, and in the November election, I was defeated by roughly 10,000 votes . . .
>
> Two years later, District Attorney Dale Tooley ran for mayor of Denver. He, too, led in that race until his opponent began to run full-page advertisements that proclaimed "Republicans! Defeat the Tooley-Barnes Bunch Again!" Although Tooley had not been active in the trial of *Keyes*, he was portrayed as linked to me as counsel for the plaintiffs . . . Tooley was also defeated.[21]

On May 25, 1971, Judge William Doyle left his position on the district court and was sworn in as a judge of the Tenth Circuit Court of Appeals. Nevertheless, for many years he continued to oversee the *Keyes* case in the district court.

Also in May, three men who were opposed to desegregation—Bob Crider, Bert Gallegos, and Ted Hackworth—were elected to the Denver school board, but Gallegos resigned and Bernie Valdez was appointed to replace him.

In June 1971, there was a very large, well-deserved testimonial dinner at the Hilton Hotel in Denver to celebrate the many contributions of retiring board member Rachel Noel. She commented later that "it was just beautiful." Her son and daughter had pictures made. "I just felt the warmth of the occasion," she said. Senator George Brown was master of ceremonies. The National Association for the Advancement of Colored People (NAACP) gave her an award. Because not all the people who came could get in, many were allowed to stand around the outside of the room. Noel was given a trip to Africa, and a scholarship in her name is still presented every year by a Black educators' group.[22] Later, in 1973, she became chair of the Metro State College Department of Afro-American Studies.

The next important stop for the *Keyes* case was a final trip to the United States Supreme Court.

13

The Supreme Court Rules

The plaintiffs filed a petition to the United States Supreme Court for a writ of *certiorari* on October 8, 1971; it was granted on February 17, 1972.[1] The plaintiffs were no longer seeking a piecemeal approach to the inequality permeating the Denver public schools (DPS). Instead, they argued for a comprehensive plan of desegregating the entire system. Before *certiorari* was granted, board member William Berge declared the board innocent of any intentional segregation:

> There has never been any action in Denver to perpetuate or encourage segregation. The makeup of predominantly minority schools results entirely from housing patterns. Denver has the fairest housing laws in the United States and people are free to move wherever they want in the city. There has been no gerrymandering of school boundaries by the board. Also, if people want to send their children to a school besides the one to which they would normally be assigned, they can do so if the transfer improves integration. The schools even provide the transportation. I don't know of any way it could be fairer.[2]

https://doi.org/10.5876/9781646422906.c013

A *Chicago Sun-Times* article in March said the case was unlikely to be heard before the November presidential election because the National Association for the Advancement of Colored People (NAACP) could only print 300 pages a week of the 2,500-page factual appendix of the plaintiffs' brief.[3]

Prior to the hearing, a study by Harvard professor David J. Armor indicated that desegregation did not improve Black students' achievement. In fact, a segregated control group did slightly better.[4] This study was quickly disputed by other scholars. Jack E. Robinson, president of the Boston chapter of the NAACP, said improved race relations was not the goal: "Mixing the races is not the issue . . . Gaining access to superior educational facilities is. This is why busing is being pursued by the NAACP." Armor's report focused on secondary school students who may resent leaving their community. Thomas Pettigrew, another Harvard sociologist, said, "All Armor is showing is that while Metco [a system for moving some inner-city students to suburban schools] may be a very fine program, it is not strong enough to compensate for what is going on in the country generally."[5]

The Plaintiffs' Brief

The plaintiffs' arguments were carefully laid out in the detailed brief they submitted for the Supreme Court's 1971 October term. After stating that the case involved the Equal Protection Clause of the Fourteenth Amendment, the plaintiffs' brief began with a series of questions:

Whether petitioners are entitled to obtain system-wide relief to desegregate the Denver public schools because:

1. The district court's findings that "during the ten year period preceding . . . [1969] the Denver School Board has carried out a segregation policy" . . . We will establish that the deprivation of constitutional rights of Black pupils in Denver is so substantial and systemic as to require the use of remedial doctrines applied to dual systems created by segregation statutes.
2. The district court erred in ruling segregation to be "innocent" and lawful in certain schools serving Denver's older Black neighborhood—including particularly Manual Training High School—because the court applied incorrect legal standards and perspectives in making its decision on intent to segregate and the causes of segregation.

3. The court below erred in holding that the sole criterion of constitutionally actionable racial segregation was segregationist intent judged by the narrow test [of] whether decisions of the school board resulting in racial separation could conjecturally be explained by any conceivable non-racial explanation.

4. The Denver Public Schools have denied equal protection of the laws to students assigned to a number of predominantly Black and Hispano schools where there is manifestly an inequality in educational opportunity, both . . . the input resources . . . and the educational achievement of the pupils.[6]

The petition reviewed the history of the case. It includes some key quotations from Judge William Doyle's opinion. For example: "We have seen that during the ten year period preceding the passage of Resolutions 1520, 1524, and 1531, the Denver School Board has carried out a segregation policy. To maintain, encourage and continue segregation in the public schools in the face of the clear mandates of *Brown v. Board of Education* cannot be considered innocent."[7]

The attorneys for the plaintiffs argued that "the record in this case shows that where race was an issue each type of decision was invariably made in Denver so that the result was racial segregation."[8] The court of appeals said that "wherever the board could show *any* 'rational neutral criteria[,] segregative intent will not be inferred.'"[9] The brief continued, "Even with this strict burden of proof, which petitioners protest as too onerous, the Denver system was found to have engaged in a decade-long segregation policy affecting a substantial portion of the black community."[10]

Then, the plaintiffs reviewed different aspects of the issue: faculty assignment, size and location of school buildings and additions, transportation policies, school attendance areas (with an emphasis on Manual High School and Cole Junior High School), optional zones and transfer devices, and the curricula of and atmosphere at segregated schools.[11]

The brief focused on the inferior education offered in minority schools compared to the education in predominantly white schools. Leading experts in the country testified "as to the intangible, subjective characteristics of the environment of these segregated schools which tend to impede and destroy the academic progress as well as the self development of the minority children."[12]

The plaintiffs stressed the importance of other students in the education of children, citing national studies:

One of the most important educational attributes of a school is the peer group with whom the student attends school. The segregated school brings together children, most of whom are poor, who come from so-called deprived home environments, and whose parents have a relatively low level of education and employment.

National studies have demonstrated that this social class composition of the school is a more important source of learning than the teachers themselves. Children learn as much or more from their peers than from the academic curriculum of the schools.[13]

The plaintiffs pointed out that next to the peer group, the quality of education is most affected by the quality, experience, and stability of teaching staffs.[14] Denver minority schools had less experienced teachers than did majority white schools. Deficiencies in facilities and achievement in minority schools were also reviewed.

The brief added that the trial court only considered schools in which Black or Hispanic membership alone was 70 percent or more and refused to consider the eight other elementary schools and Morey Junior High in which the combined Black and Hispanic population was 70 percent or more; the trial court did not order any relief for those schools.[15] In 1968, third grade students at the majority-minority schools were 1.33 years behind third graders at white schools. By fifth grade the gap was 2.2 grades. By ninth grade, when the district-wide junior high average median percentile score was 53.8, Baker and Cole, largely minority schools, were at 28.2:[16] "The trial court found, as a matter of fact, that the segregated schools were offering unequal and inferior educational opportunities to minority children. The trial court went on to find, as a matter of fact, that a cause of the inequality was the segregated condition of the school."[17] The brief quoted Doyle's opinion at length:

We cannot ignore the overwhelming evidence to the effect that isolation or segregation per se is a substantial factor in producing unequal educational opportunity.

When we consider the evidence in this case in light of the statements in *Brown v. Board of Education* that segregated schools are inherently unequal, we must conclude that segregation, regardless of its cause, is a major factor in producing inferior schools and unequal educational opportunity.[18]

Finally, Judge Doyle concluded, "The evidence in the case at bar establishes and we do find and conclude that an equal educational opportunity is not being provided at the subject segregated schools within the District . . . The evidence establishes this beyond any doubt. Many factors contribute to the inferior status of these schools, but the predominant one appears to be the enforced isolation imposed in the name of neighborhood schools and housing patterns."[19] Judge Doyle believed the remedy would require both desegregation and compensatory education, not just compensatory education alone, which, he said, had been found universally to be unsuccessful.[20]

In addition to reviewing the legal arguments in the district court, the brief reviewed the proposed remedial plans. In May 1971, at the close of the hearing, Judge Doyle had selected a plaintiffs' modification of one of the board's six alternative elementary plans and adopted the board's proposals for Baker and Cole Junior Highs and Manual High, all to be implemented in September 1971. The opinion of the court of appeals on June 11, 1971, had nullified these remedial orders.[21]

In the summary of the argument, the plaintiffs sought "system-wide relief":

Petitioners are seeking a district-wide plan of relief for segregation and inequality of educational opportunity in School District No. 1. In support of this relief, petitioners contend as follows:

The brief suggested that the findings of the trial court as to a ten-year segregation policy affecting a substantial part of the Denver system, which findings were affirmed below, justify and necessitate a plan of relief which is not limited to the few schools which were most recently and overtly affected by this policy. While the courts below thus restricted the remedy, it should be extended to the entire Denver District. Only system-wide relief promises to effectively remedy the effects of the past discriminatory policy and to prevent its reoccurrence in the future, particularly where the District's segregatory practices in the past have been carried on covertly under the cover of a racially-neutral "color blind" neighborhood school policy.

The brief asked the Supreme Court to find that the courts below employed erroneous notions of petitioners' burden of proof on the issue of purposeful segregation by not requiring that respondents justify their segregatory actions by showing them necessary to achieve a compelling, nonracial state objective . . .[22]

It asked that where the school authorities have been found guilty of intentional segregation as to some actions, other actions having a similar segregatory result should not be clothed with any presumption of legitimacy but rather should be considered prima facie illegal unless justified by the showing of a nonracial compelling state interest. Had the courts below employed this test it would have compelled a finding of more pervasive segregation throughout the system, further justifying the necessity for district-wide relief.[23]

With regard to the unequal educational opportunity systematically being provided to Denver's minority students, the brief asserted that the trial court properly held such deprivation to constitute denial of equal protection and fashioned an appropriate remedy for it, in light of the evidence and the traditional powers and duties of a court of equity. While the remedy was proper, it was improper to withhold it from other minority schools displaying the same inequalities and inferiority as those to which the trial court extended relief.

Also, in reversing, the appellate court misconceived the standards of equal protection which applied, requiring a showing that the State had deprived minorities of equal educational opportunity intentionally, that is to say with odious intent, whereas all that is required is a showing that state action has resulted in racial discrimination. If not justified by compelling state interest, the racial discrimination will deny equal protection. Furthermore, the appellate court's inability to find that the inequality was the result of any state action was derived from ignoring the variety of decisions made by the school administrators which contributed to the inequality of opportunity in and the inferiority of these minority schools.[24]

Finally, the summary of the argument says the combination of the two constitutional violations found by the trial court should be remedied together in a comprehensive, district-wide plan.[25]

The plaintiffs pointed out that systemic discrimination affected the entire Black school population. The schools in question enrolled more than a third of the Black children in the city—a substantial part of the Black community.[26] They added that it was impossible to prove discrimination in the case of every child or of every school:

Discrimination in Denver was against blacks as a group although it was manifested in different ways against blacks in different situations . . . In Park

Hill where blacks were moving into white neighborhoods in the 1960's the segregation policy was most overt and visible . . .

The piecemeal approach of trying to cure segregation at only those schools where there is proof of a deliberate policy of segregation and leaving other schools segregated is plainly inappropriate where the segregation is a part of a policy which inevitably affects all students and schools, white or Black, either directly or indirectly. Such a piecemeal approach might be appropriate if an act of deliberate discrimination was truly isolated and unconnected with the rest of a school system. But the district court's findings of a segregationist policy negate any such notion in Denver.[27]

The district court said that assigning a white neighborhood would have had only a temporary integrating effect on Manual.[28] But the plaintiffs argued that "the court's reasoning ignores the effect of such boundary decisions and decisions to designate a school as black on neighborhood residential patterns. Schools' decisions change neighborhoods . . . [A segregation policy] may well promote segregated residential patterns which, when combined with 'neighborhood zoning,' further lock the school system into the mold of separation of the races."[29]

The brief argued that the burden of proof should have shifted to the defendants once they were found guilty of *de jure* segregation in the rescission of the three resolutions. The court of appeals said such an "onerous burden does not fall on school boards who have not been proved to have acted with segregatory intent . . . This ignores that Denver *was found to have had segregatory intent.*"[30] "The record in this case discloses that no compelling state interest was present to justify the pervasive pattern of segregation in Denver."[31]

Next, the plaintiffs discussed the violation of equal protection under the Fourteenth Amendment, which the district court found in the case of certain core city schools but the appellate court overturned. This section is titled "Denver's Systematic Disparate and Discriminatory Educational Treatment of Minorities Violates Equal Protection and Entitles Petitioners to System-Wide Relief." The outline of the section follows:

A-1. The respondents' system-wide and continuously disparate treatment
of minorities . . . resulting in what amounts to a segregated and unequal
educational caste system for Negroes and Hispanos violates the Equal
Protection Clause.

A-2. We assert that the trial court's conclusion of equal protection violation
   was clearly correct under the law. The Tenth Circuit . . . wrongly [denied]
   the equal protection of the laws to Denver's black and Hispano school
   children . . .

B. We support the trial court's remedial approach to eliminate the violation
   prospectively while attempting to cure the injury already inflicted.

C. While the trial court's remedy was proper[,] it was improperly withheld
   from certain other predominantly minority schools equally afflicted with
   inequality and [we] urge that relief be extended to these schools.

[These were the schools that had a combination of 70 percent or more black
   and Hispanic students.][32]

In illustrating the unequal treatment of minorities, the brief reviewed the
evidence concerning teachers, achievement expectations, standards of performance and course contents, career expectancy, location of schools and
boundaries, transportation of students and deployment of mobile units,
neighborhood school policy, Limited Open Enrollment (LOE), and long-
and short-term planning—all used to maintain segregated schools. The brief
cited some of the testimony in the trial court, an exchange between defendants' attorney William K. Ris and plaintiffs' expert Dr. Dan Dodson during
cross-examination, which challenged the attitude of district administrators
toward minority children:

Q: Now, with regard to the handicap, a child coming from a family in a
   neighborhood and a lower socioeconomic status, you wouldn't deny
   that those children are handicapped as compared to me, would you,
   before they ever get into school?

A: I would deny that the experience that they have brought with them,
   the experience through which they have come by the time they are
   of school age, has so impaired their sensory mechanisms that they
   do not have the capacity to acquire and organize experience in ways
   comparable to what you or I might have done at a comparable stage of
   our lives. I would be planting corn in East Texas today if teachers had
   seen the low socioeconomic status kid and the limitations of him and
   his inability to learn because he didn't have all these things and had
   believed them.

Q: You aren't alone in the courtroom in that regard.[33]

The trial court found that the many deficiencies in the schools adversely affected the quality of education of minority children, as seen in low achievement and high dropout rates.[34]

The Tenth Circuit Court, the brief asserted, was wrong in overturning the district court's finding of a violation of the Fourteenth Amendment. First, "The central theme of equal protection is that where state action results in racial discrimination, the Fourteenth Amendment is violated unless the state can show a compelling nonracial reason for continuance of the discrimination." Second, the appellate court was wrong in its restrictive interpretation of equal protection: "The second pervasive error arises from the appellate court's complete disregard of the multiplicity of decisions and policies by the board and the school administration which created, contributed to, condoned and continued the educational disadvantagement of Negroes and Hispanos."[35]

Judge Doyle's remediation program was appropriate in calling for desegregation and then compensatory education because experts testified that compensatory education alone was ineffective.[36] The remedy should have been extended to all of the district's predominantly minority schools.[37]

After all of these persuasive arguments, the attorneys logically concluded that "considered together the proven racial segregation and the proven inequality of educational opportunity in Denver require a system-wide remedial approach." The brief argued that either violation of the United States Constitution would be basis enough for ordering desegregation of the entire district, but together they made a very strong case:

> The depth of the wrong inflicted on the victims of discrimination is more clearly seen when the practice of covert racial segregation is seen in connection with the operation of a caste-type separate and unequal educational system in the segregated schools. There can be no doubt that such a combination of wrongs inflicts serious injury and justifies extraordinary remedies.
>
> Conclusion: Wherefore, petitioners respectfully submit that the judgment of the Court of Appeals should be reversed in so far as it reverses the judgment of the district court, and that the case should be remanded to the district court with directions that the court grant the prayers of the complaint requesting implementation of a comprehensive desegregation plan for the Denver school system.[38]

While the city waited for the Supreme Court decision, there was more violence in Denver. First, there was a bomb threat at Ellsworth Elementary School. The school wasn't evacuated, but after the threat the policy was changed. Before school let out for the summer, there were 229 bomb threats, 164 false alarms, 3 explosions, and 7 arson fires in the city.[39]

The Supreme Court Decision

The case was argued on October 12, 1972, but the 6 to 2 decision wasn't announced until June 21, 1973, four years after the case was filed in Denver. Voting for the decision were Justices William J. Brennan, William O. Douglas, Potter Stewart, Thurgood Marshall, and Harry Blackmun. Justice Brennan wrote the opinion. Justice Douglas filed a separate opinion, and Justice Warren Burger concurred in the result. Justice Lewis Powell filed an opinion concurring in part and dissenting in part. Justice William Rehnquist filed a dissenting opinion, and Justice Byron White took no part in the decision of the case.[40]

Justice Brennan summarized the case: "The gravamen of this action . . . is that respondent School Board alone, by use of various techniques such as the manipulation of student attendance zones, school site selection and neighborhood school policy, created or maintained racially or ethnically (or both racially and ethnically) segregated schools throughout the school district entitling petitioners to a decree directing desegregation of the entire school district."[41]

Brennan said the trial court "fractionated the district and held that petitioners must make a fresh showing of *de jure* segregation in each area of the city for which they seek relief." The Court found that the core city schools were inferior to the other schools in the district and also determined that "the only program which furnishes anything approaching substantial equality is a system of desegregation and integration which provides compensatory education in an integrated environment."[42]

As the plaintiffs had requested, the Supreme Court supported their long-held contention that schools with a combined Black and Hispanic population of over 70 percent should be included in the schools to be desegregated: "We think petitioners are entitled to have schools with a combined predominance of Negroes and Hispanos included in the category of 'segregated' schools."[43] That battle had been won at last.

Plaintiffs also won on the issue of which side had the burden of proof. They had argued that once segregative acts by a district have been proven, the burden of proof, or rather the burden to disprove deliberate segregative acts, falls on the district. The Supreme Court settled this question of whether the district court and the court of appeals had used an incorrect legal standard in addressing deliberate segregation:

> Respondent School Board was found guilty of following a deliberate segregation policy at schools attended in 1969 by 37.69 percent of Denver's total Negro school population . . . We have never suggested that plaintiffs in school desegregation cases must bear the burden of proving the elements of *de jure* segregation as to each and every school or each and every student within the school system. Rather, we have held that where plaintiffs prove that a current condition of segregated schooling exists within a school district where a dual system was compelled or authorized by statute . . . the state has a duty to effectuate a transition to a racially nondiscriminatory school system.[44]

Though this case did not involve a statutory dual system "where plaintiffs prove that the school authorities have carried out a systematic program of segregation . . . it is only common sense to conclude that there exists a predicate for finding of the existence of a dual system." If the segregative acts were not isolated in a particular separate section of the district, then "proof of state-imposed segregation in a substantial portion of the district will suffice to support a finding by the trial court of the existence of a dual system."[45]

On remand, the Supreme Court ordered the district court to decide first whether the school board's "deliberate racial segregation policy with respect to the Park Hill schools constitutes the entire Denver school system a dual school system."[46] If the entire system was affected, then district-wide desegregation was required. The Supreme Court found that there was indeed *de jure* segregation in the core city schools:

> The District Court and the Court of Appeals agreed that a finding of *de jure* segregation as to the core city schools was not permissible since petitioners had failed to prove (1) a racially discriminatory purpose and (2) a causal relationship between the acts complained of and the racial imbalance admittedly existing in those schools. This assessment of petitioners' proof was clearly incorrect.[47]

. . .

Applying these principles in the special context of school desegregation cases, we hold that a finding of intentionally segregative school board actions in a meaningful portion of a school system, as in this case, creates a presumption that other segregated schooling within the system is not adventitious. It establishes, in other words, a *prima facie* case of unlawful segregative design on the part of school authorities, and shifts to those authorities the burden of proving that other segregated schools within the system are not also the result of intentionally segregative actions.[48]

. . .

Nor is this burden-shifting principle limited to former statutory dual systems.

. . .

Remoteness in time certainly does not make those actions [segregative acts] any less intentional.[49]

Finally, the Supreme Court clearly directed the next steps for the US District Court in Denver: "In summary, the District Court on remand, *first*, will afford respondent School Board the opportunity to prove its contention that the Park Hill area is a separate, identifiable and unrelated section of the school district that should be treated as isolated from the rest of the district." Next, the district court would have to decide if the school board had been operating a dual system. If it had, the board had "the affirmative duty to desegregate the entire system 'root and branch.'" Even if the district court determined that Denver did not have a dual system, the school district faced an uphill battle. The court was told to allow the school district "to rebut petitioners' *prima facie* case of intentional segregation in the core city schools raised by the finding of intentional segregation in Park Hill schools." If the school district failed to do so, the district court would have to, "as in the case of Park Hill, decree all-out desegregation of the core city schools."[50]

Then, the Supreme Court vacated the court of appeals judgment regarding the core city schools.[51]

Justice Powell concurred in part and dissented in part. He wrote with approval about the abandonment of the *de jure* and *de facto* distinction and asserted that where segregation existed, there was a *prima facie* case for which the public school officials were responsible.[52]

Justice Douglas agreed that there was no difference between *de facto* and *de jure* segregation for purposes of the Fourteenth Amendment. He stated that calling actions of segregating boards "*de facto* is a misnomer, as they are only more subtle types of state action that create or maintain a wholly or partially segregated school system."[53]

Justice Rehnquist, dissenting, wrote:

> There are significant differences between the proof which would support a claim such as that alleged by plaintiffs in this case, and the total segregation required by statute which existed in *Brown* . . .
>
> But if the school board had been evenhanded in its drawing of the attendance lines for other schools in the district minority students required to attend other schools within the district would have suffered no such deprivation.
>
> To require that a genuine "dual" system be disestablished, in the sense that the assignment to a child of a particular school is not made to depend on his race, is one thing. To require that school boards affirmatively undertake to achieve racial mixing in schools where such mixing is not achieved in sufficient degree by neutrally drawn boundary lines is quite obviously something else.
>
> The Court has taken a long leap in this area of constitutional law in equating the district-wide consequences of gerrymandering individual attendance zones in a district where separation of the races was never required by law with statutes or ordinances in other jurisdictions which did so require. It then adds to this potpourri a confusing enunciation of evidentiary rules in order to make it more likely that the trial court will on remand reach the result which the Court apparently wants it to reach. Since I believe neither of these steps is justified by prior decisions of this Court, I dissent.[54]

In July, each side tallied the cost of the case to date. Gordon Greiner said the plaintiffs had spent "about a quarter of a million dollars" on research and legal fees. Of course, four years of demanding work was donated by the plaintiffs' lawyers, who worked on a pro bono basis, though there was the prospect that if they were the winners of a civil rights case, they would eventually be reimbursed by the losers. Omar Blair estimated that the school board up to that time had spent about $280,000 in defending the case in court.[55]

There was rejoicing in Denver among the proponents of desegregation when the Supreme Court ruling came down, giving the plaintiffs nearly everything they had asked for. The plaintiffs knew it would be very hard for the Denver school board to prove that it had not operated a dual system or that the core city schools were not inferior, as they had already proven these inequities. The district court would still have the task of selecting a specific plan to desegregate DPS "root and branch."

14

The Finger Plan

Before the case returned to Denver, new members Kay Schomp, Omar Blair, and Bernard Valdez were elected to the school board in May 1973. Schomp, who was white, was the wife of a well-known Denver car dealer. She had been president of the Denver League of Women Voters and was a staunch advocate for desegregation, as was Blair, who was Black. He was the equal employment opportunity officer at Lowry Air Force Base. Valdez, a Hispanic, often mediated between the two factions on the board.[1]

The previous November, Richard Nixon had been reelected US president despite Watergate. My husband, Monte, had been elected chair of the Colorado Democratic Party. Our daughter, Sarah, was in seventh grade at Byers Junior High School; our older son, Ted, was in fifth grade at Dora Moore Elementary School; and our younger son, Will, was in preschool.

The United States Supreme Court had directed the district court to determine whether the Denver Public Schools (DPS) had maintained a dual (segregated) school system, much like those established by statute in cities in the South. The Supreme Court's decision even indicated that the DPS probably

https://doi.org/10.5876/9781646422906.c014

had maintained such a dual system. Next, the school district had the burden of proving that Park Hill and northeast Denver were separate from the rest of the city—so separate that segregative acts in schools there had no impact on the rest of the district. If defendants failed to prove that, then the district court was charged with overseeing the creation of a plan to desegregate all the schools in the district "root and branch."

The trial on remand started on December 4 and ran through December 6, 1973. At one point Gordon Greiner for the plaintiffs and even Judge Doyle became impatient with the defendants trying to argue points already decided by the Supreme Court:

> MR. GREINER: Your honor, at this time, we move to strike all of Mr. [E. Bruce] Slade's testimony and all of the exhibits with which his testimony had to do. Our motion is very simply premised on the fact that under the mandate of the Supreme Court, the issues to which Mr. Slade's testimony purportedly went with, as I understand it, whether or not there was an effect in the rest of the school district of the so-called Park Hill actions. Our position is very simple, that whether or not Denver is a, quote, "dual school system" under the Supreme Court Mandate is not a question of fact, that the only question of fact remaining to be retried at this hearing was the issue of the separateness of Park Hill.[2]

A little later, it was evident that Judge Doyle's patience with the defendants was growing thin:

> THE COURT: I mean sooner or later this case has got to come to a conclusion. We can't continue to relitigate the same—You people haven't changed your attitude since 1969 . . . The same old song. I don't know what you expect. You want to go back and back and back.
>
> MR. [THOMAS] CREIGHTON: I think Your Honor should know that we have never accepted the findings that there was—
>
> THE COURT: I know you have never accepted it. You haven't now and you never did.
>
> MR. CREIGHTON: No, sir. These were acts which were not segregated.
>
> THE COURT: And you doubt if you ever will, but, of course, this is some evidence, too, I think of attitude of viewpoint of rationale, and I regret it. I just regret that I have to observe this, but it is the truth.[3]

On December 11, Doyle ruled on the issue, determining that Park Hill was not an entirely separate part of the city and that the Denver schools had operated a dual district. First, he reviewed the many hearings and decisions in the case. Then he came to the most recent hearing: "First, we consider the question whether Park Hill is a separate, identifiable and unrelated section of the school district which is to be treated as isolated from the rest of the district. The School Board has not succeeded in establishing that it is separate. Indeed, it admits that there is no geographic separation of Park Hill from the remainder of the Denver school district."[4]

Doyle then quoted the Supreme Court again, saying the "proof of state-imposed segregation in a substantial portion of the district will suffice to support a finding by the trial court of the existence of a dual system."[5] The defendants attempted to show that "segregated conditions in individual schools outside the Park Hill area are wholly the product of external factors such as demographic trends and housing patterns, and are in no way the product of any acts or omissions by defendants. We are not persuaded by the evidence presented, nor have defendants succeeded in dispelling the presumption that the segregative intent of the School Board was clearly evidenced by its actions in Park Hill permeating the entire district. The affirmative evidence is to the contrary, that defendants' actions in Park Hill are reflective of its attitude toward the school system generally." Finally, the judge concluded that Denver was operating a dual system.[6]

A few days later, Judge Doyle ordered both the plaintiffs and the defendants to submit to the court plans for desegregating the school system.[7] Since the judge eventually rejected both sides' plans, I believe there is no need to study them both in detail except to notice the sharp contrast between them.

The plaintiffs tried to achieve as much integration as possible. At the elementary level, they used a range of 40 percent to 70 percent white as constituting an integrated school. This was roughly 15 percent above or below the district-wide percentage of whites. By this standard, twenty elementary schools were already integrated and hence not affected by the pupil reassignments. They sought a similar percentage at the secondary level. Black and Hispanic students were counted together. Younger white and minority children were affected equally. At the elementary level, minority schools and white schools were paired. All of the children attended one school in first through third grades and the paired school in fourth through sixth grades.

There were variations on this plan in which children went to either first through fourth grades or first and second grades at one school, depending on the numbers of children and the capacities of the schools. There would be an increase in busing of 12,257 elementary children.[8]

At the secondary level, white and minority children were equally affected and Black and Hispanic children were affected proportionally. At the junior high level, there would be an increase of transportation of 1,399 students. High school students would attend schools on the basis of residence, except that seniors would not be reassigned and Manual magnet program students and students who were then on voluntary open enrollment (VOE) would not be forced to change schools.[9]

The plaintiffs' plan recommended assigning minority faculty to schools that would be receiving minority students under the court order. All of the schools had more than 84 percent white teachers as of September 1973.[10]

Other sections of the plaintiffs' plan covered community education; training for school personnel; input from the community; orientation of parents, students, and school personnel; equalization of facilities; and new curricula (including a multicultural approach for Hispanics as set forth by Dr. Jose Cardenas, who had been an expert for the Hispanic intervenors). They also advocated a shift from tracking to individualized education and supportive services. The plaintiffs urged the court to continue its monitoring and evaluation of the plan.[11]

The appendix of the plaintiffs' plan provided the exact enrollment and racial composition of every school in the district. Like other parents in Denver, we immediately searched the plans as reported in the newspapers to learn where our children would be attending school if the court adopted the plaintiffs' design. At the elementary level, Moore was paired with Greenlee, Knight, and Steele Elementary Schools. Children at the mostly Hispanic Greenlee would be divided to join neighborhood children at mostly white Knight, Moore, and Steele for grades 1–3. Then, students from these schools would attend Greenlee for grades 4–6. Our son Ted, who was in fifth grade, would go to Greenlee, across Broadway in west Denver, for sixth grade in the fall. Our son Will would start kindergarten in the fall, attend Moore through third grade, and then go to Greenlee for grades 4–6. The white percentages in these schools varied from 44 percent to 57 percent. Greenlee would be 48 percent white.

Byers Junior High School, where Sarah was in seventh grade, would take students from all the schools in this elementary pairing plus those graduating from Sherman Elementary School, so Sarah would continue at Byers for eighth and ninth grades and then move to East High School, where white enrollment would be increased to 58 percent by shifting some of the mostly Black northern Park Hill students to George Washington.

There were other major changes in high school assignments. Mostly white Thomas Jefferson would exchange some attendance areas with Manual, as would largely Hispanic West High with Kennedy High. Some of the Manual and East territory would be shifted to South.[12] Though we would have had to adapt to these changes, we would not have found any of the assignments difficult for us or our children if the court had chosen to adopt them.

The school board adopted a plan on January 22 under the protest of some members who had not had time to study it and might not have approved it if they had. They also suggested that the judge include suburban districts in the plan. The district defined a desegregated school as one between 25 percent and 75 percent white, in contrast to the plaintiffs, who, as noted, had suggested a 40 percent to 70 percent required range. By this guideline, Superintendent Louis Kishkunas estimated that 69 of the district's 118 schools were already desegregated.

The most striking feature of the board's plan was the emphasis on buildings rather than on children. Eleven inner-city schools would be closed, creating an educational vacuum in the middle of the city. Each of their largely minority populations would be parceled out to four or five white schools, placing a greater burden on minority children than on white children. Four of the elementary schools would become enrichment centers where integrated activities would take place for some schools for half a day for three weeks each semester. This idea had some resemblance to the old, complex Gilberts Plan. Only seventeen schools would still be more than 75 percent minority, according to the district. The plan suggested special programs in the still segregated schools, an approach the district had been trying to implement, unsuccessfully, for years. In addition, in the new plan, the district described the entire DPS curriculum and all the existing special programs.

Schools that would still be predominantly minority, even by the defendants' very lenient standard of 75 percent minority, were Baker, Cole, and Mann Junior Highs, while Hamilton would be more than 75 percent white.

Manual High School would continue to be more than 75 percent minority. The Career Education Center would be the only school to attempt to desegregate students at the high school level.[13]

Our neighborhood school, Dora Moore, though largely white, was among those schools to be closed and partially demolished—perhaps mainly because it was old, never mind its design by noted pioneer architect Robert S. Roeschlaub in 1889 and its decoration of classical busts donated by the community (and its subsequent historic designation). The "new" part of the school was to be reopened as an enrichment center. All Moore children would be bused to Hallett Elementary, from the school at Eighth and Downing Streets to 2950 Jasmine, a thirty-minute drive when many, mostly minority schools were closer. Hallett was a school we knew well because Sarah and Ted had volunteered to enroll there for a year. Not only was our elementary school to be eliminated, our closest junior high, Morey, was also slated to be closed and reopened as a junior high enrichment center. Under this plan, Ted and later Will were slated to go to Hallett, and Sarah would continue at her current junior high, Byers.[14]

The hearings on these plans were held on February 19–22, 1974.

Greiner pointed out the shortcomings in the defendants' plans, which provided that 48 percent of minority kids at the elementary level and 45 percent at the junior high level would remain in segregated schools. Too many of the closed schools were minority or integrated schools and too many of the kids on the bus were minority kids.[15] That is, minority children carried a disproportionate burden in the attempt to desegregate the schools.

About the preparation of the defendants' plan, Assistant Superintendent Charles Armstrong was asked, "And so am I to understand then that the Denver Board of Education and its individual members gave no input whatsoever as to what the staff was trying to accomplish?" His answer: "That's right." This was a reference to the fact that the board was presented with the plan the night before it was due at the court and voted on it without an opportunity to study it.[16]

When Joseph Brzeinski, a DPS administrator who became superintendent in the 1977–1978 school year, was testifying for the defendants, Judge Doyle questioned the district's program of busing children from white areas to already overcrowded white schools when they could have gone to less crowded minority schools:

THE COURT: Well, it's all this busing for lack of schools or distance that
you do, do you not? These pick ups that occur all over the edge of
[the] periphery of the city?

THE WITNESS: Could you clarify as to where you mean under the current
plan?

THE COURT: No plan at all. I am just referring to your decision to take
these students to schools that are now 90 or 95 percent Anglo rather
than to schools, where they are already overcrowded rather than to
schools like, oh, those on the west side in which there are openings,
maybe there is a third of the capacity opened and yet they are segregated. In other words, do you know of this fact?[17]

The upshot of the presentation of these very different plans by the plaintiffs and the defendants was that Judge Doyle appointed his own expert,
Dr. John A. Finger, to attempt to design a plan. Dr. Finger had a national
reputation because he had participated in the Supreme Court case *Swann
v. Charlotte-Mecklenberg* (402 U.S.1 [1972]) and the plan for the Oklahoma City
Public Schools.[18] Doyle explained the need for an outside expert at the hearing on the new plan on March 27, 1974:

What I had in mind was that the parties would get together, and implement
those suggestions and see how it looked, at least, test it out. . . . But this
never did occur . . . The Supreme Court of the United States has repeatedly
declared that it is the job of the School District to desegregate, and I have to
give them every opportunity to do so in order to comply with the law, and it
is very plain now that they cannot—they are not going to, and so with the aid
of the Court's consultant, a plan has been prepared, or rather, he has prepared
it. I don't warrant it. He is here to present it. All right.[19]

In dialogue with William Ris, the school board's attorney, Doyle revealed his
frustration with the school board:

THE COURT: Do you think if we could wait for six months, you could
come forth with a product that was satisfactory to the Supreme Court,
or three months, or one month?

MR. RIS: I don't know.

THE COURT: Or a year?[20]

Judge Doyle showed immense courage after he became convinced that Black and Hispanic children were being denied their constitutional rights. The ordering of the Finger Plan affected every child and family in the DPS. There was tremendous backlash, including picketing and chants of "Boil Doyle in Oil." The cost to him was personal, although he was shortly appointed to the federal Tenth Circuit Court of Appeals, indicating the great respect for him within the legal community.

Many of the plaintiffs' proposals were incorporated in the Finger Plan in the judge's order. According to the plan, the white percentage in a school should range from 40 percent to 70 percent, as the plaintiffs had proposed, though that might not occur in schools offering bilingual education.[21] Support programs included adequate preparation of students, parents, teachers, administrators, and board members. The plan required that transportation be provided under current policies and that breakfast and lunch be based on need. In addition, it specified an affirmative action hiring program.[22]

One method used to desegregate was rezoning, which, especially on the west side, eliminated the need for busing. A second method was pairing, which had been suggested by the plaintiffs. Approximately thirty-three schools were desegregated by classroom or home school pairing. Classrooms were paired, and half of the minority students and half of the white students were to be bused to the paired school. The court's preference was to transport half of each class and maintain six grades in each elementary school. The minimum time spent in the receiving school was to be a half day plus lunch time. The local school was maintained as the home school. This gave the flexibility to institute special programs in the home school. Transportation took place from school to school.[23]

The third method of desegregation was assigning pupils from satellite areas. At the elementary level, these assignments mostly involved busing students from the northern section to the southern section, or one-way busing of minorities. At the secondary level this was reversed, and whites were to move to northern city schools.

Junior highs were desegregated first by rezoning. Satellite zones were created out of the Cole and Horace Mann areas, and satellites were set up for Kennedy, Merrill, and Place. Cole would become 60 percent white and Mann more than 50 percent white.[24]

At the high school level, Manual would become 56 percent white following boundary changes with East High School, the expansion of East boundary lines, and the creation of satellite zones. East would then be more than 55 percent white. East and Manual were to be consolidated as the East-Manual Complex.[25]

Doyle urged the adoption of the Bilingual-Bicultural Plan of Dr. Cardenas, which was in pilot form at Del Pueblo Elementary School. He ordered it installed at Baker Junior High and West High and at Swansea and Garden Place Elementary Schools. Del Pueblo School, he said, should not be desegregated, as that would disrupt this program.[26]

In an April 5, 1974, letter to Judge Doyle accompanying the plan, Finger said, "Despite the widespread opposition to busing, there is no evidence that it hurts anybody." He added, "The research does seem clear on one point, and that is that Anglo students attending school with minority students do just as well as their copatriots in predominately Anglo schools."[27] Finger also said nearly 10,000 students would attend integrated schools that were essentially walk-in schools, although 630 who lived more than a mile from school would have short bus runs.

In the decision, the judge first referred to the "Memorandum and Opinion" of December 11, 1973, when he determined that the acts of the school district were not isolated from the rest of the district and that the entire system was an illegal dual system.[28] Thus, a plan of desegregation "root and branch" was required. The court considered various desegregation systems submitted by the parties but decided they were all inadequate. The court directed Finger to come forward with a plan, which was presented in detail at the end of the judge's opinion.[29]

Here is a selection from the many provisions Judge Doyle "ordered and judged and decreed":

1. The defendants are enjoined from discriminating on the basis of race or color and they must take affirmative actions to disestablish all school segregation and eliminate the effects of a dual school system . . .
3. The Finger Plan shall be modified as follows:
    A. Student officers in junior high and high schools shall not be elected until the fall. Seniors who are reassigned may choose which of the two high schools they want their diplomas from.

B. Defendants should consult with Dr. Finger about moving the grid lines for attendance boundaries and to establish the boundaries between Baker and Byers junior highs which are to be maintained as separate schools. The area South of Lowry shall be assigned to Baker.

C. Anglo enrollment at Morey shall be not less than 50%.

D. Anglo enrollment at Cole shall be not less than 60%.

. . .

H. Transportation shall be provided to parents for PTA or other activities when requested by the relevant organization.

I. Kindergarten children will remain in their neighborhood schools . . .

. . .

4. The defendants shall not deviate from the Finger Plan without prior approval of the Court

. . .

6. The defendants have a continuing obligation to operate and maintain desegregated schools including proposed new schools and to prevent any school from becoming a racially identifiable school.

. . .

11. Transportation shall be provided according to the provisions and criteria set forth in the Finger Plan. The district shall submit a transportation plan to the Court which will be evaluated by a specialist designated by the Court as to the adequate provision of transportation services.

12. Defendants shall implement a plan of training of school personnel and orientation of pupils and parents substantially like that in Defendants' Exhibit ZB-III attached to the Memorandum Decision and Order of April 8, 1974.

13. A Monitoring Commission consisting of outstanding members of the community shall be appointed by the Court: the parties are invited to submit names. They shall initially serve until June 1, 1975. Defendants are ordered to cooperate with the commission and provide assistance and information as the commission may request. [This was the Community Education Council, on which I later served.]

14. The Commission shall coordinate the efforts of community agencies in implementing the plan; educate the community on the Constitutional requirement and the details of the plan; receive and consider criticism of the plan and attempt to solve problems, reporting its action to the Court;

report periodically about the implementation and provid[e] ongoing monitoring of the plan.

15. The defendants shall develop a pilot bi-lingual, bi-cultural program immediately in September of 1974 at Del Pueblo, Cheltenham, Garden Place, and Swansea elementary schools, and Baker Junior High and West High School along the lines of that proposed by Dr. Jose Cardenas. The district shall employ a specialist to help implement the program. It is expected to spread to other schools.

. . .

17. The defendants are directed to file with the Court very specific and detailed reports about the requirements above and on the following matters in September 1974:

(1)Number and percentage of students by grade, ethnicity or race in each school and district wide for elementary schools, junior highs, and senior highs.[30]

For the data on these personnel, Judge Doyle wanted numbers by grade, ethnicity, or race for each school and district-wide for teachers, students in each paired classroom, probationary teachers, tenured teachers, full-time substitutes, and the number of students suspended and expelled by grade, race, or ethnicity during the prior semester as indicated on their cumulative records.

19. The School Board shall announce and implement the following policy:

A. Effective not later than the beginning of the 1974–75 school year, the principals, teachers, teacher-aides and other staff who work directly with children . . . shall be so assigned that in no case will the racial or ethnic composition of a staff indicate that a school is intended for minority students or Anglo students.

. . .

D. The defendants are directed to implement forthwith an affirmative action plan for the hiring of minority teachers, staff and administrators on a priority basis with the goal of attaining a ratio of Chicano and black personnel within the district which reflects more truly the ratio of Chicano and black students to the total student population at the elementary, junior high, senior high levels and district-wide . . .

22. The fees of Dr. John Finger are taxed on the district since they could not come up with an acceptable desegregation plan.

23. The request of the plaintiffs for costs and attorneys' fees since the inception of the case is granted. They are asked to submit a bill by June 1, 1974.[31]

This was the final judgment and decree. The judge concluded: "The Court shall retain jurisdiction for the purpose of supervising implementation and modifying its provisions as may be necessary from time to time, until such time as the defendants have demonstrated the disestablishment of their dual school system and the maintenance of a unitary, desegregated system on a continuing basis."[32]

The awarding of attorneys' fees was not a small matter, as the plaintiffs' attorneys had worked on this case on a pro bono basis since before it was filed in 1969. Their law firms had carried them through that time.

Next, the city prepared for the desegregation of every school in the district in fall 1974, five years after the filing of *Keyes v. School District No. 1.*

15

Desegregating Denver "Root and Branch"

Citywide desegregation began in fall 1974, at the same time as elections for the US Senate and Colorado governor. Richard Lamm, the Democratic candidate for governor in the general election, was frustrated at one forum when all the questions pertained to busing. It would have been political suicide, according to Mary Jean Taylor, if he had espoused busing. Eventually, he said, "We're running for governor, not the school board!"[1] My husband, Monte, was state Democratic Party chair for this first election since the resignation of President Richard Nixon. The Democrats won in a landslide. Lamm, in fact, was the first of two Democrats who held the governor's office for the next twenty-four years. That same year, Democrat Gary Hart was elected to the US Senate.

An anti-integration amendment to the Colorado Constitution known as the Poundstone Amendment also passed that fall; it required a majority of voters of the entire county, rather than just the area concerned, to annex any part of that county to a city. The fear of suburban voters was that they would be drawn into Denver's desegregation order because Denver's school district was coterminous with the city boundaries.

https://doi.org/10.5876/9781646422906.c015

Every child in the public schools was affected in some way by the district court's final desegregation order in May 1974. They would either see new children in the "neighborhood school" or would be attending a different school outside the immediate neighborhood. And every parent was affected. If you ask any Denver person who was alive at that time, they will tell you how deeply involved they were in the changes in the schools in the early years of the desegregation order. Many schools were improved by the greater public and parental focus on them.

Our children experienced many changes. Sarah, then in eighth grade, moved from Byers Junior High, which was 3.2 miles south of our house, to Morey Junior High—a formerly majority Black school—which was slightly closer, 2.9 miles north of our house. The more distant Byers assignment had been the result of an earlier gerrymander that had kept Byers mostly white and given Morey a higher percentage of minority students. Ted, in sixth grade, continued at Dora Moore Elementary School, with more Hispanic children bused in from the Greenlee School area, and then he went to seventh grade at Morey as well. Will was in kindergarten, attended Moore Elementary School for the next six years, and then went on to Morey. All three of our children went to East High School.

Morey Junior High

The elaborate community actions to make desegregation peaceful and effective were astonishing, carried out not only by parents in favor of desegregation but also by those who opposed it, who still wanted quality education without the kind of violence that had occurred over busing elsewhere. The steps parents took at Morey are just one example of the hundreds of contributions interested citizens made all over Denver. About a month after Judge Doyle's final ruling, parents met with the Morey principal, Mr. Tilford Cole—who was Black in keeping with the district policy of assigning Black administrators to Black schools—to prepare for the new students coming in the fall. At that first meeting were Mrs. Van Jacobs, Mrs. Purcell, Sheila Cleworth, Melvin Norton, Diane Macdonald, and myself. We learned that Morey would have 1,245 students; only 342 were former students. Fifty percent would be minority. The possibility of split sessions was a concern, but the crowding was eased by staggering the starting and ending times over seven periods while students only registered for five or six courses.[2]

Among the many features Morey as a minority school lacked was a parent organization, so our first task was to create the Morey Steering Committee of teachers, parents, and students to support the educational program and provide a channel of communication between the school and the parents. Many parents and teachers came forward to help. The new parent organization immediately sponsored a series of coffees to orient new parents to Morey. Principal Cole and thirty-six teachers agreed to attend these coffees, or "beer busts." We had contact parents in nearly every school that would be sending students to Morey, including Bromwell, Moore, Kaiser, and Sabin elementary schools and Byers, Kennedy, and Cole junior highs. The steering committee had chairs for each of these activities: the newsletter, volunteers, coffees, busing, host families, and quality education. One list of steering committee members included thirty parents, the head boy and girl, and eight staff members. Volunteers helped with orientation, rode buses, served as host families, spoke at school board meetings, and tried to help in any way necessary.

In May 1975 and May 1976, the steering committee sponsored carnivals at the school, raising about $900 for the school each time. A list of volunteers indicated that fifty-two parents volunteered to run such events as "hockey puck" and "family swim." I was chair of the steering committee in 1975–1976, and Bev Yablonski and Lee Hill also served as chairs in those early years. The presence in the school of interested, active parents was an important effect of the court order. It's true that most of these parents were white, but several very active Black parents, including Wilma Webb and Mel Norton, also participated. My role was, in part, shaped by the fact that I was appointed as one of the monitors at Morey by the Community Education Council, which had been established by the court to oversee the implementation of the order (see below).

Evidence that Morey had been a separate but unequal minority school was clear in the limitations of the curriculum before the court order took effect. Morey students immediately benefited from the rule that any course offered at a student's previous school had to be offered at the new school, though I am not sure where that rule was promulgated. Previously, the only foreign language offered at Morey was Spanish; now, French 1, French 2, and

French 1A and 1B were added immediately. There had been no orchestra, so that was added, too. In addition, Morey had not offered advanced or accelerated classes, so those were added, although accelerated English and accelerated social studies were later dropped because the tracking led to resegregation in the classroom. Latin and German were also offered, perhaps for the first time.

Dora Moore Elementary School

As the desegregation order took effect, Dora Moore Elementary School's active parents pushed for better curriculum and facilities, which Moore needed. Under the court order, the school was adding mostly Hispanic students from the Greenlee and Garden Place neighborhoods.

Moore was always blessed with very active parents. Historically, its students included film star Douglas Fairbanks Sr., band leader Paul Whiteman, and First Lady Mamie Doud Eisenhower. In the modern period, active parents included Kay Schomp and Carole McCotter, both of whom became school board members; Jeanne Robb, who became a city council member; and Dick Lamm, elected governor in 1974. Sometimes, the teachers and principal might have felt they had more help than they really wanted.

The school had experience welcoming students under open enrollment from the overcrowded, largely Black Smith Elementary School area. We linked a neighborhood host family, I believe in 1971, to every incoming family that wanted one. In all, seventeen Moore families welcomed Smith families with two to four children each from northeast Denver. The host family was to provide a local home in case a child became ill or experienced some other emergency. Sometimes, the families got together for lunch or social events as well.

Moore parents, in response to the court order, requested certain changes in the school and curriculum—changes they had been seeking for years. The Budget Lay Advisory Committee, on which I served for six years, had asked nearly every one of those years for an improved library, or what was then called an Instructional Media Center (IMC). The school was overcrowded, and the so-called library was used all day as a classroom. We knew we would have room for a real library if the district-wide cataloguing division in Moore's basement, which used two classrooms, was moved to some other school building that had extra space. These two classrooms added a phantom sixty slots to the school's capacity numbers, even though no classes could use them, thus creating the illusion of space while the school was overcrowded. The school district was deaf to our requests.

In 1974–1975, the first year of the citywide desegregation order, 159 mostly Hispanic children were bused into Moore, resulting in a 54 percent white student population. The school did not qualify as a Title I school for extra educational help, which is based on the percentage of children in poverty; it also did not qualify as a bilingual, bicultural school. Ten percent of the students would have to pass a screening to qualify for a bilingual program. To address this need, in 1976, a Spanish-speaking para-professional was assigned to help eight non-English-speaking students after school.[3]

In summer 1974, the school district assigned Moore's excellent principal, Albert Rehmer, to two-fifths time at Emerson School, in addition to his responsibilities at Moore. We were expecting 570 children at Moore the following year, 200 of them new to the school from the satellites. This double burden on our principal did not seem like a recipe for success in our desegregation efforts. I wrote to Superintendent Dr. Louis Kishkunas to ask him to assign Rehmer to Moore full-time. The letter of response from Walter Oliver said they intended to assign a full-time assistant principal to work with him, which helped alleviate the problem.

In 1974–1975, students, with the guidance of teacher Keith Kirby, applied for and received landmark status for Moore from the Denver Landmark Commission. The students who testified before the commission were Ronnie Rodriguez, Valerie Wheeler, Midge Sellers, our son Ted Pascoe, Dana Atchison, and Aaron Martin.[4] Achieving landmark status was a defensive move, as the community was still recovering from the shock of the school district's first plan to close and demolish Moore and other schools in the inner city.

In spring 1975, I wrote a summary of the first year of desegregation at Moore: "Dora Moore School has enjoyed quite a tension-free year with its new bused students and its expanded district. While Moore has experienced no serious racial problems as a result of the Court-ordered plan, there are other problems due to the increased and still increasing enrollment this year. The most serious problem in the mind of the Moore community is the need for better library facilities for the students and teachers. Also the offices of the Nurse and Social Worker should be relocated."[5]

I described the library problem again. The library had a total of 4,000 volumes, or about 7 books per student. The school needed remodeling to provide an IMC, the purchase of media materials for the IMC, and the hiring of a qualified staff person for it.

Denver Public Schools (DPS) was aware of the serious needs for library facilities in the district. I cited DPS statistics dated April 7, 1975, which reported that only thirty-five elementary schools had full-time librarians, with only fourteen of those schools staffed by certified librarians. Another thirty-eight schools had part-time or half-time libraries, of which only six had certified librarians. The remaining thirty-one schools either had no library (nine) or had a library with no staff. Moore was counted as having a part-time library, even though the room so designated was a full-time classroom.

Our proposed solution to the Moore problem was to move the cataloguing room out of Moore; reduce the number of bused-in children by sixty-three, which would improve the racial balance at several schools; and, of course, develop an IMC at Moore.

There was solid evidence that the education at Moore needed improvement. Moore children were reading an average of three months below grade level and had math skills at 5.9 (five years, nine months) when they were in grade 6.7, according to a state report I cited in my 1972 annual report for the Lay Advisory Committee.[6] These areas were studied by parents in 1976: reading, Carole McCotter; music and language, Silvia Benson; math, JoAnn Burstein; art, Brad Benson; physical education, Hester Witchey; science, John VanderMiller; and social studies, Jim McCotter. The parents came to the meetings with their own curriculum summaries that we could all study, which resulted in more challenging math for some primary students, Spanish classes after school, and parental support for buying classroom science and social studies kits.

Finally, Moore parents saw some movement in the district's plans for the school. By February 1977, the curriculum committee was talking about the remodeling plans for the IMC and another room for a math lab. The desegregation of the city, which, in part, had the goal of improving minority schools, had helped Moore—a formerly white school—improve its educational program and facility.

The Community Education Council

The involvement of the whole community in the desegregation effort was greatly increased by Judge William Doyle's appointment of a large citizens' council to oversee the implementation of the order. The members were drawn from every major organization and racial and ethnic group in the city. At the first meeting of the Community Education Council (CEC), in his chambers in May 1974, the judge started by introducing the diverse members, including absentees:

> I think we did succeed in bringing together the leaders of this community. Temporary chair: Chancellor Maurice Mitchell . . . Arthur Glenn, manager of Channel 7; Dr. Harold Haak, vice president of the University of Colorado; Dean Robert Yegge; Charles Leasure, station manager at Channel 9; Richard Wright, board of Chamber of Commerce; John Hasselblad, president of Van Schaack; Rex Jennings, President and General Manager of Denver Chamber of Commerce; Rev. Williams of New Hope Baptist Church; Rachel Noel, professor at Metro State; Mary Baca; Senator Roger Cisneros; William Roberts, councilman; Bruce Rockwell, President and CEO of Colorado National Bank; Rabbi Earl Stone of Temple Emanuel; Larry Varnell, Vice President Central Bank; Gerald Phipps, President of Gerald H. Phipps, Inc.; Salvador Carpio, professor at Metro State, Hispanic Educators; Conrad Romero, Hispanic Educators; Jean Emery and Lorie Young, League of Women Voters; Dean Herbert M. Barrall of St. John's Cathedral; Monseigneur William H. Jones, vicar for education of the Archdiocese of Denver; Robert Anderson, President-Elect Denver Classroom Teachers Association; Rev. Richard S. Kerr, Rector of Church of the Holy Redeemer; Michael B. Howard, managing editor of the Rocky Mountain News; Jeanne Kopec, president of Denver County Parent, Teachers, and Students Association; Jean Bain; Senator George L. Brown; Robert Wright, Dean of the Center for Urban Affairs, Metropolitan State College; Marjorie Hornbein, board member of Temple Emanuel; Martha Radetsky; David Williams, Colorado Department of Education; and Sheldon Steinhauser, Anti-Defamation League.[7]

The judge observed that when he had ordered the first modest desegregation five years earlier, many problems arose due to the failure to prepare.

He hoped he had learned a lesson from that experience and that parents would be more prepared. Then, he explained the reasons why the court order was necessary:

> I think experience has shown, and it is pointed out in this work [desegregating the schools], that the busing itself, although it is often said by the opponents that it is the great problem, it doesn't prove to be ordinarily, once it starts. The great problem is spirit and apprehension, and so I picture the work of this group as being an educational one, if you can bring the facts to the community, as a necessity for the program that we are operating under the law of the land, I don't think they realize in many instances the role of the Court in this, the Federal Courts . . . In the *Brown* case the old doctrine of "separate but equal" being in accord with the Constitution was discarded, and for the past twenty years, then, the Federal Courts have had this responsibility of entertaining cases. This is not a process that you enjoy, particularly anybody who participates in it, and yet it is an activity and an effort which is lawful, solidly so. It is in accord with the letter and the spirit of the Constitution of the United States . . .
>
> I do believe that this group should have the responsibility of two things: One, dealing with the School District, where the citizenry has not had a reception, you know. It seems to me that this group can serve to be the liaison with the School District in some instances, so these problems can get some attention before they become so big that they can't—that they are difficult to handle. That's what I have in mind.
>
> As I said, I think the great problem is the quieting of the fears and apprehensions in some areas. At this point, though, I believe it is kind of isolated . . . the antidote for this is really the need to get the facts. If parents can be persuaded to go into the community and examine where the kids are going to go to school and take a part in it, support the school and become interested, involve themselves in it, there is not going to be any great problem, any big one, you know.[8]

Maurice B. Mitchell, chancellor of the University of Denver and the CEC's first chair, established rules and order that allowed the council to function. First, it was agreed that only members of the CEC would be allowed to speak at meetings unless a nonmember was invited to speak for some reason. When groups opposed to busing came to meetings to harass the council,

Mitchell requested US marshals from Judge Doyle, and the meetings were able to proceed uninterrupted. After Mitchell stepped down as chair, Jean Bain, a former state representative who had been vice chair, became chair. Bettye Emerson, a Black teacher at Morey, was the council's secretary.

In the first year of the order, I served under the CEC as a monitor at Morey Junior High. The first problem I observed there was the apparent loss of between seventy-five and ninety-five mostly Black students who simply never appeared at the school in the fall. Many people I talked with believed this was because of the dangerous neighborhood, the drug addict-ridden Arapahoe Housing Project north of Park Avenue, the students had to walk through. I rode with Dr. Gerald Elledge, the district head of transportation, to measure the distance to see if the students were far enough away to be entitled to bus transportation. The intersection at Thirtieth and Larimer Streets was beyond two miles, at 2.01. Dr. Elledge agreed that anyone living on Larimer between Twenty-ninth and Thirtieth Streets would be entitled to bus transportation, but we checked with two men living in that block and they said no junior high children lived there.

Since under district policy children in most of this area would not be entitled to bus transportation, I suggested that the area be designated a satellite and that the 125 students in the area be bused to either Morey or another white school. Chancellor Mitchell wrote a letter to the judge urging him to order a bus to reclaim the children who had been lost due to the new attendance boundaries. Judge Doyle replied that he was reluctant to change the order on a piecemeal basis, and he attached John Finger's report, which was more conciliatory. Finger said there were 125 students in the Arapahoe Housing Project, all just inside the two-mile area. On public transportation, the children would have to change buses downtown, and bus transportation would cost each child eight dollars a month, which would be a hardship for low-income families. It was Finger's opinion that "whenever, as a result of a desegregation order the distance that children must travel to school is significantly increased, the School Department should provide transportation. This is especially true when a hardship is created as in this instance." As I recall, a bus was provided by the district, and most of the children returned to school.[9]

Monitoring was a key part of the function of the CEC, and Judge Doyle's May 10, 1974, order called the CEC a monitoring commission. More than

200 monitors were required to make one visit per month to classes, lunchrooms, and other activities in each school. The school district was not always supportive of the role of the monitors. In fact, the district balked at nearly every step of implementation of the court order. In a letter in October 1975, Chancellor Mitchell reminded the superintendent that he had requested on July 25 that the superintendent send a letter to all patrons of the school district to introduce the new CEC monitors at each school and that this had been subsequently discussed with him on the phone. Superintendent Kishkunas said that this request was made on September 25, and he asked principals to make a reference to the CEC in the first mailing home to parents, but some CEC members did not think all the principals were doing this.[10]

I was appointed to the CEC in the second year of the court order, 1975–1976, becoming a member of the junior high monitoring subcommittee. Altogether, sixty-three people were listed as members of the council, with various assignments. My responsibility for that school year was to coordinate monitors at four junior highs in west Denver: three monitors at Kepner, two at Kunsmiller, three at Horace Mann, and three at Rishel.[11] One form asked the monitors to measure classroom atmosphere, student attitudes toward each other and the teacher, whether teachers encouraged all students to participate regardless of ethnicity, whether students sat in racially isolated groups, and whether the curriculum seemed to meet the needs of all students. There was room on the form for comments on each question.[12] At other times the judge asked for the racial and ethnic percentages in each school, the racial and ethnic distribution of teachers, extracurricular activities, parent involvement, bus schedules and supervision on buses, in-service training, and activities for new students. Much of this statistical information was to be furnished to the court by the school district.[13]

In one report I noted that Kepner was overcrowded; consequently, faculty morale was low. Classes were even meeting in the lunchroom. When Kepner was allotted two more teachers, there were no classrooms for them, so they did not come. Projected enrollment for the 1974–1975 school year was 1,530, though somewhat fewer came. Bused children did not have the same opportunities to participate in after-school activities as did the children who were not bused.[14]

The work of the CEC was variously evaluated by the parties. On the positive side, the CEC had been the single most important factor in the implementation process, according to Gordon Greiner, attorney for the plaintiffs, and George Bardwell, lead statistician for the plaintiffs. Judge Doyle attributed the success of the program "in large measure to the magnificent leadership furnished by Chancellor Mitchell," and he lauded the CEC members and 200-plus volunteer monitors for their efforts. In contrast, Superintendent Kishkunas said the monitoring was totally unnecessary. Monitors, he said, were highly critical and eager to discover problems, and their reports were selective and prejudiced. According to the council's own evaluation, monitors gave "the closest view possible of what is actually happening in the district, schoolhouse by schoolhouse."[15] I believe the CEC bolstered the confidence of Denver parents and children during a time of new experiences that aroused fear in some.

By fall 1976, I was chair of the CEC public relations committee. Some members felt the CEC had not done enough to educate the community about the necessity for and purpose of the court order, as directed in the court's mandate, or about the many positive programs in the Denver Public Schools. Our committee worked with the public relations director for the district. In small groups we visited the *Rocky Mountain News*, the *Denver Post*, and all five major TV channels. The committee members were Mary Holleman, Harrison Hudson, Daniel Lynch, John McCall, Martha Radetsky, Jim Reynolds, Sheldon Steinhauser, Jim Voorhees, Joan Wohlgenant, and Lorie Young.[16]

Prior to the 1977–1978 school year, the CEC itself began questioning its value and how long it would be continued. There was a general feeling that the council would soon be terminated by the court, so as early as October 1976 the council began to talk of sponsoring a citywide conference to form an education support organization that would continue some of the CEC's mission when it was discontinued.[17] Such a conference was sponsored on March 25, 1977, with assistance from the federal General Assistance Center for Region VIII and the Colorado Department of Education Community Services Department.

"The committee will make every effort to establish a desire for and the need for a continuing organization capable of working to improve the quality of education in the Denver Schools while maintaining equality of opportunity for all students," the CEC reported to the judge. However, the conference attendees did not want to form another organization, which was seen by some attendees as potentially competing with existing organizations.[18]

In March 1976, Judge Doyle, who had been appointed to the Tenth Circuit Court of Appeals, turned the case over to Judge Richard P. Matsch, who was praised as "off the scale intellectually" in the *Almanac of the Federal Judiciary*, which rates judges: "He's the leading legal figure, and there's no one that comes close . . . he's beyond excellent."[19] Soon thereafter, the council expressed frustration at what it saw as a lack of support from the judge in the face of a sometimes recalcitrant school district. Judge Matsch explained that changes in the court order could only be made as a result of pleadings by the parties and a court hearing. Finally, the council requested a meeting with the judge. The Black members of the council strongly urged its continuation, and a memorandum from the council called attention to the continuing need for monitoring and in-service training. A summarized joint statement had some very pointed questions for the judge, such as "Does the Court intend to act on reports and recommendations of the CEC? If not, is there a reason for continuing" and "Is there to be any action on the part of the Court when a violation of the existing Court Order is reported to the Court by the Council?"[20]

One area of concern was the lack of compliance with the order for in-service education. Although the court ordered in-service training each semester following hearings on August 8 and 15, 1975, the Denver Classroom Teachers Association newsletter in January 1977 announced that in-service training was no longer required by the court. Only about a third of the schools had submitted the required plans for their in-service programs.[21]

Meanwhile, the monitoring of every school continued. The most important information in the June 1977 report of the monitoring committee concerning suspensions was that Black and Hispanic students were overrepresented. In the elementary schools, 57 percent of suspensions were of Blacks while only 20.2 percent of the students were Black. Similarly, at the junior high level, 42 percent of suspensions were of Black students while only 22 percent of the students were Black; 32 percent of suspensions were of Hispanics but only 29.5 percent of the students were Hispanic, so they were slightly overrepresented. At the senior high level, 41 percent of suspensions were of Black students but only 19.8 percent of the students were Black. Again, Hispanics were only slightly overrepresented, at 25 percent of total suspensions for 22.1 percent of the student population. The report, which was provided by the district, gave school-by-school statistics as well.[22]

FIGURE 15.1. Judge Richard P. Matsch. Photo by Andrew Dieringer. Used with permission of Marti Matsch.

Also in June, the CEC unanimously adopted a statement for Judge Matsch:

> The normal instruments of government . . . and the various citizens' organizations have had three years of decreasing pressures from the Court to demonstrate that they are able and willing to implement the letter and the spirit of the Court Order to desegregate the schools.
>
> It is the conclusion of the Court's Community Education Council that these agencies have not shown that ability and/or willingness, and that on the contrary there has been a process of erosion in the quality of compliance with the Court Order in direct proportion to the relaxation of pressure from the Court.[23]

On October 14, 1977, Judge Matsch reduced the size of the CEC from sixty to nineteen members, appointed for two years, and he initiated a process for the CEC or the school district to use a magistrate of the court to mediate disputes. If disputes could not be settled by the magistrate, he could refer them to the court. Matsch explained that the CEC concerns had not resulted in any court action because they were not the subject of any formal pleadings in court. He reviewed the fact that in August, Judge Sherman G. Finesilver had determined that fees were to be paid by the defendants for the professional services of the counsel for the plaintiffs. He mentioned the need to move for "the termination of judicial involvement in the operation of the Denver Public School system." This was overly optimistic, as the supervision by the court continued until 1995, twenty-six years after the case was filed.[24]

At the end of November, I received a letter from Judge Matsch explaining that I was no longer on the CEC, a letter he probably sent to more than forty terminated members when he reduced the size of the council. He said, "The reduction in the size of the CEC was necessary for effective performance of the role prescribed in the October order." The letter continued:

> Please accept my sincere thank you for your past participation in the work of the CEC. You have made a very significant contribution to the implementation of the desegregation orders and the entire Denver community has been helped by your efforts.
>
> The selection of the members of the new CEC was entirely my personal decision and it was very difficult. I hope that you are not offended by my failure to name you.
>
> In the confidence that you will continue to be an interested, informed and active citizen, I am, Most appreciatively yours,
>
> Richard P. Matsch.[25]

It was difficult to give up activities that I believed would help children achieve equal educational opportunity, but it was probably best for me because I was in the third year of coursework for my doctoral degree. Nevertheless, our family continued to be concerned about the success of desegregation in the Denver schools.

16

The Tenth Circuit Court Rules Again

Although the entire school district was implementing the Finger Plan in fall 1974, the school district appealed the case once again to the Tenth Circuit Court of Appeals, which ruled on August 11, 1975. The United States Supreme Court denied *certiorari* on January 12, 1976, which was the end of the appeals process.[1]

First, in its decision, the appeals court gave a very complete summary of the case from its inception in 1969.[2] It considered whether the district court had properly concluded that the school board's segregative acts made Denver an illegal dual system, and it agreed that Denver had maintained a dual school system. Then, the court of appeals considered the order concerning reassignment and transportation. Finally, it dealt with the order on bilingual, bicultural education, the East-Manual Complex, and faculty and staff desegregation.

On the issue of Denver Public Schools creating a dual system, the court said, "Rather the courts must presume the existence of a dual system from school authorities' segregative acts, the burden then shifting to those authorities to prove the absence of any causal relation between those acts and current levels of racial segregation."[3]

https://doi.org/10.5876/9781646422906.c016

Next, the appeals court summarized the district court's desegregation plan. It said that twenty-four schools were rezoned, twenty-three more schools were both rezoned and received students from satellite areas, and thirty-seven schools were organized in pairs or clusters for the purposes of part-time reassignment of students on a classroom basis. However, the pairing program, already under way, was rejected by the court of appeals. This was the program that involved students moving half days or alternate days from their neighborhood school to another school. The appeals court, in rejecting this idea, said, "We hold that the part-time pairing component of the court's remedy for desegregation of elementary schools is not constitutionally acceptable as a basic and permanent premise for desegregation but deem that practicality negates the necessity of invalidating in toto this aspect of the trial court's judgment at this time."[4]

The court saw this part of the plan as only a step toward the future. The appeals court objected because among the eighteen predominantly minority schools in the part-time program, thirteen had 10 percent or fewer white students.[5] In addition, in the paired schools, basic subjects such as math and reading were taught in segregated classrooms.[6] This part of the order was remanded to the district court for implementation of a full-time desegregation order.[7]

Next, the appeals court took up the issue of the still segregated Hispanic elementary schools—Cheltenham, Del Pueblo, Elyria, and Garden Place—which were left out of the desegregation plan because of their bilingual, bicultural programs. As part of the reversal of the Cardenas Plan, the court said this segregation could not be continued because "bilingual education . . . is not a substitute for desegregation."[8] The issue was remanded to the district court, which was to desegregate these schools. The appeals court vacated the entire portion of the order that required implementation of the Cardenas Plan and directed the court to find ways to ensure the transition of Spanish-speaking children to English.[9]

The appeals court also vacated the part of the order establishing the East-Manual Complex, not because it might not be a good idea but because the court lacked the power to order it as part of the remedial jurisdiction.[10] The court's orders on faculty and staff desegregation were upheld by the court of appeals.[11]

The district court said another hearing was not necessary if the two sides agreed on changes to carry out the directive of the court of appeals. In

March 1976, the Denver Public Schools staff presented two plans to the board. Member Ted Hackworth moved to adopt the plan that had the least amount of busing, but that motion died 4 to 3. Ginny Rockwell, who had been elected to the board in May 1975, next moved the alternative plan, which passed. This led to some harsh words about Rockwell from another new board member, segregationist Naomi Bradford, according to the *Denver Post*:

> After the desegregation resolution passed, Mrs. Bradford verbally lambasted its author, Board Member Virginia Rockwell, as "the most despicable person I've ever met" and accused her, among other things, of buying her seat on the board.
>
> As soon as the meeting adjourned, Mrs. Bradford sailed over to Mrs. Rockwell and repeated her denunciation, leaving Mrs. Rockwell white-faced and in tears. This prompted Black Board Member Omar Blair, standing nearby, to upbraid Board President Bernard Valdez for not silencing Mrs. Bradford. "One way or the other, we're going to shut that woman up," Blair insisted.[12]

Rockwell was the wife of prominent Denver banker Bruce Rockwell. Her election to the board gave the integrationist forces a 4 to 3 majority for the first time since 1969. It led to the eventual change of superintendent when Kishkunas was forced out in 1977.[13]

Most of the district court's order for the desegregation "root and branch" of the Denver public schools had been endorsed by the court of appeals. The legal struggle to integrate the schools that had begun in 1969 ended six years later with the court of appeals decision, but the court supervision ordered in the *Keyes* case continued until 1995.

17

Effects of Desegregation

Desegregation had a major effect on student achievement in Denver, as it did in other districts throughout the country. At the same time, it changed the racial balance in the schools and accelerated white flight.

White Flight

Undeniably, many white families chose to leave the city during the desegregation order rather than live alongside and go to school with Black families, but desegregation merely accelerated an existing trend. Such population movements were recorded at least as far back as the eighteenth century in England near the time of the publication of Daniel Defoe's *Robinson Crusoe* (1719), as noted by Ian Watt in his landmark *Rise of the Novel*: "Very soon, however, the movement of the prosperous into the suburb became very marked, and indeed caused a decline of the population within the city limits."[1] In modern times, some authors see the trend of whites leaving cities as beginning after World War I and accelerating following World War II. This

https://doi.org/10.5876/9781646422906.c017

pattern preceded desegregation by many years.[2] Urban economists suggest that the decline in white public school enrollment that began in the 1960s was in large part a function of the post–World War II white suburbanization trend. Another cause of decline in white school enrollments is the declining white birth rate, which dropped 1 percent a year starting in 1968 and almost 2 percent annually by 1983. The Black school-age population began to decline more recently.[3] To allay some fears concerning white flight, the League of Women Voters pointed out that white enrollment had increased in Berkeley, California, following integration and that housing values had increased in Evanston, Illinois, after integration.[4]

Denver did experience the relocation of some white students to the suburbs and to private schools. In 1968, Denver Public Schools (DPS) student enrollment topped 95,000. By the time busing ended in 1995, enrollment had dropped below 60,000, largely the result of white families moving to the suburbs. Though DPS was at that time the fastest-growing urban school district in the country, by 2015 it had not regained its pre-busing enrollment numbers. The school population dropped by 8,365 students in 1974 when the citywide desegregation plan was first implemented. In fall 1974, only 80 percent of the projected elementary enrollment and 76 percent of the projected secondary enrollment showed up for classes.[5]

Most national studies show a doubling in the relocation of white students in the years in which desegregation was implemented (from 4 percent to 8 percent). In the average big-city school system with about 35 percent minority students, a district could expect that 35 percent to 50 percent of white students assigned to minority schools would not show up. In another study, the average rate of whites assigned to Black areas who did not attend classes was 24 percent. These white reassignments to Black schools produced two to three times more white flight than did Black reassignments to white schools.[6]

Calvin Trillin commented on the deterioration of the desegregation effort in Denver twenty years after the court order and then twenty years after that: "Twenty years later [in 1995], the court allowed the abandonment of the plan. At that point, largely because of white flight to the suburbs, the schools were, according to *The New York Times*, 'more racially segregated than ever'—a phrase that could have served as a succinct summary of a report that the school board received twenty years after that, in 2015. That report said that only twenty-nine of Denver's one hundred eighty-eight schools could be considered integrated."[7]

White flight has little long-term effect, however. In general, the extent of white flight in desegregation efforts depends on the extent of the impact, the size of the minority population, the number of white students bused into formerly Black schools, and the distance students are bused.[8] In an article replying to a Coleman study, political science professor Christine H. Rossell showed that by the second and third years of desegregation, districts had an average rate of reduction in the proportion of their white population, which was less than both their own pre-desegregation rates and the rates of other districts. In eighty-six northern school districts, "School desegregation has little or no effect on white flight, as measured in percentage of white students enrolled in public schools. Even in the two highest desegregating school districts, white flight is minimal and temporary."[9]

Craig Barnes, who wrote some of the first *Keyes* briefs for the plaintiffs, had a mixed evaluation of the results, in part because of white flight:

> The *Keyes* victory may not have succeeded. The early successes appear to have been substantially vitiated by white flight. Further, when measured in terms of educational improvement the contest over whether racial integration succeeds in raising achievement levels may also be contested. My own children eventually attended East High School in Denver and even though the school had been "integrated" in terms of the overall student population, classes at East High tended to gather students along racial lines with higher numbers of Anglos and Asians attending college preparatory classes while blacks and Hispanics attended these classes in much fewer numbers. It cannot be said that Keyes solved this problem.[10]

The critics of resegregation in schools and of the disproportionately small number of minority students in advanced classes, though this is regrettable, fail to recognize that without court-ordered integration of the schools, there would have been no minority children in such classes because those courses were seldom offered in minority schools.

In Mary Jean Taylor's 1990 thesis on the subject of the leadership in the desegregation case, Assistant Superintendent Richard Koeppe described the success or failure of Denver's desegregation:

If success or failure is to be measured by the degree of current satisfaction with the Denver Public Schools and the integrative rulings still in effect, then desegregation in Denver must be considered a failure. If, however, success or failure is measured by the extent to which students in Denver come into contact with and learn to cope with students of other races, ethnic and socio-economic backgrounds, then desegregation in Denver must be considered a success. If success is measured by a national reputation, or the local stature of the district and the number of elite schools it contains, then desegregation has been detrimental. If, on the other hand, success is measured by the extent to which educational resources are distributed equitably throughout the community, then desegregation has been beneficial.[11]

Years later Koeppe said, "Desegregation didn't work. The definition of desegregation changed several times. At first there had to be 50 percent Anglo [students]; then under the court order a range of 40 percent to 70 percent was allowed."[12] He believed desegregation did provide equal educational opportunity to minority students. Some minority parents said, "You have to put my kid beside a white kid to learn? Baloney." Others thought, he said, that white parents, who had more time and influence with the school board, would demand good education in every school. He said he would rather have assertiveness than apathy from parents.[13]

Koeppe believes the plan did reduce segregation, but it did not bring integration. At lunch and on the playground, students were still in self-selected racial groups. When asked to describe the relationship between the school board and the administration, he said it was strained: "The board resented the court, and the court resented the board's obstinacy." Few administrators supported the court, although he did. The administration was caught between the two.[14]

In a 1990 interview, Koeppe said that many teachers and principals still in the system longed for the good old days: "The district has lost a lot of students and the composition of the students has changed. The new student body is more difficult to teach. We have a higher concentration of special ed, we have a higher concentration of the poor, and that makes their job more difficult. I think the majority of central administrators are people who really wanted to make it work."[15]

One can ask whether Judge William Doyle believed desegregation worked. According to his grandniece, Sheila Macdonald, "they put bombs on his porch. He had a lot of threats. In the early '70s . . . they threatened my grand-father. He felt strongly that it was the right thing to do, but it didn't achieve the quality [education] he thought it would. Students didn't have books in every class. Where advanced students read the whole story, regular classes only got an excerpt from the story and they couldn't take books home."[16] As a biography pointed out:

> His opinions in *Keyes* are examples of judicial craftsmanship. A threshold issue in that case was whether the school board had ever been guilty of segregative action. Doyle wrote, "Segregative purpose may be overt, as in the dual system maintained in some states prior to *Brown v. Board of Education* . . . or it may be covert in which case purpose normally must be proved by circumstantial evidence." He goes on to say that intent to segregate may be just one of the motives of the school board. He said it is clear that "the Constitutional rights of children not to be discriminated against in school admission on the grounds of race or color . . . can neither be nullified openly . . . nor nulli-fied indirectly by them through evasive schemes for segregation whether attempted geniously or ingeniously."[17]

Many years later, board president Jim Voorhees, who had to be persuaded to support desegregation and was subsequently defeated in his bid for reelection in 1971, said the board did the right thing. He said there was credible evidence that "we had to get rid of some of the inequities in educational opportunity that existed in the schools . . . It was perfectly clear that the lower-achieving schools were located in the segregated and lower economic areas of the city."[18]

In evaluating the effects of the desegregation order, former board member Ed Benton said, "It established and validated constitutional equality under the law and validated equal educational opportunity. If the board had put its full faith and credit into it, it would have had a much greater effect."[19]

Rachel Noel, whose resolution began the Denver effort to desegregate, thought desegregation was poorly implemented by the school board. Doyle's order could have been implemented to work or not to work. Rachel was repeatedly called about the ways the board and administration were sabo-taging the order. Management dragged its heels and deliberately sought a strategy that upset everyone.[20]

Nationally, an "overwhelming proportion" of both Black and white parents reported satisfactory experiences with desegregation and with the quality of their schools. In addition, Rossell suggests that "reductions in school segregation have been followed by reductions in racial intolerance."[21]

Racial Balance

According to the Benton-Pascoe school board campaign, true racial balance in Denver in 1969 would have produced schools close to 70 percent white, 13 percent Black, and 17 percent Hispanic, reflecting the district-wide student population.[22] In the Finger Plan adopted by Judge William E. Doyle in 1974, the percentage of white students in each school was allowed to range between 40 percent and 70 percent, though the judge recognized that in schools with bilingual education, a larger percentage of Hispanics might be desirable.[23]

National Measures of Student Achievement

The effect of desegregation on student achievement can best be measured by comparing test scores before the court order, during the court's supervision, and after the end of the court order.

Prior to the court order, using 1968 data, the Benton-Pascoe campaign observed low scores in minority schools, particularly elementary schools: "Facts to think about—about one-half of elementary schools have achievement scores at grade five which are ten points below [the] national norm."[24] That is, when tests were given in the eighth month of fifth grade, when achievement at grade level would be expected to be 5.8, about half of the elementary schools—schools that were majority-minority—scored around 4.8, indicating that the students were one year behind. On another test, with national norms at the 50th percentile, the composite score in minority schools in grade 5 was at the 22nd percentile, in grade 9 at the 30th percentile, and in grade 11 at the 28th percentile. In contrast, the scores for schools over 90 percent white in grade 5 were at the 66th percentile, in grade 9 at the 73rd percentile, and in grade 11 at the 74th percentile. The city averages for all students were at the 43rd, 62nd, and 59th percentiles, respectively.[25] These achievement levels are represented in table 17.1.

Most of the ninety-three studies reviewed by two scholars found that desegregation improved minority achievement. The most important factor

TABLE 17.1. Achievement levels, 1968

Percentile Scores

	Grade 5	Grade 9	Grade 11
Majority Black or Hispanic	22	30	28
Over 90 percent white	66	73	74
City average	43	62	59
National norm	50	50	50

leading to improvement was the age of the students when desegregation started; desegregation was most effective if it started in kindergarten. When it started in secondary school, less than half of the samples saw positive effects. Hispanics showed similar improvement, although there were few studies of Hispanics.[26]

After desegregation, the National Assessment of Educational Progress (NAEP) found that changes in achievement were strongest in the desegregated US Southeast and that the difference between Black students and white students was narrowing. In 1991 the NAEP reported that seventeen-year-old Black children had reduced the difference between themselves and whites in reading scores—the most important indicator of educational achievement—by about 50 percent over the previous twenty years, which is exactly the period of greatest desegregation in the public schools in both the North and the South. The mathematics gap was reduced about 25 percent, to 40 percent, and the science gap by 15 percent, to 25 percent. NAEP concluded optimistically that if these trends continued, the reading disparity should end within fifteen to twenty years.[27] Unfortunately, that progress did not continue in Denver. Denver Hispanics now have one of the biggest achievement gaps in the country on the NAEP assessment, though bilingual students score better in Denver than in other districts.[28] The largest gains during the period of desegregation appeared consistently in IQ, with an average increase of four IQ points.[29]

Research professor and education historian Diane Ravitch also cites NAEP results. Because this is a long-term test assessment that has been given every four years since 1973 to students ages nine, thirteen, and seventeen and many of the questions have been repeated in every test, it is a good measure of long-term change. The scores show a steady improvement in achievement in reading and mathematics for all racial groups from 1973 to 2008. In mathematics for age nine, white students' scores improved by 25 points, Black students' scores by 34 points, and Hispanics' scores by 32 points. For age thirteen, the scores of whites increased by 16 points, Blacks' scores increased by 34 points, and those of Hispanics increased by 29 points. For age seventeen, whites' scores increased by 4 points, those of Black students increased by 17 points, and Hispanics' scores increased by 16 points. In reading for age nine, the scores of whites increased by 14 points, those of Blacks increased by 34 points, and those of Hispanics increased by 25 points. For age thirteen, whites' scores increased by 7 points, Blacks' scores increased by 25 points, and Hispanics' scores increased by 10 points. For age seventeen, whites' scores increased by 4 points, those of Black students increased by 28 points, and Hispanics' scores increased by 17 points. Even though minority groups' scores have improved, it has been impossible to eliminate the achievement gap—the persistent distance between the scores of white students and those of minority students—although the gap became smaller. This is the case in part because the scores of white students are also improving. Ravitch says that an analysis of the achievement gap over the twentieth century showed that it narrowed the most in the 1970s and 1980s in response to such things as desegregation, class size reduction, early childhood education, the addition of federal resources to schools that enroll poor children, and wider economic opportunities for Black families. Since that period, there has been no sharp reduction in the gap.[30]

Research shows that when Black children have access in integrated schools to advanced courses, well-trained teachers, and other resources, they begin to catch up. A 2014 study by Rucker Johnson, professor at the University of California at Berkeley, found that

> Black Americans who attended schools integrated by court order were more likely to graduate, go on to college, and earn a degree than Black Americans who attended segregated schools. They made more money: five years of integrated schooling increased the earnings of Black adults by 15 percent. They were significantly less likely to spend time in jail. They were healthier.
>
> This progress did not come at the expense of white students[,] who did just as well as the whites in segregated schools.[31]

There is evidence that desegregated schools have other positive effects for children, such as reduced prejudice, increased civic engagement, and engagement in more complex thinking.[32]

A feature on National Public Radio made a persuasive case for the effectiveness of school desegregation. The narrator declared:

> There was just one generation of integration in the country. It was the one
> reform that worked. Integration cut the achievement gap in half. In 1971
> before widespread integration began black students achieved about 39 points
> less than whites [on achievement tests in reading and math]. In 1988, at the
> height of integration, that gap had been reduced to 18 points, and that was
> for all black students, not just those who had been bused. Just one generation
> of students were integrated.
>
> People think, we tried that [integration] and it didn't work. But it does
> work, not because there is something magical about black students sitting
> next to white students, but it gives black kids access to quality teachers and
> the best instruction and there isn't as large a concentration of those who
> grew up in poverty.[33]

Denver Improvements in Achievement

Professors Catherine L. Horn and Michal Kurlaender, in a 2006 paper comparing math scores in Denver schools during and following the court order (1994 to 2000), found that the research generally showed that Black students in integrated schools increased their achievement levels. They had higher educational and occupational aspirations and attainment. This was greater for Black males than for Black females. Achievement levels for Hispanics were also higher in integrated schools.[34]

Overall, racial proportions also shifted in DPS between 1994 and 2003. The percentage of whites fell from 29 percent to 22 percent, and the proportion of Hispanics rose from 45 percent to 57 percent, while there were slight changes in Black and Asian percentages. There was a surprising rise in the number of whites in racially isolated schools. The relationship between race and socioeconomic status is so strong that the authors categorized schools according to the level of change in white enrollment, which is a proxy for socioeconomic level. This relationship was especially true in Denver where, the study showed, a school's percentage of white enrollment was very highly inversely correlated with the percentage of students eligible for free or reduced-price lunches. There were many more schools with very low white enrollments and correspondingly high levels of students eligible for free and reduced-price lunches in 2000 than there had been in 1994.[35]

Horn and Kurlaender found that there was much more segregation in Denver schools in 1998 than there had been in 1994 when the court order was still in effect: "In fact, in 1994, there had been virtually no elementary schools with fewer than 10 percent Whites enrolled; by 1998, that proportion had jumped to one-third of all elementary schools."[36]

The scores on math tests became more highly correlated with the presence of white students during this period. For purposes of the study, the authors classified elementary schools as having little change in white enrollment (0–10 percent), moderate increases in white enrollment (10–20 percent increase), substantial increases in white enrollment (20 percent or more), moderate decreases in white enrollment (10–20 percent decrease), and substantial decreases in white enrollment (20 percent decrease or more). An increase in white students was usually accompanied by a corresponding decrease in minority students, and vice versa. Six elementary schools gained 20 percent or more white students: Asbury, Bradley, Bromwell, Cory, Kaiser, and Steele. Two schools, Phillips and Whiteman, gained more than 20 percent Black students; Smith was close, with a 17 percent increase in Black students. Amesse, Ashley, Cheltenham, Del Pueblo, Fallis, Godman, Harrington, Johnson, McGlone, and Schenck all gained 20 percent or more Hispanic students. Several other schools were close to that 20 percent gain. At Hallett the increase in Blacks and Hispanics combined was 23 percent; at Smith, 27 percent; at Whittier, 24 percent.[37]

In studying achievement, Horn and Kurlaender found no substantial change in achievement for whites in schools that experienced either moderate or substantial gains in the numerical percentage of whites. They found moderate declines in achievement scores of whites where the numerical percentage of white students declined. However, modest minority student achievement gains occurred in schools that had moderate or substantial gains in the white enrollment percentage. Scores for Black students declined where there were moderate to substantial declines in the percentage of white students. Hispanics experienced more gains than any other group when white enrollment increased moderately or substantially.[38]

Because of the decline in white enrollment, one would expect a decrease in the number of racially isolated white schools. Instead, the number of mostly white schools increased, "suggesting that the racial/ethnic neighbor-hood isolation off-set through busing was no longer being addressed." White segregation—and minority segregation—is growing in DPS, or at least it was at the time of the Horn and Kurlaender study in 2006.[39]

Test scores of white students were no better after busing ended, though many expected that they would improve. There were modest improvements in Black students' test scores where there was a substantial increase in the number of white students.[40]

The success of desegregation when Denver was under the court order was recognized by former superintendent Tom Boasberg, who said the Denver desegregation plan produced strong improvements in achievement. Boasberg contrasted those gains with the more recent failure to close the academic gap: "While we saw significant progress in narrowing gaps between white students and students of color in the 1960s and 1970s (whether measured by high school graduation, college enrollment or performance on state and national assessments), that progress has slowed dramatically. We continue to see very large gaps, locally and nationally, on all academic measures."[41]

Given all we know about the positive effects of desegregation on both minority and majority children, the Denver school board should insist on a plan to desegregate Denver schools again.

18

The End of Court Supervision

Twenty-six years after Gordon Greiner and his team of lawyers filed *Keyes v. School District No. 1*, on September 12, 1995, Judge Richard P. Matsch ended the case. He granted the defendant's motion to terminate jurisdiction and dismiss the action. His ruling said: "It is now determined that defendant School District No. 1 . . . has complied in good faith with the desegregation decrees entered in this case and that the vestiges of past discrimination by the defendant have been eliminated to the extent practicable. The defendant's second motion to terminate jurisdiction is granted and full authority is restored to the District's Board of Education for governance of Denver's schools under applicable laws of the State of Colorado and the United States. This civil action is, therefore, closed with a final order of dismissal."[1]

The plaintiffs agreed that segregation had been eliminated regarding student assignments, faculty, staff, transportation, extracurricular activities, and facilities; but they had asked the court to retain some residual control because of racial disparities in discipline, dropout rates, and participation in gifted and talented programs that might be remaining vestiges of the dual

https://doi.org/10.5876/9781646422906.c018

system. The court said that to obligate the district further would go beyond remediation of past discriminatory conduct.[2]

In the opinion, the judge denied any conflict between the state constitutional amendment against busing and the Fourteenth Amendment of the US Constitution: "The busing clause of the state constitution is not inconsistent with the Fourteenth Amendment." The Colorado amendment, passed in 1974, says, "No sectarian tenets or doctrines shall ever be taught in the public school, nor shall any distinction or classification of pupils be made on account of race or color, nor shall any pupil be assigned or transported to any public educational institution for the purpose of achieving racial balance."[3] Matsch continued, "There is nothing in the Colorado Constitution or in the other statutes which will now be in full force and effect in Denver to prohibit the Board from pursuing pluralism and racial integration as positive objectives of public education . . . The limitations are as to the means which may be used to meet these goals. What is prohibited is assignment and transportation of public school pupils according to a preconceived plan of racial mixture."[4]

The judge cited changes in Denver that caused him to believe that minority children would be protected and represented: "The Denver now before this court is very different from what it was when this lawsuit began." He noted Denver's Black and Hispanic mayors, a Black female superintendent of schools, and Black and Hispanic men and women on the city council, the school board, the state legislature, and other political positions, adding "they are active players in the political, economic, social and cultural life of the community."[5]

Districts Resegregate

What happens to the schools when court orders are lifted? There have been several studies of such situations across the country. A 2012 Stanford study examined school districts with at least 2,000 students that had been released from court order since 1990. It found that, typically, these districts became steadily more segregated after their release. A separate study found that within ten years of being released, school districts on average undid about 60 percent of the integration they had achieved under court order.[6]

The Denver story reveals even more resegregation. The reversal of much of the desegregation effort occurred almost immediately after the court order ended. The school board voted for a return to the neighborhood school policy, a policy to send students to schools close to their homes, which was described as making every neighborhood school a good school. This policy switch occurred despite earlier resolutions recognizing the policy's segregative impact; the move also ignored the Noel Resolution passed by the board in 1968 and never rescinded, aimed at integrating every school. The arguments for the neighborhood school policy were echoes of the arguments against integration in the 1969 Benton-Pascoe campaign: "This was what the majority wanted," "Children should not ride a bus for an hour," "We want to be close to our children," "We chose the house we live in because of the neighborhood school," and so on. Despite Judge Matsch's optimistic predictions, integrating the schools was no longer the stated goal of the board or the administration.

At the same time as this change in policy, the racial proportions of the student population shifted. The number of whites decreased, and the number of Hispanics increased even more rapidly. The number of Black students decreased slightly. Concentrations of minority and majority children were even greater than would be expected by the numbers. By 2003–2004, 84 percent of all Hispanic students, 74 percent of Black students, and 52 percent of Asian students but only 27 percent of white students attended schools with more than 70 percent minority students.[7]

Radical Segregation

Some policymakers believe there are now legal barriers to integrating schools. But these barriers do not prohibit a variety of plans that would lead to more integrated schools. A United States Supreme Court case that is seen as a hurdle to integration is the 2007 decision in *Parents Involved in Community Schools v. Seattle School District No. 1*. It said, in part, "What the government is not permitted to do, absent a showing of necessity not made here, is to classify every student on the basis of race and to assign each of them to schools based on that classification."[8] However, the dissenting justices in that case argued that the US Constitution permits such desegregation, even though it does not require it.

Today, the factor most often used to measure segregation is the percentage of children eligible for the federal free or reduced-price lunch program (FRL).

This is also a good proxy for the number of children living in poverty. A US Government Accountability Office study looked especially at schools that were 25 percent to 75 percent Black and/or Hispanic and in which 25 percent to 75 percent of the students were on FRL; such a condition in a school was labeled radical segregation. The study stated that a clear link exists between family socioeconomic level or income and student academic outcomes. As income increases, so does academic achievement.[9]

There was a large increase in schools in the United States that are isolated by both poverty and race between 2000–2001 and 2013–2014. The percentage of these impoverished and Black and Hispanic schools increased during this period, from 9 percent to 16 percent. These minority schools represented 61 percent of all high-poverty schools. They offered fewer opportunities to students than did non-poverty, non-minority white schools. For example, fewer of the high-poverty schools offered the full range of math and science courses. While only 29 percent of high-poverty schools offered calculus, 71 percent of low-poverty schools did. While only 55 percent of high-poverty schools offered physics, 80 percent of low-poverty schools offered the course.[10]

A very influential study conducted by the UCLA Civil Rights Project reported the effects of schools with a high percentage of children on FRL, especially those that also had a high percentage of Black and/or Hispanic children.[11] There was a striking rise in double segregation between 1991 and 2016: segregation by both race and poverty. The number of intensely segregated non-white schools rose during that period, from 5.7 percent to 18.6 percent of all public schools.[12]

The authors of the study defined intensely segregated schools as those that have 0 percent to 10 percent white enrollment. The number of such schools more than tripled in the period 1991 to 2016, corresponding to the twenty-five years after the end of most court-ordered desegregation. But the number of white schools with 0 percent to 10 percent non-white enrollment fell by half. In Denver, many majority white schools have a very low percentage of minority students; thus, white students, like minority students, are racially isolated.

The rights of Hispanic students were first recognized by the United States Supreme Court in Denver's *Keyes* case in 1973. Nationally, cases focusing on Hispanics have mostly been dismantled, according to the study. In Colorado, 18.7 percent of Hispanic students in 2013–2014 were in schools that were

90 percent to 100 percent non-white. Only 37.3 percent of Hispanic students had "exposure to white students."[13]

Nationally, Black and Hispanic students attend schools with substantial majorities—two-thirds—of poor classmates. This double segregation means serious isolation from racial and class diversity and exposure to the many problems that systematically afflict poor families and communities. Between 1993 and 2013, the percentage of low-income students in schools attended by Black students changed from 36.7 percent to 67.9 percent. For Hispanics it increased from 45.6 percent to the same level, 67.9 percent.[14]

Desegregating Denver

There are many policies that any district could use that would lead to more integration, according to Gary Orfield and colleagues. The Civil Rights Division of the US Department of Justice made several suggestions: "The Administration released important guidance in 2011 clarifying that districts could implement race-conscious student assignment policies, although much more technical assistance is needed to help districts, advocates and states understand how to design district and state policies (including those for charter schools) to further diversity in a comprehensive manner."[15]

The Civil Rights Division explained that in *Parents Involved in Community Schools v. Seattle School District 1*, the Supreme Court struck down the school district's use of individual racial classifications in assigning students to schools. In concurring, Justice Anthony D. Kennedy said the decision should not be interpreted as prohibiting schools from considering a school's racial makeup. In other words, they can adopt race-conscious measures to address the problem. The schools must have flexibility in designing ways to achieve diversity. Schools should consider ways that do not rely on race before those that do, but race can be a criterion if it is not specifically relied upon. The district might use zone-based selection that would affect a group of students. Schools may use socioeconomic data, parental education, single-parent household status, students' socioeconomic status, and geography and composition of neighborhoods—whether single-family homes, high-density public housing, or rental housing. Neighborhoods can be identified with a generalized racial identification without identifying the race of individual students. If all else fails, race may be used as one factor in evaluating a student.[16]

Examples were given of strategies that can be used to improve diversity without violating civil or constitutional rights, such as school and program siting decisions, grade realignment and feeder school decisions, school zoning decisions, open and choice enrollment decisions, admission to competitive schools and programs, and inter- and intra-district transfers. These strategies can all be managed in ways that increase diversity.[17]

Denver Schools Today

Some of these strategies are being employed in Denver, but they are not widespread enough to affect the entire district. The research of Catherine L. Horn and Michal Kurlaender on the changes in Denver suggests that even a little integration is beneficial to minority students, as it results in improved achievement for them without lowering achievement for white students (see chapter 17).

In 1998–1999, when the district's new neighborhood school policy had been in effect for three years (1995–1996, 1996–1997, 1997–1998), the scores on the Iowa Test of Basic Skills revealed the detrimental effects of segregation on the education of minority children. In 1998–1999, when third grade students would not have experienced desegregation, the average median achievement score for third grade Black students district-wide was 42 in language, 39.2 in math, and 41.6 in reading; Hispanics scored 34.9 in language, 38 in math, and 36 in reading. In contrast, whites scored 59.7 in language, 62.4 in math, and 60.5 in reading.[18]

Two very recent studies evaluate where the Denver Public Schools (DPS) are today in providing equal educational opportunity to all students. The first was an effort initiated by the school administration, the Strengthening Neighborhoods Committee.[19] The citizens' committee called for high-quality schools in every neighborhood and insisted that greater integration was an important step toward that goal. It called for the board to set a specific quantitative goal for the integration of each school and for a communication campaign to educate the public about the benefits of integration and the work of the committee: "The Committee believes that prioritizing enrollment access for underrepresented students in charter schools is a lever to promote school integration and increase enrollment equity."[20] No school should use tests to limit admission (as does the Denver School of the Arts), and new charters should be designed to appeal to diverse students, it said. The committee added that integration should be promoted through the district's new school approval process and also recommended expanding transportation to make more options available and affordable for low-income students. Not surprisingly, the committee called for recruitment, retention, placement, and support of diverse staff and for the district to share demographic data about its employees.[21]

Most of what the committee recommended, except for suggestions related to charter schools, was asked for and won by the plaintiffs in the *Keyes* case, including the percentage targets for integration, the provision of transportation, the effort to include minority students in advanced classes, education of the public, the goal of a diverse faculty, and transparency about the number of minority faculty by school.

The second recently completed major study of the Denver schools was "Learn Together, Live Together: A Call to Integrate Denver's Schools" by A+ Colorado.[22] Its objective is stated at the beginning of the study: "The report will present the most compelling arguments for socioeconomically integrating Denver's schools, and making them centers of inclusion, where all cultures and communities are honored, and everyone feels they have a strong voice in key decisions."[23] Gentrification creates an opportunity to integrate schools, according to Richard Kahlenberg, a senior fellow at the Century Foundation and a leading expert on school integration who is quoted in the report.[24] But the danger is that the middle- and upper-middle-class families moving into a neighborhood will eventually overwhelm the original population, such that the school is no longer integrated, as was the case described by Nikole Hannah-Jones.[25] The A+ Colorado report goes on to observe that integration is not the responsibility of the schools alone. Everyone must also be committed to integrated housing, including elected officials and funders.

This report briefly argues for the benefits of integration, citing several studies. Why does the achievement of low-income students rise in integrated schools, the report asks. It continues: "Integrating schools leads to more equitable access to important resources such as structural facilities, highly qualified teachers, challenging courses, private and public funding, and social and cultural capital."[26]

Graduation rates are also heavily affected by school integration. A study of rates in sixteen states and Washington, DC, discovered that the rate was 10 percentage points higher in the most socioeconomically integrated schools than in schools that were at the national average and 20 percentage points higher than in extremely segregated schools.[27]

In studying Denver's integrated schools, it was clear that such schools can be effective for both lower-income and more affluent students, but that isn't always the case: "The quality of the school itself matters—not simply the students."[28] The A+ Colorado study praises the DSST system (originally the Denver School of Science and Technology but now a system of eleven charter schools emphasizing the STEM subjects: science, technology, engineering, and math). Though 69 percent of its students are eligible for free or reduced-price lunch, the DSST system boasts excellent academic achievement. However, it offers little school-by-school information to gauge whether each one is integrated. The report also praises Highline Academy Southeast, Denver Green Schools, and Odyssey School of Denver for their high achievement.

In contrast, East High School is named as one school where segregation happens at the classroom level, giving minority students few academic benefits. Though overall test scores were above state averages, there was a large gap in scores between low-income students and those not of low income: "In 2017, in English Language Arts, just 19 percent of low-income 9th grade students met or exceeded expectations, compared to 73 percent of non-low-income students." For the entire district, "25 percent of low-income 9th graders met or exceeded expectations . . . and 60 percent of the more affluent students did."[29] The report concludes that tracking (ability grouping), which results in segregation at the classroom level, is the cause of the ineffectiveness of much school integration.

The report cites other benefits of integration, one noted by the American Educational Research Association: diversity makes students smarter: "The novel ideas and challenges that such exposure brings leads [*sic*] to improved cognitive skills, including critical thinking and problem-solving."[30]

A brief from the American Psychological Association, cited by the Century Foundation, added, "White students in particular benefit from racially and ethnically diverse learning contexts in that the presence of students of color stimulates an increase in the complexity with which students—especially white students—approach a given issue. When white students are in racially homogeneous groups, no such cognitive stimulation occurs."[31]

The A+ Colorado report urges affluent parents to consider that racially and economically integrated schools will have great long-range benefits for their children in gaining admission to top colleges and succeeding in the workplace. Jobs are going to require very different skills in the future. Citing the 2017 report *The Age of Agility* by America Succeeds, A+ Colorado says these important new skills are sense making, novel and adaptive thinking, cross-cultural competence, and design mind-set. Design mind-set is explained as "the ability to represent and develop tasks and work processes for desired outcomes."[32]

The report suggests that one way to overcome group biases and fears is to experience individuation. That is, parents must see the parents from another group as individuals and no longer just as members of a group. Both privileged and marginalized parents need to support each other.[33] Denver, the report says, should call on the persons who experienced desegregated schools in the 1970s and 1980s to help as advocates for desegregation.[34]

There are many strategies the school board and the administration could use to provide more socioeconomic integration, which would also lead to more racial integration in the Denver schools, although 69 percent of the students citywide qualify for free or reduced-price lunches. But this must become a priority for the schools. The A+ Colorado report describes how two high-poverty schools within the old Smiley Middle School, which were 82 percent FRL, became only 22 percent FRL when affluent McAuliffe International Middle School was moved there from the Stapleton area. The idea of an international emphasis would naturally appeal to socioeconomically higher parents under Denver's elaborate choice system.[35] The school could have been integrated if the district had set a floor for a minimum percentage of seats for students qualifying for FRL. In fact, every charter school or magnet school for which students must "choice in" could set minimum and maximum percentages of FRL students. DPS has a pilot group of twenty-six more affluent schools where students on subsidized lunch have priority to "choice in" after the neighborhood students are accommodated. It is ironic that the district established a pilot to test desegregation, considering that it was thoroughly tested for twenty-six years when every school in Denver was desegregated under the *Keyes* court order. In another strategy, neighborhood zones could be used more effectively to broaden the diversity of student bodies simply by redrawing the zone boundaries.[36]

The report also calls for the creation of magnet schools that have broad community appeal. One current example is the Academia Ana Marie Sandoval School, which combines dual-language Spanish-English instruction with a Montessori teaching approach. Though it is in the Highland neighborhood, where just 12 percent of neighborhood students are on FRL, the school itself has 34 percent students on FRL. A less integrated school, the Denver School of the Arts, has been a powerful magnet, even for students living in suburban districts, but it doesn't have an integrated student body because the entrance tests set too high a bar in talent screens for students whose parents cannot afford private lessons. There is no public feeder elementary school for middle and high school.[37] The report proposes that Denver create a network of magnet schools in low-income neighborhoods where a good portion of the places are reserved for neighborhood children and the rest are assigned by lottery. This was a very successful approach in Raleigh, North Carolina.[38]

The A+ Colorado report ends with a call to action for a coalition of business interests, civil rights groups, teachers, faith leaders, elected officials, and school district leaders to become "champions for change." The recommendations echo many of those of the Strengthening Neighborhoods Committee:

1. It suggests that DPS set a goal of no more than 90 percent of students per school qualifying for free and reduced lunches, with results by school to be reported annually to the public.
2. DPS should educate the community on the need for integration.
3. The district should use the school choice process to reserve seats in economically segregated schools to intentionally integrate them. It should create enrollment zones that are intentionally diverse. Transportation must be provided to ensure that enrollment zones work for all students, allowing them to access the programs of their choice whether they are within or outside the enrollment zones.
4. "Construct feeder patterns that prioritize students who have historically been left out of specialized programs." The programs cited here are the Denver School of the Arts, International Baccalaureate (IB) programs, and gifted and talented programs.
5. Support new diverse-by-design schools. This refers to establishing schools in low-income areas but reserving space for the neighborhood children; it also refers to new schools that feature diversity as part of their charters.[39]

In addition to these calls to action, the report suggests some policy changes at the board level, including de-tracking schools so they don't become segregated by classroom inside an otherwise integrated building. The district should also focus on relationship building at the school level: PTO and PTA membership should look like the school's membership. The report cautions against complete gentrification of the city under which long-standing communities will be displaced.

Both reports on the current situation in the Denver Public Schools are sobering, yet they offer solid suggestions and hope for the way the board could direct the district to improve the education of all Denver children. Knowing the harmful effects of racial isolation and the inferiority of education in a racially and economically isolated school, how can we shortchange the children? The district talks a lot about making every school a good school—effectively, compensatory education—but we know from experience and from the Supreme Court that separate but equal is not only ineffective, it is unconstitutional.

I once asked Robert Connery, an early *Keyes* plaintiffs' attorney, if he thought we would ever have another *Keyes* case. He said we would need another George Bardwell and Paul Klite for that to happen. That was true in the era when computers were the privilege of college professors only. Today, with powerful computers in general use, the years of analyses that Bardwell performed could be done in a few months (or less). However, we do not need another twenty-six-year lawsuit to learn what has already been well demonstrated: compensatory education in a segregated setting does not work. Judge Doyle found that it did not work, and the Supreme Court concurred. What we do need is a new team of courageous board members like Rachel Noel and Ed Benton and fearless candidates like Monte Pascoe to lead the fight for justice for all children. And we need persuadable board members like John Amesse and Jim Voorhees.

During the desegregation struggle, I developed great admiration for those I met—Black, Hispanic, and white—who had an unwavering commitment to improve the education of all the children in Denver. These people "showed up" for meeting after meeting and donated their time to make the plan work for all. I soon realized that these were the finest people I would ever meet. Unfortunately, our dream of justice has not been fully realized, even though equal educational opportunity is a necessary step toward a just society.

The Denver school board and administration did not do all they should have to make desegregation work, but, in spite of that, the education of Black and Hispanic children improved during the time the desegregation order was in effect. Though some students, particularly minority students, had painful experiences in their new schools, those experiences should be weighed against the lifelong consequences of segregated education: an inferior education, greater poverty, limited opportunity, higher unemployment, a higher crime rate, more welfare, and poorer health.

There is plenty of evidence that segregated education is inferior education, that it destroys both the mind and the self-image of minority children. This has been affirmed by scholars and by the courts, from the Federal District Court to the United States Supreme Court.

The current board and administration are responsible for segregation each time they adopt policies that result in the separation of students by race. It should not take another twenty-six-year court order to desegregate Denver schools as required by the Noel Resolution—a resolution that has never been rescinded. Given all the evidence of the harmful effects of segregation, the Denver school board has the moral duty and the legal requirement to desegregate our schools. Justice under the law must be more than a dream.

Afterword

While the *Keyes* case moved slowly through the courts and during the period of the court order, a lot of life went by. In the twenty-six years after the case was filed and while Denver schools were under the court order (1969 to 1995), our three children experienced integrated education in the Denver Public Schools at Moore Elementary School, Morey Junior High School, and East High School. Their integrated school experience was an advantage with admissions officers when they applied for college. By 1995, Sarah had graduated from Colorado College and completed a master's degree at Brown University. She became a teacher of teachers in Douglas County, Colorado. Ted graduated from Dartmouth College and spent three years with the Peace Corps in a village in Senegal. He continued his education with an MBA at the University of Denver. For many years, he has been the executive director of a day shelter for homeless and indigent seniors. Will graduated from Stanford University and later the University of Colorado Law School. He fought courageously against cystic fibrosis until, at age forty-nine, he lost the battle in

https://doi.org/10.5876/9781646422906.c019

June 2018.

All three of our children benefited from the broadening experience of attending integrated schools. They were more tolerant and appreciative of differences, and they learned how to work alongside people of different backgrounds.

Monte and I remained proud of our support for integrated schools as a matter of basic justice for children and for their parents who had dreams for those children. We cherished the friendship of the people we met—Black, white, and Hispanic—who were fervent about that cause.

This is a story that needs to be a part of our community history, whether we look at the deprivations of segregated schools or at the changes brought about by the court order. It is necessarily incomplete because of the omission of the narratives of many good people of Denver whose contributions I was unable to include, but I urge them to tell their stories and continue to work for equal educational opportunity for all of our children.

APPENDIX A

Supporting Materials

Chapter 1

The Noel Resolution, May 16, 1968

RESOLUTION NUMBER 1490

Part I

Policy 5100, Denver Public Schools, recognizes that the continuation of neighborhood schools has resulted in the concentration of some minority racial and ethnic groups in some schools and that a reduction of such concentration and the establishment of an integrated school population is desirable to achieve equality of educational opportunity.

Therefore, in order to implement Policy 5100, the Board of Education hereby directs the Superintendent to submit to the Board of Education as soon as possible, but no later than September 30, 1968, a comprehensive plan for the integration of the Denver Public Schools. Such plan then to be considered by the Board, the Staff and the community and, with such refinements as may be required, shall be considered for adoption no later than

https://doi.org/10.5876/9781646422906.c020

December 31, 1968.

Part II

1. The Board of Education is faced with a serious social crisis. We believe a majority of citizens of Denver have confidence in the ability of this Board to meet the complex, difficult and controversial issues involved in this crisis. However, the Board is aware of wide and deep distrust of its motives and actions by certain racial and ethnic groups, and individuals within these groups. It is accused of injustice, of perpetuating, without concern, the educational and social evils occurring with de facto segregation in schools. These groups have been promised much by society in general. Repeated failures of performance have alienated good friends, have created wide distrust of motives and have created an atmosphere where responsible leadership and concerned citizen support are being lost to the schools and to the community. We are increasingly aware of feelings of antagonism, of isolation, of hopelessness, of deep and unyielding bitterness, real and intense. These feelings are strongly held and are not subject to easy communication to those who do not have a similar background. The Board now states that its policy will be to eliminate distrust of its motives and performance by the minority community.

2. Also, the Board is aware of a different and widespread community distrust of Board motives and actions. This is evidenced by a substantial credibility gap, based on the fears of many citizens that their freedom of choice of home location and concurrent school selection is or will be threatened by proposed Board actions, particularly actions in the solution of the educational problems of de facto minority ethnic and racial segregation. The words "bussing," or "reverse bussing" (meaning the transportation of white children into minority populated schools), express the undefined fears of large numbers of Denver citizens that somehow the Board and its policies threaten deeply felt sensibilities. Here there is abroad in Denver a degree of distrust that is frightening in its intensity and has many ramifications. Expressions of such feelings are frequently prefaced by express denials of prejudice, racial or otherwise, and the Board accepts such denials at face value and as evidence of the existence of good will towards the minority communities of Denver. The Board recognizes that the voluntary support of citizens who presently hold such views is necessary to the proper functioning of the school system.

3. A third source of distrust of Board motives and performance is the body of citizens of all races, including many whites, who recognize and accept

that segregated education is harmful to both minority and majority children and who now insist that the Board increase its efforts to eliminate the educational evils of de facto segregation. The Board has obviously failed to convince these people that its past actions, and particularly the recent approval of major junior high school construction and the proposed voluntary movement of elementary minority pupils[,] represent good faith efforts in this area. The confidence of these citizens must be restored and the Board proposes to seek their active support.

4. A fourth force presently apparent and widely communicated to the Board is a reluctance throughout the city to see the tax load—primarily the real estate tax load—increased in any degree. In this area, the Board has apparently failed to communicate to the community the validity of the financial needs of the District. Increased State aid, if and when forthcoming, will be welcome but realistically can do little to reduce the real estate tax levy and will, in the long run, create a further class of concerned taxpayers to whom the function, purpose, method and objectives of the school system must be explained and whose understanding of such matters must be obtained. The Board states that its policy is and will be to foster such understanding.

5. The death of Dr. Martin Luther King has focused the attention of concerned people of good will upon the deep and festering injustice of modern urban existence, with its contradictions of opportunity and achievement, in an America dedicated, at least in theory, to the equality of opportunity for all men. Particularly in the area of public education, Dr. King's death has caused thoughtful persons of all races, particularly whites, to reassess beliefs long and dearly held and to question the pace of change and even its direction.

A. The Board is resolved to act as a unifying agency for Denver in these times. To this end, it requests the Superintendent[,] in implementation of the purposes of Resolution No. 1490 and in response to the community concerns stated above, to include within the plan required by Resolution No. 1490, or to submit separately but at the earliest practical time or times, a further plan, or a series of plans, including specific timetable, to accomplish the following:

1. The reduction of concentrations of minority racial and/or ethnic groups in schools and the integration of school populations.

2. The actual existence of equality of educational program in all schools, regardless of location, including, without limitation, faculty quality, training, experience and attitude, course offerings, equipment and facilities.

3. The active participation in programs within the metropolitan Denver area to establish more diverse or heterogeneous racial and/or ethnic school populations.

4. The emphasis at all instructional levels of the individual and group contributions of ethnic and racial minorities.

5. The maximum involvement, consistent with maintenance requirements, of the school plant in the community activities of the Denver metropolitan area, to commence during the forthcoming summer.

6. Human relations and sensitivity training for all teaching and administrative personnel and assurance that personnel recruitment and assignment policies are consistent with the realities of our multiracial and multiethnic world.

7. The establishment of citizen community support to accomplish the widest possible community understanding of the aims, purposes, motives and affairs of the School District.

B. To Consider, among other factors as appear proper, the following:

1. The use of transportation and the degree to which transportation should be mandatory or voluntary.

2. The desirability of temporary or permanent closing of certain schools.

3. The existence of community attitudes and opinions.

4. The requirement for all children of course offerings in minority group cultural, historical, social and economic contributions to our society and of qualified minority group member teachers.

5. The development of "magnet" or "laboratory" schools in core areas, including attendance policies for such schools.

6. The use of community resources and resource people.

7. The availability to all children at all levels of textbooks and other instructional materials which fairly and favorably represent minority groups and individuals.

8. The availability for use by persons in all parts of the District of school facilities for extracurricular educational, recreational and community purposes.

9. The feasibility of some form of extended school year.

10. The degree to which present vocational, technical and job oriented course offerings meet the needs of the children of this District.

11. The active extension of intercultural and interracial experiences for children, including the expansion of the cultural art center program and similar programs.

C. The Board is impelled by a sense of urgency in these matters. To this end, it has requested the Superintendent to submit his plan responsive to Part I of this resolution within the periods therein provided. The plans required by Part II should be submitted as and when prepared for Board and public consideration and for adoption at the earliest possible time. As an example only, plans for the fullest use of school facilities for community summer programs are obviously needed now. Also preliminary plans for community organizations can properly be expected shortly. In any event, the Board requests the Superintendent to present plans responsive to Part II of this resolution not later than the regular meeting of the Board in September 1968 and periodically thereafter until complete plans are forthcoming.

APPENDIX

The Segregation Index presented in Chapter 6

EXPLANATION OF
THE CONSTRUCTION OF
THE SEGREGATION INDEX

This index measures the departure of the racial and ethnic distribution of students among a group of schools from a standard whereby Anglo, Negro and Hispano students are assumed to be uniformly distributed among all schools in the group. The index ranges from 0, denoting total desegregation, to 100, denoting total segregation.

The rationale for the formulation of this index is as follows:

Consider the proportion of Anglo students for m schools. The deviation of each school from the Denver mean multiplied by the enrollment in each school reflects the relative contribution of each school to total segregation in the District. The total "amount" of segregation is the sum of these products. To "normalize" this sum for indexing purposes, it is divided by that number which would represent a totally segregated situation.

Let

p_i = proportion of Anglo students in school i, $(i=1,2,\ldots,m)$, where m is the number of schools comprising the index,

P = proportion of Anglo students in the School District. (the number of schools may or may not be equal to m),

t_i = total enrollment in school, i,

Then

Segregation Index = SI

$$= \frac{\sum\limits_{i=1}^{m} \left| p_i - P \right| t_i}{P\left(\sum\limits_{1}^{m} t_i - 2 \sum\limits_{1}^{m} p_i t_i\right) + \sum\limits_{1}^{m} p_i t_i}.$$

The vertical bars in the numerator refer to absolute value.

1222

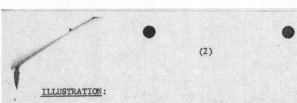

(2)

ILLUSTRATION:

School	Anglo Students	Total Enrollment	Proportion of Anglo Students	Absolute Deviation Of Proportion From District Proportion	Weighted Absolute Deviation
A	20	200	0.10	0.55	110
B	360	400	0.90	0.25	100
C	285	300	0.95	0.30	90
	665	900	0.739		300

Proportion of Anglo students in School District = 0.65.

Hence,

$$SI = \frac{300}{0.65 \quad (900 - 2 \times 665) + 665}$$

$$= \frac{300}{- 279.5 + 665} \quad \frac{300}{385.5} \quad = \quad 0.78$$

Remarks:

The index can be near 100 even in cases where the proportion of Anglo students in the School District is small or large. The index takes into account concentrations of Anglos as well as concentrations of minority students.

The index in the example above refers to a sub-group of schools in a District. It is equally applicable to the entire District.

While the index has some intrinsic merit standing alone, it is especially useful when used for purposes of comparison; for example, in assessing the effectiveness of plans for desegregation of schools, or for measuring the increasing or decreasing segregation of a group of schools over time.

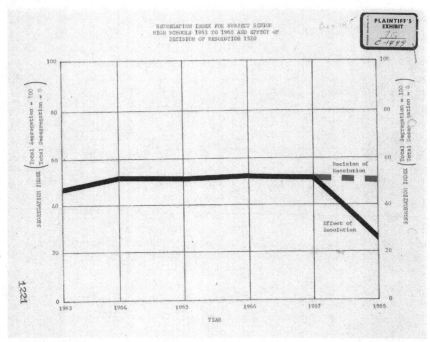

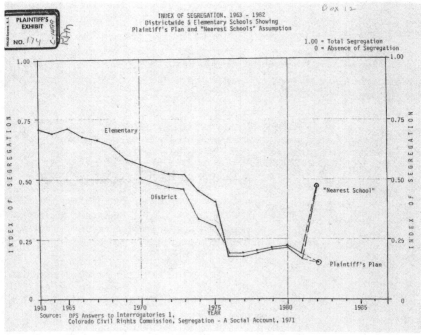

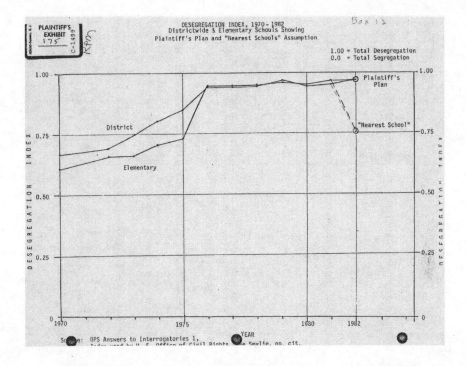

DESEGREGATION INDEX, 1970-1982
Districtwide & Elementary Schools Showing
Plaintiff's Plan and "Nearest Schools" Assumption

Box 12

1.00 = Total Desegregation
0.0 = Total Segregation

Plaintiff's
Plan

"Nearest School"

District

Elementary

DESEGREGATION INDEX

DESEGREGATION INDEX

YEAR

Source: OPS Answers to Interrogatories 1,
Index used by U.S. Office of Civil Rights, see Smylie, op. cit.

Chapter 9

Exhibit A.2 shows achievement scores in minority versus white schools, described in chapter 9.

EXHIBIT A.2. Plaintiffs' Exhibit 82: Composite percentile scores of students in minority schools and more than 90 percent Anglo schools in Denver, May 1968

	Composite Percentile		
Composition of School	Grade 5	Grade 9	Grade 11
Majority Black and Hispano students*	22	30	28
More than 90% Anglo students	66	73	74
City average	43	62	59
National norm	50	50	50

* Extreme cases include 96.9% Black at Barrett Elementary; 82.8% Hispano at Elmwood Elementary; 72.5% Black and 22.2% Hispano at Cole Junior High.

Source: "Denver Public Schools Look at Themselves," Supplementary Information, 1968.

Chapter 11

Exhibits A.3, A.4, A.5, A.6, and A.7 contain data as presented in plaintiffs' exhibits, described in chapter 11.

EXHIBIT A.3. Plaintiffs' Exhibit 501-A: Table 1, after transporting, 1970, court schools

Number	School	Total Students	Percent Anglo	Percent Capacity	Average Achievement
3	Asbury	644	60	102	44
4	Ashgrove	750	59	105	56
11	Berkeley	344	60	104	34
13	Bradley	985	59	102	51
16	Bryant-Webster	697	55	105	31
22	Columbine	1,054	55	94	49
23	Cory	596	60	99	53
27	Doull	923	59	99	52
31	Ellis	946	59	105	53
33	Elmwood	426	54	94	50
37	Fairmont	513	55	106	32
38	Fairview	924	55	94	42

continued on next page

EXHIBIT A.3—*continued*

Number	School	Total Students	Percent Anglo	Percent Capacity	Average Achievement
39	Fallis	364	60	101	65
45	Greenlee	969	55	105	34
46	Gust	808	59	103	47
47	Hallett	728	57	105	40
48	Harrington	539	54	94	41
51	Knight	617	59	97	46
54	Mcmeen	881	59	104	63
55	Mitchell	994	55	94	41
66	Pitts	448	60	99	59
69	Sabin	1,292	59	97	46
73	Slavens	677	60	98	61
75	Smith	941	54	106	55
77	Stedman	664	55	98	49
83	Traylor	784	59	104	55
84	University Park	1,027	59	106	58
86	Washington Park	491	60	90	52
89	Whittier	993	55	94	45
Total		22,039	57	100	48

EXHIBIT A.4. Plaintiffs' Exhibit 503-A: Table 1, after transportation, court and target schools

Number	School	Total Students	Percent Anglo	Percent Capacity	Average Achievement
3	Asbury	639	58	101	43
4	Ashgrove	752	56	104	55
11	Berkeley	337	58	102	32
12	Boulevard	393	54	100	31
13	Bradley	974	56	101	47
14	Bromwell	277	58	102	58
16	Bryant-Webster	696	53	105	33
17	Carson	714	59	95	67
22	Columbine	1,043	52	92	48
23	Cory	592	58	98	53
25	Crofton	337	51	93	42

continued on next page

EXHIBIT A.4—*continued*

Number	School	Total Students	Percent Anglo	Percent Capacity	Average Achievement
26	Denison	552	58	96	41
27	Doull	915	57	98	51
29	Ebert	389	52	92	36
31	Ellis	938	57	104	52
32	Ellsworth	202	61	96	53
33	Elmwood	421	52	93	49
34	Elyria	141	51	94	32
37	Fairmont	515	52	107	30
38	Fairview	911	53	93	40
39	Fallis	361	57	100	64
40	Force	825	58	90	37
41	Garden Place	689	52	106	23
42	Gilpin	832	53	92	43
45	Greenlee	957	53	105	28
46	Gust	800	57	102	46
47	Hallett	728	55	105	37
48	Harrington	533	51	93	42
51	Knight	857	57	97	46
52	Lincoln	588	58	108	29
54	Mcmeen	867	56	103	60
55	Mitchell	976	52	92	41
57	Montclair	576	60	91	51
58	Montan	176	60	97	48
62	Palmer	472	59	104	58
66	Pitts	443	57	98	56
68	Rosedale	451	58	107	34
69	Sabin	1,279	56	96	45
73	Slavens	674	58	97	62
74	Smedley	701	53	106	27
75	Smith	936	51	105	52
77	Stedman	657	52	97	48
80	Swansea	673	54	101	33
82	Thatcher	350	59	97	27

continued on next page

EXHIBIT A.4—*continued*

Number	School	Total Students	Percent Anglo	Percent Capacity	Average Achievement
83	Traylor	756	55	102	54
84	University Park	1,018	57	106	56
86	Washington Park	486	57	90	51
89	Whittier	975	52	92	42
90	Wyatt	477	51	106	44
91	Wyman	394	54	93	35
	Total	32,020	55	99	45

EXHIBIT A.5. Plaintiffs' Exhibit 505-A: Junior high schools' ranking by 1967 Iowa Test scores, with 1969 capacity and enrollment

School	1967 Iowa Score (9th grade)	Percent Anglo, 1969	Capacity, 1969	Enrollment, 1969	Percent Capacity, 1969
Hill*	80	74.0	1,485	1,319	89
Thomas Jefferson	79	94.5	1,065	1,266	119
Merrill	77	78.6	1,455	1,576	108
John F. Kennedy	74	97.2	1,050	1,417	135
Gove	65	66.5	730	800	110
Byers	64	81.1	1,200	1,204	100
Kunsmiller	64	81.9	1,815	1,831	101
Rishel	59	70.5	1,230	1,302	106
Grant	56	74.1	810	902	111
Skinner	56	78.7	1,185	1,285	108
Kepner	50	68.6	1,710	1,546	90
Lake	49	48.2	1,380	1,249	90
Smiley*	44	61.2	1,635	1,393	85
Horace Mann	30	23.2	1,155	1,110	96
Morey	25	26.8	1,200	801	67
Baker	24	11.6	1,050	885	84
Cole	20	1.4	1,725	989	58
Hamilton**	—	84.8	1,560	1,544	99
Citywide	62	66.1	23,440	22,419	—

* These schools were included in the court's injunction.

** Opened second semester of the 1969–1970 school year.

EXHIBIT A.6. Plaintiffs' Exhibit 509: Court-designated elementary schools—ethnic and racial data, teacher experience, and median achievement

| | Enrollment, Percent, 1969 | | | Teacher Data, Percent, 1968 | | | Median Achievement, 1968 |
	Anglo	Negro	Hispano	New	Proba-tionary	Median Experience	Percentile, Grade 5
Bryant-Webster	23	1	76	14	35	8.0	23
Columbine	1	97	2	27	50	2.5	20
Elmwood	8	—	92	39	39	3.0	28
Fairmont	20	—	80	25	79	1.0	16
Fairview	7	8	83	10	33	6.0	18
Greenlee	17	9	73	13	40	4.0	17
Hallett	38	58	3	25	46	3.0	32
Harrington	2	76	20	30	74	1.0	14
Mitchell	2	71	27	26	44	4.0	12
Smith	4	92	3	26	49	3.0	30
Stedman	4	93	3	24	40	4.0	28
Whittier	1	94	5	27	57	2.0	19
Average	11	52	37	23	48	3.5	21

EXHIBIT A.7. Plaintiffs' Exhibit 510: Target schools—ethnic and racial data, teacher experience, and median achievement

| | Ethnic Enrollment, Percent, 1969 | | | Teacher Data, Percent, 1968 | | | Median Achievement, 1968 |
	Anglo	Negro	Hispano	New	Proba-tionary	Median Experience	Percentile, Grade 5
Gilpin	3	36	60	25	42	4.5	23
Crofton	7	38	52	21	43	4.0	18
Ebert	11	35	52	21	42	3.0	18
Wyatt	2	46	52	14	27	6.0	15
Boulevard	30	1	68	17	50	3.0	20
Garden Place	17	17	65	18	37	4.0	16
Wyman	28	38	30	22	50	4.0	24
Smedley	20	2	77	21	57	2.0	19
Elyria	27	—	73	33	50	2.5	23
Swansea	29	4	67	18	36	3.5	22
Average	16	20	64	20	42	3.7	20
Average court schools	11	52	37	23	48	3.5	21
City average	60	15	24	16	37	5.6	43

APPENDIX B

Interviews of Students and Parents

Students

Edmond (Buddy) F. Noel Jr., Rachel Noel's son,[1] graduated from East High before the court-ordered desegregation plan took effect, but he had a first-hand view of the conditions that led to the order. He did not think the plan worked as well as it should have because it was sabotaged from the beginning by the board and the administration, and "integration" became merely desegregation. He said, "Most white people became afraid, and only the strongest kept their convictions. Being anti-busing would never get you in trouble, and the people who thought busing was right became quiet. It vanished."

When asked if desegregation efforts changed his views, he replied, "My views were honed as a young person. I am more willing to live with my optimism of '62 to '64 than [with] the realism of the 1980s and 1990s. After my sixty-six years I choose not to be guided by the Reagan or Clinton years but by the optimism of '63 and '64, when we really believed in integration

https://doi.org/10.5876/9781646422906.c021

and believed it could happen in our society." When asked if it was all worth it, Buddy replied, "I still think an integrated society is better. I still want to stick to that more optimistic period of my life." He doesn't think the current school board worries about integrated schools, a fact that had saddened his mother.

Paul Lewis, who is Black, said busing at the time it occurred was about hanging out with his friends who were on the bus. Because of busing, his personal view of the world changed for the better. He said, "I realized that the world was not fair, but it didn't have to be for me to succeed."[2] He was bused to Dora Moore Elementary School under the Voluntary Open Enrollment plan. From that experience he learned later in life that "it's not what you have, it's what you do with what you have." He added, "I fully believe that the experiences learned, as a result of busing, helped me fully understand that we as a people have more in common than our differences. We all have happy, sad, joy, pain, fear, anxiety, good stress and bad stress, moments of curiosity, minutes of enlightenment, emotions that take us all over the place. The difference is what triggers those feelings and the honesty of why we are expressing them."

He concluded: "I did not always believe that desegregation was in the best interest of Blacks or America. As I've matured spiritually, emotionally, and mentally, I have come to the conclusion that it is because of these life experiences and opportunities that I have grown to be the person I am. [I have been] learning to accept the things that I cannot change and fight for the things that I believe in. If I had to do it all over again, I would hope that my parents would make the same decisions to support the desegregation and to bus me."

Sheila Macdonald, who is white, remembers that when she went to Bromwell Elementary School, busloads of Black kids arrived at the school. When I asked Sheila if desegregation worked, she replied, "It worked for me. It should have been the first step in about ten steps. We should have made sure every school had the same resources. And there should have been a campaign about getting [minority] kids in honors classes. There shouldn't be just one kid in honors classes."[3] Sheila is now a political campaign consultant.

Kadija Haynes, who identifies herself as biracial Latino and Chicano, said busing was arguably the most negative experience in her young life.[4] Under the busing plan she was sent to Carson, a formerly white school, where racism, she said, extended from the bus rides to the classrooms. For junior high, she needed a change and went to an independent study school with a more diverse student body. Then she spent a year at Gove Junior High before finishing at East High School, which she called one of the most heterogeneous schools in the district, with minority kids in advanced classes. Kadija did not see any benefits from attending integrated schools. She believes that instead of busing the students, they should have bused the teachers. She said they took "the voiceless, the innocent and the young and threw them into the fire. They were wrong in thinking they are doing something special. Instead they should actually fight the fight. Move the teachers; change the redlining of the homes. That's the fight . . . It is easy to do petri dishes with the kids. They were cowards."

Kadija's sister, Mary Haynes, who identifies herself as Black and Chicano and who also went to Carson, recalls having fewer negative experiences.[5] She recounts one example of a racial incident in the sixth grade:

> In sixth grade we sat in rows according to how we scored on a math test each week. The highest scorer was the first person in the first row, the second highest scorer sat behind him or her, and after the first row was full, the next highest scorer was at the front of the second row and succeeding rows were filled in that manner. I always ended up in the second row, but I was determined to get in the first row. Finally, I got the highest score, but then the teacher changed the rules. She said, "We are going to do something different this week." She put me, the highest scorer, in the last seat in the first row, much to my disappointment.

Another teacher asked each student to pick a country and report on it in front of the class. Mary said they had books all over their house, including a set of encyclopedias. She invited all of her Black classmates to come over to her house and pick a country and then take home the relevant volume of the encyclopedia to write their reports. She then invited them back to her house to practice their oral presentations. When they presented the reports to the class, she was coaching some of them with the words because she had them memorized. She was crushed when the teacher accused them all of cheating. The teacher claimed Mary had written the reports of which they were all so proud. She never cried about these experiences as a kid, but she sometimes cries about them now because some of the teachers displayed overt racism. She felt the white students were better than the teachers were at accepting students.

The music teacher, Miss Althouse, was popular with the Black students. She chose Mary to be an angel, in effect the moderator, in a dramatic production. Mary also remembers one very positive experience with a white art teacher, who cut off the end of her finger with a paper cutter. She told Mary, who didn't realize what had happened, "I'm leaving you in charge of the class," which Mary found affirming.

Mary saw the Carson kids again in high school. One of her white friends was Nelson Rangell, a saxophone player. She and Nelson have reconnected. Another white girl tried to give her some diet recipes, which she appreciated. At Carson there was ability grouping, and Mary and one other student were the only Black students in the top group. She said there were probably five minority kids in the top classes.

Mary's junior high years were spent at Gove. There were only a couple of years when all of the students got along. Gove had been naturally integrated until citywide busing began in 1974. The district would not provide a bus for Black students who lived within one mile of the school, but the students convinced the public bus company to provide service. In another struggle, the choir director divided the singers into an A Choir and a B Choir. All of the white students and a few Black students were in the A Choir and most of the Black kids were in the B Choir. Mary confronted the teacher about this in class. After he explained his rationale for the division, Mary said "f— you!" The next day the director said to the class that he had never been so disrespected, and Mary apologized. The segregated choir sections, nevertheless, remained.

The tracking at Gove created some segregation. Theater was integrated because the productions required a lot of people. There was an all-Black gospel choir. As far as discipline was concerned, Mary says she thought Black kids were in trouble more than white kids were.

A group of nine to twelve Black ninth graders invited the entire class to a barbecue. They moved a lot of grills into Mary's backyard and bought all the food. They invited all of the white kids, whether they were bused in or lived in Park Hill. The parents of the bused-in kids wouldn't let their children go to the Black neighborhood, even though the kids said they wanted to go.

When she was at East High School, Mary said, she had a different life at home than she did at school. At school she was a leader, while on weekends she was going to house parties. Mary was elected head girl at East, which she says was an election she engineered. The students who hung out on the south lawn told her she was better than they were because they spent their days getting high and smoking cigarettes. Her brother and sister hung out there, so she had some friends among them. She went out and asked the kids there to vote for her. Everybody went into the building to vote and then went back out to the south lawn [instead of going to class].

When I asked Mary about the benefits of attending integrated schools, she responded with a question: "Is it better to be in a school that has inferior materials or go to a school where teachers do terrible things to you?" The drawback was being bused, she said. "First and Grape [where Carson School was located] seemed clear across the city," she said. Neither the teachers nor the kids knew what to expect: "I don't know what preparation they provided teachers and [their] expectations of behavior."

Was it all worth the effort? I asked. She answered, "Speaking very personally, I think overall it was worth it. I wouldn't have the friends that I have to this day. I would have many of them, but not all. Several of the alumni found a time capsule at Gove and through Facebook they connected. It really changed all of our lives. It allowed us to be friends with people we would never have had a chance to know."

Mary went to Stanford University, where she later worked in admissions and as assistant dean of students. She has worked at three institutions of higher education. Now she works half-time for the Daniels Fund and privately as a life coach.

A Stapleton-area neighborhood newspaper interviewed several former Manual students about their experiences with desegregated education. Dr. Jason F. Kirksey, who is Black, said: "It was a transformative experience not just for us, as students, but for parents and for the communities involved. My parents would have never interacted with these people under any other scenario. They were from two distinct communities, but they were able to come together for the good of their children and for the good of Manual." At the time, Kirksey was chief diversity officer and associate vice president at Oklahoma State University.[6]

The white students bused into Manual "have overwhelmingly positive memories. In fact, the majority of Manual graduates interviewed credit the experience of attending Manual at its most diverse with transforming their lives," according to the author of the neighborhood newspaper article, Maegan Parker Brooks.

Most important, the experience changed the students' expectations. Jim Hoops, a math teacher and football coach, said it changed the question for students of color from "will I go to college" to "where will I go to college?"

White student Megan Lederer wrote her college application essay about being bused to a Black school, which she considered an amazing experience. Both she and Hoops said colleges were impressed by the experience the students were getting. Many of the white graduates went on to attend prestigious colleges.

Lainie Hodges, who is white, said that interacting with students from various backgrounds taught her "how to survive in the world." Another white former student, Jody Hansen, also said she "learned how to live in the world." She can "walk into any job, talk to any person . . . I really learned how to be with people in the world."[7] Tim Tribbett, also white, loves telling people he went to Manual. He graduated, Brooks says, "with confidence to engage a diverse world."

The former students noted some limitations to desegregation, though. Lorenza Munoz Scott said there wasn't much interaction between groups. Scott's mother recalled that her [minority] son entered an Advanced Placement (AP) classroom and the teacher asked if he was in the wrong place. Dr. Kirksey said that even when students tested well enough to be in AP classes, they were not always placed there. Scott said some students "fell through the cracks."

In spite of the limitations she cited, Scott said Manual "has had a huge impact on my life now . . . and has made me more culturally sensitive." Alexis McClain, similarly, credits her years at Manual with her "ability to go out and deal with real situations." Kendrick Lane, a white student who was bused from Crestmoor Park, said, "I feel I gained a broader perspective on life, race, and culture at Manual than through any other experience in my life. I feel the experiences I had at Manual, specifically the interactions with such a diverse student body, served me well in my current line of work seeing and relating to patients from all walks of life." She is now a physician's assistant.[8]

Parents

Connie Platt recalled that she was active in the parents' group at Park Hill Elementary School during the early days of the desegregation order. She said: "I worked with parents of our daughters' schoolmates, black and white. We inherited a history of white assumptions about whites' right to lead, and the most valuable lesson I took from my experience was to do a lot of listening in heterogeneous groups. I was also grateful for the opportunity to test my abstract belief in racial justice against my own actions . . . principles in practice. That belief is still important to me, and still I act on it."[9]

Anna Jo Haynes, who described herself as Latina, was first active as the Denver chair of the desegregation efforts of the Congress of Racial Equality (CORE). Anna Jo said, "We published data sheets about what was happening in the school district. We sent white members to the white schools, Black members to Black schools to collect information." CORE published the contrasting data anonymously. "We found," she said, "that 'ski-bunnies' would come to teach short term in Black schools and leave after the ski season ended."

Anna Jo's daughter Happy went to Park Hill for kindergarten and returned to Barrett for first grade when it opened. According to Anna Jo, the white principal at Barrett, "Carl Barnhart, was very welcoming and he had all Black teachers. He wanted all of the families there." Anna Jo said that in general, teachers and administrators were lukewarm toward minority children: "The teachers were always surprised if Mary did well, which Mary found painful."

Under the court order, Anna Jo's daughters Mary and Kadija went to Carson Elementary School and then Gove Junior High and East High. Desegregation, she thought, did not provide equal educational opportunity, but it provided an improved education: "Poverty will always make education of children unequal." In the new schools, they had the needed resources under the court order, but they weren't treated equally. Anna Jo believed the effort was worth it, although the Latino community did not want desegregation for their kids. They wanted their community to be whole. They wondered, "Why put our kids through that?" Anna Jo concluded, "I think it was the right thing to do, absolutely. They learned lessons about how to get along with one another and that we are all equal. It made Denver a great city, and it was really hard to do."[10]

The fight for desegregation began for lawyer Richard E. Young and his wife, Lorie, when Dick chaired Denver's Commission on Community Relations. In 1964–1965 he started the Fair Housing Center, which worked with realtors to end the use of the red line that prevented Black people from buying beyond a certain street. By 1967 the center was well funded with a staff of eighteen, having received a $500,000 grant from the Ford Foundation. Lorie was appointed to the Community Education Council along with Jean Emery to represent the League of Women Voters, where she reported to the council on the desegregation efforts in junior highs and served on the public relations committee. Lorie "was trying to get all the media to report the true picture [of desegregation]."

When asked if he saw discrimination in course offerings, teacher experience, facilities, and achievement, Young answered, "Yes, yes, yes, and yes." At Smiley Junior High, there was "unevenness of equipment and teacher experience." He said, "The Lowry parents objected to the plant [and the fact that there was] no language lab [and the fact that the] whole building and grounds were dirty." On the very first day the students were moved to Smiley, the parents went downtown to the administration building to object. Shortly thereafter, they picketed Smiley in a general strike, and the kids walked out of school. The expectations for minority children were different from those of white children. Lorie said that at minority Morey Junior High before the desegregation order, "only shop and cosmetology were offered to prepare students for work."

To prepare for the desegregation order at Park Hill Elementary School, pairs of teachers, one Black and one white, visited the homes of every child at one grade level. Then teachers could see that many of their minority students were middle-class people who came from lovely homes, changing some of their stereotypes.

What came out of integration, Lorie said, was that the students were able to get along with persons of another race. Schools are more segregated now, Lorie said, so she believes integration was not successful in the long term. It was successful for the children who were there at the time, though. Dick, in contrast, said it was successful: "Now there are more mixed marriages. We are no longer a white Christian country. In twenty to thirty years there won't be that many people who are unfamiliar with people of another race. Park Hill is more integrated than it was then. There are still just two Black families in our block. Housing prices have slowed any migration."

Dick added that their lives are much better because they were involved in the desegregation effort. For two years he chaired the Park Hill Action

Committee, dedicated to integrating their community. Roy Romer (later governor of Colorado) and he were the two delegates from Montview Boulevard Presbyterian Church, and Ed Lupberger, also from Montview, was the committee's first chair.[11]

Parent Palecia Lewis, who is Black, said desegregation was a mixed experience for her family: "I was a parent at Smith Elementary, and the school was overcrowded by a very large number of students. The district acquired twelve or thirteen mobile units . . . Mrs. Davis, principal of Smith School, sent [her children] Camellia, Pam, and Paul to Moore School on Voluntary Open Enrollment. They had a host family at Moore. Families on VOE and host families had outings and activities together, sometimes a school event, sometimes just the two families. Camellia had several bad experiences at Moore. She hated school after going there."[12]

Palecia said the teachers at Moore were more experienced and the variety of things they taught the children was broader than was the case at Smith. They had more field trips, including a trip to the zoo. As far as facilities go, Moore was much older, but the children enjoyed learning about its history. Her children liked the environment and the community around the school. And there were no mobile units used as classrooms at Moore, as there were at Smith.

In junior high, Palecia's children first went to Kunsmiller in southwest Denver. "They were not wanted there," Palecia said. "They were discriminated against . . . by teachers and students. Sometimes they would say mean things to them and laugh at them." Some of the good students got better treatment, though. Her children finished junior high at Hill, which was all right, Palecia said. For one thing, they had a greater variety of sports there.

Finally, her children went to Thomas Jefferson High School. "Every school they went to there were some negative experiences," Palecia said. She added: "Children are different. They do and say things and make comments. [It was] not always the children who were troublesome that did negative things. Sometimes kids get in the wrong place with the wrong bunch of kids and something negative was said to them because of things other members of the group did. Maybe they just laughed and edged the misbehaving child along. [They are] put into the group by teachers who see all Blacks the same and address them as 'you-all.' The teacher might scold the wrong child in the group."

Sometimes a student would raise her hand and not be called on, which looked like discrimination. Children were also disappointed when they weren't selected, say, for a drama part. If they had been in their neighborhood school, they were sure they would have been selected. Sometimes they did not get into accelerated classes, or lighter-skinned Black students were treated fairly but darker-skinned Black kids were not. They had good sports coaches at Thomas Jefferson. Paul played basketball, while Pam spent more time in the classroom. A niece of Palecia's was a cheerleader.

When I asked Palecia how the court order affected her children, she replied, "They would have preferred to stay where they were, that was their preferred choice. They learned to make good choices. Now they see that it gave them an opportunity that they would have missed otherwise."

Then I asked her how the desegregation efforts affected her. She replied:

It helped me to make better choices, [to] listen and think. I didn't care whether they wanted to be there or not. I felt they had a right to be there. I felt goodwill enough from some people but not too goodwill from other people. I'm a country girl, and we worked hard. I always wanted to be the best. I grew up in Oklahoma on a farm. My parents told me I could be anything I wanted to be. I went to segregated schools. I was [at] the top of my class. Then I went to Langston College, which was segregated. I was at the top of my class and graduated with honors. I had been active in the Park Hill Action Committee.

Finally, I asked her if the desegregation order worked. She replied:

It provided opportunity for Black young people and some adults to wake up to see they could get what they wanted if they pressed for it, worked for it. Some took advantage of it and many did not.

I believe that the way desegregation ended, it was not finished. It stopped, but it was not finished. I think we did not learn what was intended. I don't know how better to say it. I don't think you and people whose feelings are more like I would want them to be are working toward it . . . We should treat people as we want to be treated. People like you practice where we ought to be. If we are Christians we should live differently. Both sides failed.

Black educator Loretta Richardson described her experience as a parent during the desegregation era as well. She mentioned Black children going to Slavens, Alcott, and Dora Moore Elementary Schools on Voluntary Open Enrollment. She worked with groups trying to address inequality in the schools, such as Black Educators United, the Urban League, the Denver Classroom Teachers Association, and other community groups.[13]

On the quality of faculty in Black schools, she said: "Newly hired teachers were usually placed in neighborhoods with children who were most deficient in their skills. These newly hired, particularly white teachers, were not given help with working with children of minority groups. Many of them were not very successful in their efforts to teach our children. Their excuse was a lack of understanding about the culture. The children needed teachers with some background and experience in working with minority children."

She said she had been told that today there are fewer minority teachers in the schools than in the past, and she urged a strong effort to recruit and train more minority teachers to teach minority children. Salaries have to be competitive to acquire quality teachers in the classrooms, she added.

Expectations for minority children were quite low, Loretta stated. Some people believed minorities did not possess the same learning capacity as many of their white counterparts. Some experts believed they were inherently inferior, and many misinformed people in education believed that theory. During the course of integration, the accomplishments of minorities became apparent, and this myth has proven inaccurate.

The court order provided Black children with more choices to obtain quality education, Loretta said. It was apparent that the neighborhood schools in certain areas such as Bromwell and Slavens were providing the best education possible. There were some incidents and some problems from the neighborhood children and their parents and, in a few cases, serious situations developed, but they were resolved. The white children, in most cases, seemed much more tolerant and sincere in their relationships with people of different races than their parents were.

The desegregation order, Loretta added, affected her family, her friends, and her. They thought it was about time for this to happen. Her husband and her friends had the same sincere desire: that their children would receive the quality of education they deserved. Like her parents, she wanted her children to become the best people they could be. She wanted them to be able to contribute to society in a highly productive way.

Loretta believes

the desegregation order accomplished a small measure of what it was expected to do . . . Part of the problem is that attitudes and opinions cannot be legislated. Individuals involved in the education of our children have to decide for themselves that all people are created equal and deserve equal opportunities to become successful persons in our society. My opinion is that it did not work in the manner that it should have worked . . . The district should make it clear that its major purpose is to educate all of the children to achieve at their highest level.

Notes

Preface

1. To view the complete text, see Martin Luther King Jr., *Why We Can't Wait* (New York: Signet Books, 1963, 1964), 76–95.

Introduction

1. Regis Groff, *When a King Came to Town*, PBS documentary, 2006.

Chapter 1: Separate and Unequal

1. Miller Hudson, "Bob Allen Left Legacy as Liberal Lion in Colorado House," *Colorado Statesman*, February 13, 2015, 5. Representative Bob Allen and Senator George Brown were the bill's sponsors. Colorado was the first state in the nation to outlaw covenants and mortgage redlining and to restrict the sale of a home to any willing purchaser.

2. Mary Jean Taylor, "Leadership Responses to Desegregation in the Denver Public Schools: A Historical Study, 1959–1977," PhD thesis, University of Denver, 1990, 53, 55.

3. Edgar Benton, interview by Pat Pascoe, October 16, 2013.

4. A Special Study Committee on Equality of Educational Opportunity in the Denver Public Schools, Jim Voorhees, chair, "Report and Recommendations to the Board of Education, School District Number One, Denver, Colorado" (Voorhees Report), March 1, 1964.

5. Voorhees Report, E-4, E-17–E-18.

6. Voorhees Report, 6–7.

7. Voorhees Report, D-3–D-4, C-28–C-30.

8. Voorhees Report, C-8.

9. Voorhees Report, B-14, D-11

10. Voorhees Report, B-8–B-9.

11. Voorhees Report, C-8, C-11.

12. Voorhees Report, C-10–C-11, C-21–C-22.

13. Voorhees Report, C-34–C-35, C-37.

14. Voorhees Report, C-3–C-4, C-38.

15. Voorhees Report, D-12–D-14.

16. Voorhees Report, D-11.

17. Voorhees Report, D-9.

18. Voorhees Report, D-4–D-5.

19. Voorhees Report, D-2–D-4.

20. Voorhees Report, D-7–D-8.

21. Voorhees Report, D-19–D-20.

22. Voorhees Report, D-4–D-5.

23. Voorhees Report, E-6–E-7.

24. Voorhees Report, E-20.

25. Voorhees Report, A-2, A-5.

26. Voorhees Report, A-11, table 19.

27. Voorhees Report, A-13, A-10.

28. "Volunteer Open Enrollment Gain," *The Review* (Denver Public Schools, February 1970), 4.

29. Voorhees Report, 7.

30. Quoted in *Denver School Buildings . . . Today and Tomorrow: A Proposal for Meeting the Most Urgent School Building and Site Needs of the Denver Public Schools* (Denver: Denver Public Schools, August 1967), 65.

31. Judge William E. Doyle, "Memorandum Opinion and Order," *Keyes v. School District No. 1*, No. C-1499, 303 F. Supp. 279 (D. Colo., July 31, 1969), at 283.

32. "Equality of Educational Opportunity," summary, US Department of Health, Education, and Welfare (Washington, DC: US Government Printing Office, July 2, 1966).

33. William G. Berge, chairman, and Bernard Valdez, vice-chairman, et al., "Final Report and Recommendations to the Board of Education School District Number One" (Berge Report), Advisory Council on Equality of Educational Opportunity in the Denver Public Schools, Denver, School District Number 1, 1967.

34. Edgar Benton, interview by Pat Pascoe, January 30, 2012.

35. Berge Report, 16.

36. Berge Report, 9–10.

37. Excerpted from "Characteristics of Negro Residences in Park Hill Area of Denver, Colorado, 1966," George E. Bardwell, Consultant to the City and County of Denver, April 20, 1966.

38. Berge Report, 29.

39. Berge Report, 36.

40. Berge Report, 129.

41. Berge Report, 89.

42. Doyle, "Memorandum," 2.

43. Charles Carter, "Berge Quizzed on School Plan: Integration Trial," *Denver Post*, February 11, 1970.

Chapter 2: The Noel Resolution

1. Edgar Benton, interview by Pat Pascoe, January 30, 2012. In pronouncing *Noel*, the accent is on the first syllable.

2. Quoted in Jenny Brundin, "40 Years since Keyes," Colorado Public Radio, February 4, 2013, report on the first day of a symposium sponsored by the University of Denver Law School.

3. Edmond F. Noel Jr., interview by Pat Pascoe, June 6, 2013.

4. Juanita Gray, Jim Davis, and Rachel Bassette Noel: *Oral History*, 1973 (Denver Public Library, October 11, 1973), Tape 2, Side A.

5. Gray, Davis, and Noel, *Oral History*, Tape 2, Side A.

6. Noel interview, June 6, 2013.

7. Gray, Davis, and Noel, *Oral History*, Tape 2, Side B.

8. Minutes, Denver Board of Education, Denver Public Schools, May 6, 1964.

9. Minutes, Denver Board of Education, Denver Public Schools, May 16, 1968.

10. Edgar Benton's personal file of letters.

11. 347 U.S. 483 (1954).

12. *Keyes v. School District No. 1*, 413 U.S. 189, 217 (1973).

13. All the letters cited in this section are from Edgar Benton's personal file.

14. Gray, Davis, and Noel, *Oral History*, Tape 2, Side B.

15. "'Integration' Aid Is Education Aid That Schools Need Right Now," *Denver Post*, February 25, 1971.

16. Mary Jean Taylor, "Leadership Responses to Desegregation in the Denver Public Schools: A Historical Study, 1959–1977," PhD thesis, University of Denver, 1990, cited in Robert T. Connery, "Keyes v. School District No. 1: A Personal Remembrance of Things Past and Present," *Denver University Law Review* (January 1, 2013): 1099–1100.

17. Wymond J. Ehrenrook and Lloid B. Jones, "The Denver Public Schools Look at Themselves" (Denver: Denver Public Schools, Division of Instructional Services, May 1968). The test scores were in the supplement, which is not available from the Denver Public Library or the Denver Public Schools. The release of the scores was covered in Charles Carter, "Test Scores Dip for Some City Pupils," *Denver Post*, September 8, 1968.

18. Ehrenrook and Jones, "Denver Public Schools Look at Themselves," 35.

19. Ehrenrook and Jones, "Denver Public Schools Look at Themselves," 35.

20. Ehrenrook and Jones, "Denver Public Schools Look at Themselves," 36.

21. Ehrenrook and Jones, "Denver Public Schools Look at Themselves," Supplementary Information.

22. Charles Carter, "Negro School Setup Told by Researcher: Integration Hearing," *Denver Post*, July 17, 1969, 3.

23. Brundin, "40 Years since Keyes."

24. Brundin, "40 Years since Keyes," 85–86.

25. Robert D. Gilberts, *Planning . . . Quality Education: A Proposal for Integrating the Denver Public Schools* (Denver: Denver Public Schools, October 1968), 106.

26. Gilberts, *Planning*, 34.

27. Gilberts, *Planning*, 40–41.

28. Gilberts, *Planning*, 93–94.

29. Gilberts, *Planning*, 55.

30. Gilberts, *Planning*, 111–112.

31. Gilberts, *Planning*, 17–18.

32. Edgar Benton's personal file of letters.

33. Edgar Benton's personal file of letters.

34. "Mixed Reactions Greet Gilberts' Integration Program," *Denver Post*, September 5, 1968, 35.

35. "Mixed Reactions," 35.

36. "Mixed Reactions," 35.

37. "Panel Hears Talks Backing Integration," *Denver Post*, September 27, 1968.

38. Arlynn Nellhaus, "Park Hill Meeting Rejects Gilberts' Proposal: School Plan 'Inadequate,'" *Denver Post*, November 1, 1968 [?].

39. "Alternate Proposal Suggests Six North-South 'Cluster' Units," *Denver Post*, November 13, 1968.

40. For an explanation of the segregation index, see chapter 6.

41. George Bardwell, "Looking Ahead: Racial and Ethnic Distribution of Students in the Elementary Schools and the Proposal for Integrated Education," November 12, 1968, Suzanne Palmer Notebook file, private collection.

Chapter 3: The Benton-Pascoe Campaign

1. Calvin Trillin, "U.S. Journal Denver: Doing the Right Thing Isn't Always Easy," *New Yorker*, May 31, 1969, 86.

2. Monte's later civic activities included four years as chair of the Colorado Democratic Party, twelve years on the Denver Water Board, twelve years as trustee of the Colorado School of Mines, and three years as director of Natural Resources under Governor Richard Lamm. He ran unsuccessfully for Denver mayor in 1983. Since his death in 2006, the mayor of Denver has annually presented the Monte Pascoe Award for Civic Leadership.

3. 163 U.S. 537 (1896).

4. *Brown I*, 347 U.S. 483 (1954).

5. *Denver Public Schools Look at Themselves*, Supplementary Information, 1968. The supplement is not available at the Denver Public Library or from the Denver Public Schools, but I have one page from it showing a table titled "Composite Percentile Scores of Students in Minority Schools and over 90% Anglo Schools in Denver, May, 1968." The terms *Negro*, *Hispano*, and *Anglo* were used by the Denver Public Schools at that time.

6. "Here's Schedules for Campaign," *Denver Post*, date unavailable.

7. "Monte Pascoe Announces Candidacy," press release, March 8, 1969, Pat Pascoe file.

8. Martin Moran, "Benton Sees Integration as City School Solution," *Rocky Mountain News*, May 11, 1969.

9. "Denver Board of Education Election May 20, 1969," Pat Pascoe file.

10. Liz Wing, "Community Relations for Benton-Pascoe School Board Campaign," campaign document, March 11, 1969.

11. Edgar Benton and Monte Pascoe, "Statement of Position—2," Pat Pascoe file.

12. "Beliefs Strong Enough to Stand On," Benton-Pascoe Campaign, Pat Pascoe file.

13. "We Elect School Boards to Make Tough Decisions," Benton-Pascoe Campaign, February 1, 1969, Pat Pascoe file.

14. Edgar Benton and Monte Pascoe, "Statement of Position—A Summary—1," Benton-Pascoe Campaign, 2–3, Pat Pascoe file.

15. "Denver's Problem," Pat Pascoe file.

16. Press release, William Kostka and Associates, Inc., May 6, 1969.

17. Pat Collins, "Bused Families Have a Change of Heart," *Contemporary, Denver Post*, May 18, 1969, 8. See also Art Branscombe, "How Berkeley Integrated Schools," *Denver Post*, January 12, 1969.

18. Richard Tucker, "Dems, GOP Active in School Board Race," *Rocky Mountain News*, May 19, 1969, 5.

19. Trillin, "U.S. Journal Denver," 85.

20. James C. Perrill, Perrill Campaign card, n.d.

21. "School Board's Main Job Is Education: Perrill," *Rocky Mountain News*, May 12, 1969.

22. Trillin, "U.S. Journal Denver," 86.

23. "Stop the Buses—Vote Tuesday," *Rocky Mountain News*, May 19, 1969.

24. "Imagination . . . Edgar Benton and Monte Pascoe Have It!" Doctors for Benton and Pascoe, signed by 324 doctors, *Rocky Mountain News*, May 19, 1969, 6; "Denver Physicians for Better Schools," Perrill and Southworth advertisement, cited in Mary Jean Taylor, "Leadership Responses to Desegregation in the Denver Public Schools: A Historical Study, 1959–1977," PhD thesis, University of Denver, January 1, 1990, 129.

25. Frank Southworth and Jim Perrill, Letter to Denver Police and Fire Departments, Denver Better Public Schools Committee, May 1, 1969[?].

26. "School Board Candidates Address the Issues," Chamber of Commerce, May 1, 1969[?].

27. "Two School Candidates Get Backing," *Denver Post*[?], May 16, 1969.

28. "Parochial Integration Policy Given," *Rocky Mountain News*, May 15, 1969, 5.

29. George Kane, "School Bus Drivers Seek Control over Unruly Riders," *Rocky Mountain News*, May 19, 1969; "Union Disavows School Bus Drivers' Statement," *Rocky Mountain News*, May 20, 1969.

30. Robert Gilberts, Superintendent, "A Proposal for Stabilization of Memberships of Elementary Schools in Northeast Denver and for Further Integration of the Denver Public Schools: For Study and Discussion," Denver Public Schools, April 1, 1969.

31. Craig Barnes, "The School Board Suit," unpublished memoir, January 6, 2017, 3. I am indebted to Craig's wife, Michaela Barnes, for sharing this unpublished memoir with me.

32. "For School Board: Benton, Pascoe," *Denver Post*, May 11, 1969.

33. "A Time to Vote Our Faith," *Denver Post*, May 18, 1969.

34. "The School Board Election," *Rocky Mountain News*, May 16, 1969.

35. Edgar Benton, interview by Pat Pascoe, July 28, 2015.

36. Thirteen staff members of RMN, "Staffers Speak Up," *Rocky Mountain News*, May 17, 2012.

37. Edgar Benton, interview by Pat Pascoe, January 30, 2012; Trillin, "U.S. Journal Denver," 86.

38. Taylor, "Leadership Responses," 153, citing interviews with Edgar Benton, Jim Voorhees, and Rachel Noel.

39. Charles Carter, "Perrill, Southworth Win; City Pay Raises Okayed," *Denver Post*, May 21, 1969, 1.

40. Carter, "Perrill, Southworth Win," 1.

41. Carter, "Perrill, Southworth Win," 1.

42. Anthony Ripley, "Denver School Vote Ends a Dream for Negroes," *New York Times*, May 22, 1969.

43. Jesse Wagner, "Citizen's Thanks to Benton, Pascoe," letter to the families of Edgar Benton and Monte Pascoe *Denver Post*, May 22, 1969.

44. "High Hopes, Apprehensions Mark Evaluations by Others: Other Board Members," *Denver East News*, May 29, 1969.

45. Robert T. Connery, "Keyes v. School District No. 1: A Personal Remembrance of Things Past and Present," *Denver University Law Review* 90, no. 5 (2013): 1101.

46. Craig Barnes, "Forty Years since *Keyes v. School District No. 1*," seminar presentation, Thursday, January 31, 2013; Craig Barnes, "A Personal Memoir of Plaintiffs' Co-Counsel in *Keyes v. School District No. 1*," *Denver University Law Review* 90, no. 5 (2013): 1059–1081.

Chapter 4: The New Board Moves to Resegregate

1. The minutes of the meeting show ten more votes for Benton than the newspaper article had, at 31,108. Kenneth R. Gher, "Minutes of the Special Meeting (69–11) of the Board of Education of School District No. 1 in the City and County of Denver and State of Colorado Held in the Board Room, 414 Fourteenth Street, 2:00 p.m., Tuesday, May 27, 1969," Denver Public Schools, 1.

2. Gher, "Minutes of the Special Meeting (69–11)," 3–4. See also "Benton Charges Play on Fears," *Denver Post*, May 28, 1969.

3. Kenneth R. Gher, "Minutes of the Special Meeting (69–12) of the Board of Education of School District No. 1 in the City and County of Denver and State

of Colorado Held in the Board Room, 414 Fourteenth Street, 2:30 p.m., Tuesday, May 27, 1969," Denver Public Schools, 2; Edgar Benton, interview by Pat Pascoe, July 29, 2015.

4. Charles Carter, "Forced Busing Plan Killed; 'Voluntary' Program OKd," *Denver Post*, June 10, 1969.

5. Kenneth R. Gher, "Minutes of the Special Meeting (69–13) of the Board of Education of School District No. 1 in the City and County of Denver and State of Colorado Held in the Board Room, 414 Fourteenth Street, 7:30 p.m., June 9, 1969," Denver Public Schools, 2–3.

6. Gher, "Minutes of the Special Meeting (69–13)," 4.

7. Gher, "Minutes of the Special Meeting (69–13)," 5.

8. Gher, "Minutes of the Special Meeting (69–13)," 5.

9. Gher, "Minutes of the Special Meeting (69–13)," 5–6.

10. Gher, "Minutes of the Special Meeting (69–13)," 6–7.

11. Gher, "Minutes of the Special Meeting (69–13)," 7.

12. Gher, "Minutes of the Special Meeting (69–13)," 8.

13. Gher, "Minutes of the Special Meeting (69–13)," 9–10.

14. Gher, "Minutes of the Special Meeting (69–13)," 10.

15. Gher, "Minutes of the Special Meeting (69–13)," 10–11.

16. Gher, "Minutes of the Special Meeting (69–13)," 11–12.

17. Gher, "Minutes of the Special Meeting (69–13)," 12.

18. Gher, "Minutes of the Special Meeting (69–13)," 16.

19. Gher, "Minutes of the Special Meeting (69–13)," 17.

Chapter 5: The *Keyes* Case Is Filed

1. Robert T. Connery, "Keyes v. School District No. 1: A Personal Remembrance of Things Past and Present," *Denver University Law Review* 90, no. 5 (2013): 1083–1114.

2. 269 F. Supp. 401 (D.D.C. 1967).

3. Connery, "Keyes," 1097–1098.

4. Connery, "Keyes," 1103–1104.

5. 163 U.S. 537 (1896).

6. Connery, "Keyes," 1104–1105.

7. Connery, "Keyes," 1105–1106.

8. Craig Barnes, "The School Board Suit," unpublished memoir, January 6, 2017, 4–5.

9. Barnes, "School Board Suit," 7.

10. Barnes, "School Board Suit," 7.

11. Connery, "Keyes," 1107.

12. Fred Thomas and L. Douglas Hoyt, letter to "Dear Friend," officers of the Denver Equal Educational Opportunity Fund, August 23, 1971, Janet Bardwell file, private collection

13. Mary Jean Taylor, "Leadership Responses to Desegregation in the Denver Public Schools: A Historical Study, 1959–1977," PhD thesis, University of Denver, 1990, 142.

14. Wilfred Keyes et al., Plaintiffs, Congress of Hispanic Educators et al., Plaintiff-Intervenors, School District No. 1, Denver, Colorado, Defendants (313 F.Supp. 90, Denver, Colo., 1970).

15. Connery, "Keyes," 1110.

16. Barnes, "School Board Suit," 10.

17. Craig S. Barnes and Gordon G. Greiner, "Keyes v. School District Number One, Denver, Colorado, et al., Motion for Preliminary Injunction," June 19, 1969.

18. Craig S. Barnes, Gordon G. Greiner, Jack Greenberg, James M. Nabrit III, and Conrad K. Harper, "Keyes v. School District Number One, Denver, Complaint for Permanent Injunction and Declaratory Judgment," June 19, 1969, 5. In presenting this complaint, I have frequently used language from this source in paraphrased form; un-paraphrased direct quotes are indicated with quotation marks or indented extracts.

19. Barnes et al., "Complaint for Permanent Injunction," 8–14.

20. Barnes et al., "Complaint for Permanent Injunction," 15.

21. Barnes et al., "Complaint for Permanent Injunction," 15.

22. Barnes et al., "Complaint for Permanent Injunction," 15–16.

23. Barnes et al., "Complaint for Permanent Injunction," 16.

24. Barnes et al., "Complaint for Permanent Injunction," 16–17.

25. Barnes et al., "Complaint for Permanent Injunction," 18.

26. Barnes et al., "Complaint for Permanent Injunction," 18.

27. Barnes et al., "Complaint for Permanent Injunction," 19.

28. Barnes et al., "Complaint for Permanent Injunction," 20.

29. Barnes et al., "Complaint for Permanent Injunction," 21–23.

30. Barnes et al., "Complaint for Permanent Injunction," 23–24.

31. Barnes et al., "Complaint for Permanent Injunction," 25.

32. Barnes et al., "Complaint for Permanent Injunction," 25.

33. Barnes et al., "Complaint for Permanent Injunction," 26.

34. Barnes et al., "Complaint for Permanent Injunction," 26.

35. Barnes et al., "Complaint for Permanent Injunction," 27.

36. Barnes et al., "Complaint for Permanent Injunction," 27–28.

37. Barnes et al., "Complaint for Permanent Injunction," 28–30.

38. Barnes et al., "Complaint for Permanent Injunction," 30–31.

39. Barnes et al., "Complaint for Permanent Injunction," 32.

40. "Meeting on Research Needs," June 22, 1969, Janet Bardwell file, private collection.

41. Chuck Green, "Three Steps on Schools Supported at East Denver Meeting," *Denver Post*, June 11, 1969.

42. Charles Carter, "HEW Asked for Denver School Probe: Complaint," *Denver Post*, June 13, 1969.

43. Letter from Ted Stockin, co-chairman of the Southwest Denver Human Relations Council, to Robert H. Finch, Secretary of Health, Education, and Welfare; quoted in article by Tom Bailery, "S.W. Denver Group Asks Federal Action for School Integration," *Denver Post*, June 12, 1969, 15.

44. "Individual Complaints with HEW Revealed by Regional Office: New Discrimination Charges," *Denver East News*, June 26, 1969.

45. "Angels with Bitter Tongues," editorial, *Denver Post*, June 13, 1969[?].

46. "Mayor Promises Help in Integration," *Rocky Mountain News*, June 11, 1969.

47. Charles Carter, "Hallett School Busing Situation Is Evaluated," *Denver Post*, June 15, 1969.

Chapter 6: The First Court Hearing

1. Sheila Macdonald, interview by Pat Pascoe, May 9, 2017.

2. The Honorable John L. Kane Jr. and Sharon Marks Elfenbein, "William E. Doyle," in *The Federal Courts of the 10th Circuit: A History*, ed. James K. Logan, chapter 7, 69–71 (Denver: US Court of Appeals for the Tenth Circuit, 1992). All of this biographical information, except the quotes from Sheila Macdonald, is from this source.

3. Macdonald interview, May 9, 2017.

4. Kane and Elfenbein, "William E. Doyle," 70.

5. Craig Barnes, "The School Board Suit," unpublished memoir, January 6, 2017, 11.

6. Barnes, "School Board Suit," 15. Bardwell did not escape harassment for his support of integration. His daughter, Janet Bardwell, an elementary school student, once answered the phone to hear someone tell her they were going to blow up their house. Janet Bardwell, interview by Pat Pascoe, June 19, 2014.

7. Andrew Bardwell, interview by Pat Pascoe, June 21, 2014.

8. Barnes, "School Board Suit," 14.

9. Trial transcript, *Keyes v. School District No. 1*, No. C-1499 (D. Colo., vol. II, July 17, 1969), 185. The transcripts are on file at Norlin Library Archives, University of Colorado at Boulder. I am indebted to Bob Connery, who shared his copies with me. See the reproductions of some of the exhibits in appendix A. One map of

Denver, beautifully colored, showed the density of the Black population on a very large map of the city, based on data for each census tract. Charts were presented in color, with shiny tape showing the changes over the years. Other maps had plastic overlays to show the potential changes under different plans.

10. Barnes, "School Board Suit" 12.

11. Robert T. Connery, "Keyes v. School District No. 1: A Personal Remembrance of Things Past and Present," *Denver University Law Review* 90, no. 5 (2013): 1111.

12. Trial transcript, *Keyes v. School District No. 1*, No. C-1499 (D. Colo., vol. I, July 16, 1969), 39.

13. Connery, "Keyes," 1111; Trial transcript, vol. I, 75–76.

14. Trial transcript, vol. I, 65.

15. Trial transcript, vol. I, 72.

16. Trial transcript, vol. I, 90–93. Though the exhibits were introduced at these pages in the transcript, they are not accessible in the thirty-nine boxes of records of the trial available through the Federal District Court, as the exhibits were stored separately from the transcripts and are not inventoried or readily available.

17. Trial transcript, vol. I, 114–115.

18. Connery, "Keyes," 1111–1112; Trial transcript, vol. I, 130–144.

19. Trial transcript, vol. I, 156.

20. For an example of how the formula operates, see in appendix A "Explanation of the Construction of the Segregation Index" (District Court, Box 14, 2 pages). The Sigma stands for the total of the absolute deviations from each of the three schools in the group in the example. Following the rest of the formula yields the segregation index of 0.78 for the group of three schools in the example; in other words, this group of schools is rather highly segregated. Also see "Index of Segregation, 1963–1982, Districtwide and Elementary Schools Showing Plaintiff's Plan and 'Nearest Schools' Assumption," Plaintiff's Exhibit No. 174 (District Court, Box 12) and "Segregation Index for Subject Senior Highs" (District Court, Box 14).

21. Trial transcript, vol. II, 189–197; Judge William E. Doyle, "Memorandum Opinion and Order," *Keyes v. School District No. 1*, No. C-1499, 303 F. Supp. 279 (D. Colo., July 31, 1969), at 285. The opinion is on file at Norlin Library Archives, University of Colorado at Boulder. I am indebted to Bob Connery, who shared his copy with me.

22. Connery, "Keyes," 1112.

23. Trial transcript, vol. II, 309–313.

24. Trial transcript, *Keyes v. School District No. 1*, No. C-1499 (D. Colo., vol. III, July 18, 1969), 355–356.

25. Trial transcript, *Keyes v. School District No. 1*, No. C-1499 (D. Colo., vol. IV, July 21, 1969), 464–466.

26. Trial transcript, vol. IV, 501.

27. Trial transcript, vol. IV, 512–522.

28. Trial transcript, vol. IV, 543–544.

29. Trial transcript, vol. IV, 549.

30. Trial transcript, *Keyes v. School District No. 1*, No. C-1499 (D. Colo., vol. V, July 22, 1969), 599–622.

31. Trial transcript, vol. V, 689.

32. Trial transcript, vol. V. The closing argument is on unnumbered pages of the Xerox copy of the transcript. Some of the following summary uses the exact words of the closing argument.

33. Trial transcript, vol. V, unnumbered pages.

34. Trial transcript, vol. V, unnumbered pages.

35. Trial transcript, vol. V, unnumbered pages.

36. Doyle, "Memorandum Opinion and Order."

37. Doyle, "Memorandum Opinion and Order," at 281.

38. Doyle, "Memorandum Opinion and Order," at 283–284.

39. Doyle, "Memorandum Opinion and Order," at 284.

40. Doyle, "Memorandum Opinion and Order," at 286.

41. Doyle, "Memorandum Opinion and Order," at 287.

42. Doyle, "Memorandum Opinion and Order," at 287–288.

43. Doyle, "Memorandum Opinion and Order," at 288.

44. Richard O'Reilly, "School Board to Consider Court Integration Order," *Denver Post*, July 24, 1969. The *Denver Post* printed the full text of the order on July 27, 1969, 49.

45. George E. Bardwell, letter to Mr. Howard A. Glickstein, Acting Staff Director, United States Commission on Civil Rights, July 28, 1969.

46. Charles Carter, "School Board Asks Stay on Court Order," *Denver Post*, July 30, 1969.

47. "Views Heard on Integration: U.S. Court in Denver," *Denver Post* [?], August 4, 1969.

48. "Views Heard on Integration."

49. Charles Carter, "Schools Case Renewed: Suit Returned to Doyle," *Denver Post*, August 7, 1969.

50. Invitation "To Friends of Edgar Benton," the Campaign Committee, July 20, 1969.

51. "Church of Black Cross Gives Awards," *Denver Post*, July 27, 1969. Also see "Pascoe, Dwight Receive Awards," *Rocky Mountain News*, July 27, 1969.

52. Richard O'Reilly, "Integration Voice Leaving: Rev. Jesse Wagner," *Denver Post*, August 3, 1969.

Chapter 7: The United States Supreme Court

1. "Panel Vacates Doyle's Rule on Busing," [*Denver Post*, 8/6/69?]; *Keyes v. School District No. 1*, 396 U.S. 1215 (1969); Charles Carter, "Schools Case Renewed; Suit Returned to Doyle," *Denver Post*, August 7, 1969.

2. Charles Carter, "School Order Stopped: Case Goes to Supreme Court," *Denver Post*, August 27, 1969, 1, 4.

3. Robert T. Connery, "Keyes v. School District No. 1: A Personal Remembrance of Things Past and Present," *Denver University Law Review* 90, no. 5 (2013): 1087.

4. Craig Barnes, "The School Board Suit," unpublished memoir, January 6, 2017, 23.

5. Connery, "Keyes," 1084–1085. The account of the events at the Supreme Court that day is from Connery's article.

6. Edgar Benton, interview by Pat Pascoe, November 19, 2015.

7. Barnes, "School Board Suit," 25.

8. *Keyes v. School District No. 1*, 396 U.S. 1215 (1969). See also Dan Bell, "Judge Brennan Orders Integration of Schools," *Rocky Mountain News*, August 30, 1969, 5; Charles Carter, "Integration Order Restored: Justice Brennan Backs Doyle Opinion," *Denver Post*, August 29, 1969, 1.

9. Charles Carter, "Board Moves to Void Order on Integration," *Denver Post*, August 30, 1969.

Chapter 8: Desegregation Begins

1. Robert Saile, "'Tinkerers' Threaten Schools—Southworth," *Denver Post*, September 12, 1969.

2. James Crawford, "Park Hill Unit Honors Five Attorneys," *Rocky Mountain News*, September 30, 1969.

3. Daniel P. Moynihan, "Text of the Moynihan Memorandum on the Status of Negroes," *New York Times*, March 1, 1970.

4. Cindy Parmenter, "Concerned Denverites Aid Busing Plan," *Denver Post*, September 5, 1969.

5. "Hallett Exchange Plan Enrollment Is Growing," *Denver Post*, August 27, 1969.

6. "Voluntary Open Enrollment Gains," *The Review*, Denver Public Schools, February 1970, 4.

7. Sarah Pascoe, interview by Pat Pascoe, December 4, 2015; Ted Pascoe, interview by Pat Pascoe, December 15, 2015.

8. Charles Carter and John Dunning, "School Busing's Reality Changes Few Minds," *Denver Post*, December 14, 1969, 33–35.

9. Charles Carter and John Dunning, "Social Implications of Busing Assessed," *Denver Post*, December 16, 1969, 60.

10. Dick Koeppe, interview by Pat Pascoe, April 15, 2013.

11. John Dunning and Charles Carter, "Integration Complicates Some Discipline Problems," *Denver Post*, December 17, 1969, 49.

12. Don Goe, interview by Mary Jean Taylor, September 5, 1989, in Taylor, "Leadership Responses to Desegregation in the Denver Public Schools: A Historical Study, 1959–1977," PhD thesis, University of Denver, 1990, 147.

13. Edgar Benton, interview by Pat Pascoe, February 28, 2015.

14. Koeppe interview, April 15, 2013.

15. Koeppe interview, April 15, 2013.

16. Koeppe interview, April 15, 2013.

17. Koeppe interview, April 15, 2013.

18. Martin Moran, "Student Fight Closes George Washington High School," *Rocky Mountain News*, September 25, 1970.

19. Moran, "Student Fight."

20. Cindy Parmenter, "Transfers to GW High Called Upset," *Denver Post*, September 26, 1970

21. Parmenter, "Transfers to GW High Called Upset."

22. "Police Patrols Set at GW High School," *Denver Post*, September 26, 1970.

23. Koeppe interview, April 15, 2013.

24. Martin Moran, "GW Vows to Make Integration Work," *Rocky Mountain News*, September 30, 1970.

25. Richard Maes, ". . . Blamed on Integration," *Rocky Mountain News*, September 30, 1970.

26. "GW Wednesday Classes Closed," *Denver Post*, October 21, 1970.

27. "West Closes after Fights in Corridors," *Denver Post*, October 23, 1970.

28. George Lane, "Removing Police at GW Urged," *Denver Post*, October 21, 1970.

29. Edgar Benton, interview by Pat Pascoe, April 28, 2017.

30. Benton, interview, April 28, 2017. Also see photo, *Denver Post*, October 23, 1970; "Board Will Try to Remove Police at GW," *Denver Post*, October 23, 1970.

Chapter 9: The Trial on the Merits: The Plaintiffs' Case

1. Trial transcript, *Keyes v. School District No. 1*, No. C-1499 (D. Colo., vol. I, February 2, 1970), 7. These transcripts of the trial on the merits are in thirty-nine boxes of records of the *Keyes* case administered through the Federal District Court in Denver. As noted later, no transcripts are available for some days of the trial.

2. Trial transcript, vol. I, 9.

3. Trial transcript, vol. I, 10.

4. Trial transcript, vol. I, 10–11.

5. Trial transcript, vol. I, 11.

6. Trial transcript, vol. I, 12.

7. Trial transcript, vol. I, 16–17. Judge Doyle was evidently referring to another case in the Fifth Circuit rather than the Tenth Circuit.

8. Trial transcript, vol. I, 19.

9. Trial transcript, vol. I, 25–27.

10. Trial transcript, vol. I, 36.

11. Trial transcript, vol. I, 38.

12. Trial transcript, vol. I, 63–64.

13. Trial transcript, vol. I, 89–90, 93.

14. These exhibits have not yet been located in the thirty-nine boxes of trial materials at the Federal District Court in Denver. See appendix A for examples of exhibits.

15. Trial Transcript, vol. I, 126.

16. Trial transcript, vol. I, 135–136. These numbers probably reflect LOE totals in 1967–1968, the last year of LOE.

17. Trial transcript, vol. I, 156.

18. Trial transcript, *Keyes v. School District No. 1*, No. C-1499 (D. Colo., vol. II-A, February 3, 1970), 2.

19. Trial transcript, *Keyes v. School District No. 1*, No. C-1499 (D. Colo., vol. II, February 3, 1970), 184–186. Janet Bardwell kindly shared with me a massive book of the computer printouts of the many analyses performed by her father, Dr. George Bardwell; these were the source of Klite's information.

20. Trial transcript, vol. II, 193.

21. Trial transcript, vol. II, 197.

22. Trial transcript, vol. II, 242–244.

23. Trial transcript, vol. II, 273–294. He said this information was in the *Denver Post* on January 13 or January 19, 1956 (the date in the transcript is illegible).

24. Trial transcript, vol. II, 291–294. See "Schools Face Segregation Suit," *Denver Post*, July 11, 1956. Articles dated July 12, 1956, and June 21, 1956, were also entered as exhibits, 301.

25. Trial transcript, vol. II, 305–307.

26. Trial transcript, vol. II, 348.

27. Trial transcript, vol. II, 357; Charles Carter, "Faculties Allowed to Vote on Negroes, Witness Says," *Denver Post*, February 4, 1970.

28. Trial transcript, *Keyes v. School District No. 1*, No. C-1499 (D. Colo., vol. III, February 4, 1970), 380–390. The 1968 pamphlet is available from the Denver Public

Library and the Denver School District, but the supplement that contained the scores by school is not available at these locations.

29. Trial transcript, vol. III, 391.

30. Trial transcript, vol. III, 397–405.

31. Trial transcript, vol. III, 440–454.

32. Trial transcript, vol. III, 463.

33. Charles Carter, "Boundary Bent, Witness Says: School Integration Trial," *Denver Post*, February 5, 1970.

34. Trial transcript, vol. III, 468–488.

35. Trial transcript, vol. III, 488.

36. Trial transcript, vol. III, 503.

37. Trial transcript, vol. III, 517–525.

38. Trial transcript, *Keyes v. School District No. 1*, No. C-1499 (D. Colo., vol. IV, February 5, 1970). This transcript, if it exists, has not been located in the thirty-nine boxes of court records at the US District Court, Colorado.

39. Marten Moran, "Statistics 'Testify' in Integration Suit," *Rocky Mountain News*, February 7, 1970.

40. Moran, "Statistics."

41. Charles Carter, "Segregation Trial Half Over," *Denver Post*, February 8, 1970.

42. David Jenkins, "38 School Buses Bombed: Cronin Says Arsonists Involved," *Denver Post*, February 6, 1970.

43. Craig Barnes, "The School Board Suit," unpublished memoir, January 6, 2017, 31.

44. Trial transcript, *Keyes v. School District No. 1*, No. C-1499 (D. Colo., vol. V, February 6, 1970), 734–745; for Mrs. Rollins's testimony, see Trial transcript, vol. II, 357.

45. Trial transcript, vol. V, 763–768.

46. Trial transcript, vol. V, 788.

47. Trial transcript, vol. V, 806–841.

48. Trial transcript, *Keyes v. School District No. 1*, No. C-1499 (D. Colo., vol. VI, February 9, 1970), 842.

49. Trial transcript, vol. VI, 840–847 (Exhibit 338A).

50. Trial transcript, vol. VI, 849–850.

51. Trial transcript, vol. VI, 851–854.

52. Trial transcript, vol. VI, 854–858.

53. Trial transcript, vol. V, 867–870.

54. Trial transcript, vol. V, 870–871.

55. Trial transcript, vol. V, 876.

56. Trial transcript, vol. V, 877.

57. Trial transcript, vol. V, 877–885.

58. Trial transcript, vol. V, 922–923.

59. Trial transcript, vol. V, 950.

60. Trial transcript, vol. V, 954–956.

61. Trial transcript, vol. V, 958.

62. Trial transcript, vol. V, 961.

63. Trial transcript, vol. V, 962.

Chapter 10: The Trial on the Merits: The Defendants' Case

1. Trial transcript, *Keyes v. School District No. 1*, No. C-1499 (D. Colo., vol. VI, February 9, 1970), 962–965.

2. Trial transcript, vol. VI, 962.

3. Trial transcript, vol. VI, 965.

4. Trial transcript, vol. VI, 965.

5. Trial transcript, vol. VI, 966.

6. Trial transcript, vol. VI, 967. He cites *Whitus v. George*, 385 U.S. 545 (1967), 542, note 2, where probability analysis was used to shift the burden of proof to the defendants.

7. Trial transcript, vol. VI, 968–969.

8. Trial transcript, vol. VI, 969. Exhibit 241 has the rest of the schools affected.

9. Trial transcript, vol. VI, 971.

10. Trial transcript, vol. VI, 971.

11. Trial transcript, vol. VI, 972–973. The cited quote is from page 2400 in the Pasadena case.

12. Trial transcript, vol. VI, 987–1002.

13. Trial transcript, vol. VI, 1015–1021.

14. Trial transcript, vol. VI, 1025–1026.

15. Trial transcript, vol. VI, 1036–1039, Plaintiffs' Exhibit No. 416. This exhibit is not in the appendix.

16. Trial transcript, vol. VI, 1034.

17. Trial transcript, vol. VI, 1058.

18. Trial transcript, vol. VI, 1058.

19. Trial transcript, *Keyes v. School District No. 1*, No. C-1499 (D. Colo., vol. VII, February 10, 1970), 1066–1071.

20. Trial transcript, vol. VII, 1078–1079.

21. Trial transcript, vol. VII, 1089–1093.

22. Trial transcript, vol. VII, 1097–1110.

23. Trial transcript, vol. VII, 1111–1112.

24. Trial transcript, vol. VII, 1113–1114.

25. Trial transcript, vol. VII, 1115–1117.

26. Trial transcript, vol. VII, 1120–1128.

27. Trial transcript, vol. VII, 1133.

28. Trial transcript, vol. VII, 1139–1143.

29. Trial transcript, vol. VII, 1156–1159. There appears to be an error in the number of students enrolled in Byers, either in the transcript or in my recording of the number. The point Greiner was making was that minority and majority students were separated even when enrollments would have been more appropriate to capacities, and schools could have been integrated if the boundaries had been redrawn with that in mind. This citation applies to the rest of the paragraph, as well.

30. This was Intervenor's Exhibit U, Burch's own "Confidential Copy." Trial transcript, vol. VII, 1166–1171.

31. Trial transcript, vol. VII, 1172–1174. See Special Study Committee on Equality of Educational Opportunity in the Denver Public Schools, Jim Voorhees, chair, "Report and Recommendations to the Board of Education, School District Number One, Denver, Colorado," Denver Public Schools, March 1, 1964, 43.

32. Trial transcript, vol. VII, 1178–1193.

33. Trial transcript, vol. VII, 1197–1203.

34. Trial transcript, vol. VII, 1205.

35. Trial transcript, vol. VII, 1206–1209.

36. Trial transcript, vol. VII, 1210.

37. Trial transcript, vol. VII, 1212–1214.

38. Trial transcript, vol. VII, 1216–1237.

39. Trial transcript, vol. VII, 1222.

40. Trial transcript, vol. VII, 1239.

41. Trial transcript, vol. VII, 1239–1246; Advisory Council on Equality of Educational Opportunity in the Denver Public Schools, William G. Berge, chair, and Bernard Valdez, vice chair, et al., "Final Report and Recommendations to the Board of Education School District Number One," 1967, 135.

42. Trial transcript, vol. VII, 1255.

43. Trial transcript, vol. VII, 1258–1260.

44. Trial transcript, vol. VII, 1278.

45. Trial transcript, vol. VII, 1279–1981.

46. Trial transcript, vol. VII, 1283–1285.

47. Trial transcript, *Keyes v. School District No. 1*, No. C-1499 (D. Colo., vol. VIII, February 11, 1970), 1294–1295.

48. Trial transcript, vol. VIII, 1304.

49. Trial transcript, vol. VIII, 1308.

50. Trial transcript, vol. VIII, 1321–1322.

51. Trial transcript, vol. VIII, 1335.

52. Trial transcript, vol. VIII, 1339.

53. Trial transcript, vol. VIII, 1342–1344.

54. Trial transcript, vol. VIII, 1361.

55. Trial transcript, vol. VIII, 1361–1362.

56. Trial transcript, vol. VIII, 1377–1381.

57. Trial transcript, vol. VIII, 1392.

58. Trial transcript, vol. VIII, 1393.

59. Trial transcript, vol. VIII, 1398–1399.

60. Trial transcript, vol. VIII, 1422–1427.

61. Trial transcript, *Keyes v. School District No. 1*, No. C-1499 (D. Colo., vol. IX, February 16, 1970), 1446.

62. Trial transcript, vol. IX, 1464.

63. Trial transcript, vol. IX, 1463–1473.

64. Charles Carter, "Denver Efforts to Hire Minority Teachers Told," *Denver Post*, February 17, 1970.

65. Trial transcript, vol. IX, 1487–1509.

66. Trial transcript, vol. IX, 1529.

67. Trial transcript, vol. IX, 1536–1557.

68. Trial transcript, *Keyes v. School District No. 1*, No. C-1499 (D. Colo., vol. X, February 17, 1970), 1569–1570.

69. Trial transcript, vol. X, 1591–1598.

70. Trial transcript, vol. X, 1601–1615.

71. Trial transcript, vol. X, 1616, 1621.

72. Trial transcript, vol. X, 1632–1634.

73. Trial transcript, vol. X, 1653–1654.

74. Trial transcript, vol. X, 1685–1686.

75. Trial transcript, vol. X, 1688–1700.

76. Trial transcript, vol. X, 1701–1704.

77. Trial transcript, vol. X, 1729.

78. Trial transcript, vol. X, 1760–1765.

79. Charles Carter, "Oberholtzer Final Witness for School Board," *Denver Post*, February 19, 1970, 2.

80. Charles Carter, "Board Concludes Its Defense: Denver School Trial," *Denver Post*, February 20, 1970.

81. Charles Carter, "Closing Arguments Due in School Trial: Segregation Issue," *Denver Post*, February 22, 1970.

82. "Jim Perrill Home Firebombed," *Denver Post*, February 22, 1970. See also "Explosive Rips Denver Home," *Denver Post*, February 25, 1970.

83. "Plaintiffs Complete School Suit Arguments," *Denver Post*, February 24, 1970.

84. Martin Moran, "Attorneys Conclude Final Arguments in School Suit," *Rocky Mountain News*, February 25, 1970.

85. "Explosive Rips Denver Home."

86. Mary Jean Taylor, "Leadership Responses to Desegregation in the Denver Public Schools: A Historical Study, 1959–1977," PhD thesis, University of Denver, 1990, 152.

87. "Nixon to Push Integration Only as an Education Aid," *New York Times*, March 8, 1970.

Chapter 11: Judge Doyle's Decision and the Remedy Plans

1. "Suit Dismissal Is Sought: School Integration Brief," *Denver Post*, March 14, 1970.

2. Judge William E. Doyle, "Memorandum Opinion and Order," *Keyes v. School District No. 1*, No. C-1499, 313 F. Supp. 61 (D. Colo., March 21, 1970), at 63 See leagle .com.

3. Judge William E. Doyle, "Memorandum," at 64.

4. Doyle, "Memorandum," at 64.

5. Doyle, "Memorandum," at 65.

6. Doyle, "Memorandum," at 66.

7. Doyle, "Memorandum," at 67.

8. Doyle, "Memorandum," at 68.

9. Doyle, "Memorandum," at 69.

10. Doyle, "Memorandum," at 69–73.

11. Doyle, "Memorandum," at 73.

12. Doyle, "Memorandum," at 73.

13. Doyle, "Memorandum," at 73–74.

14. Doyle, "Memorandum," at 74.

15. Doyle, "Memorandum," at 75.

16. Doyle, "Memorandum," at 75.

17. Doyle, "Memorandum," at 75.

18. Doyle, "Memorandum," at 76; see *Board of Education, etc. v. Dowell*, 375 F. 2d 158 at 166 (10th Cir. 1967); *Downs v. Board of Education*, 336 2d 988 (10th Cir. 1964).

19. Doyle, "Memorandum," at 76. Doyle is quoting *Board of Education v. Dowell*.

20. Doyle, "Memorandum," at 77.

21. Doyle, "Memorandum," at 77. This is called the third count of plaintiffs' second claim, but on the next page after III the following issue is also called "The third count of plaintiffs' second claim for relief."

22. Doyle, "Memorandum," at 77.

23. Doyle, "Memorandum," at 77.

24. Doyle, "Memorandum," appendix I, at 86.

25. Doyle, "Memorandum," appendix II, at 88.

26. Doyle, "Memorandum," at 80.

27. Doyle, "Memorandum," at 81.

28. Doyle, "Memorandum," at 81.

29. Doyle, "Memorandum," at 81–82.

30. Doyle, "Memorandum," at 82.

31. Doyle, "Memorandum," at 83.

32. Doyle, "Memorandum," at 84.

33. Doyle, "Memorandum," at 84.

34. Doyle, "Memorandum," at 84.

35. Doyle, "Memorandum," at 85.

36. Doyle, "Memorandum," at 85.

37. Doyle, "Memorandum," at 85.

38. Bill Myers, "Judge Rules Denver Busing to Continue," *Denver Post*, March 22, 1970, 1.

39. President Richard Nixon, "Nixon Gives Policies on Desegregation of Schools," *Denver Post*, March 25, 1970, 56.

40. Charles Carter, "Hearing Ordered May 11 on School Plan," *Denver Post*, April 17, 1970, 2. All the information here about the April 17 meeting is from the *Denver Post* article.

41. Carter, "Hearing Ordered," 2.

42. Martin Moran, "Doyle Orders 17 Area Schools Desegregated," *Rocky Mountain News*, April 22, 1970, 5. Doyle seemed unaware that the number of Hispanic students was much greater than the number of Black students.

43. Gordon G. Greiner and Craig S. Barnes, "Plaintiffs' Memorandum for the Hearing on Relief," *Wilfred Keyes, et al., Plaintiffs, vs. School District No. One, Denver Colorado, et al, Defendants*, US District Court for the District of Colorado, May 7, 1970. As noted, the memorandum is over fifty pages long. It was provided to me by Janet Bardwell, the daughter of Dr. George Bardwell. For the plans of both sides, see also Cindy Parmenter, "Integration Key in School Plans: 15 'Minority Schools,'" *Denver Post*, May 10, 1970.

44. Cindy Parmenter, "Board OKs Upgrading Plan for 15 Minority Schools," *Denver Post*, May 8, 1970, 16.

45. Parmenter, "Board OKs Upgrading Plan," 16.

46. Parmenter, "Board OKs Upgrading Plan," 16.

47. "School Board Divided on Quality Plan Merits," *Denver Post*, May 8, 1970, 16.

48. "School Board Divided," 16.

49. "School Board Divided," 16.

50. Cindy Parmenter, "'Single Answer' Doubted by Gilberts," *Denver Post*, May 11, 1970, 34. The information about the hearings is taken from newspaper articles because no transcripts are available of the hearings on the remedy at the district court.

51. Parmenter, "Single Answer," 34.

52. Parmenter, "Single Answer," 34.

53. Cindy Parmenter, "Integration Best Schooling: U.S. Court Witness," *Denver Post*, May 12, 1970, 8[?]. All of the information about Coleman's, Sullivan's, and Bardwell's testimony is from this article.

54. Parmenter, "Integration Best Schooling," 8[?].

55. Judge William E. Doyle, "Opinion and Decision," *Keyes v. School District No. 1*, No. C-1499, 313 F. Supp. 90 (D. Colo., May 21, 1970).

56. Doyle, "Opinion," at 96–97.

57. Doyle, "Opinion," at 97.

58. Doyle, "Opinion," at 91.

59. Doyle, "Opinion," at 93.

60. Doyle, "Opinion," at 94.

61. Doyle, "Opinion," at 94.

62. Doyle, "Opinion," at 95.

63. Doyle, "Opinion," at 96.

64. Doyle, "Opinion," at 96–97. The guidelines are summarized here.

65. Doyle, "Opinion," at 97–98.

66. Doyle, "Opinion," at 98.

67. Doyle, "Opinion," at 98–99.

68. Doyle, "Opinion," at 97–98.

69. Doyle, "Opinion," at 99.

70. Doyle, "Opinion," at 99.

71. Doyle, "Opinion," at 100.

Chapter 12: The Court of Appeals

1. "Desegregation Plan Will Wait until Fall," *Denver Post*, May 22, 1970, 1.

2. Cindy Parmenter and Robert Pattridge, "Year-Round School Classes 'Inevitable': Denver's Departing Superintendent," *Denver Post*, July 26, 1970, 1.

3. Gordon G. Greiner, letter to Michael Jackson, defendants' attorney, August 25, 1970. Janet Bardwell provided this letter, which I marked Exhibit B.

4. Judge Delmas Carl Hill, *Keyes v. School District No. 1*, 445 F. 2d 990 (US Court of Appeals, Tenth Circuit, June 11, 1971).

5. Hill, *Keyes*, at 995.

6. Hill, *Keyes*, at 996.

7. Hill, *Keyes*, at 999.

8. Hill, *Keyes*, at 1000.

9. Judge William E. Doyle, "Memorandum Opinion and Order," *Keyes v. School District No. 1*, No. C-1499, 313 F. Supp. 61 (D. Colo., March 21, 1970), at 65.

10. Hill, *Keyes*, at 1001.

11. Hill, *Keyes*, at 1001; *Board of Education, etc. v. Dowell*, 375 F. 2d 158 (10th Cir. 1967); *Downs v. Board of Education*, 336 2d 988 (10th Cir. 1964).

12. Hill, *Keyes*, at 1002.

13. Hill, *Keyes*, at 1003.

14. Hill, *Keyes*, at 1003–1004; *Brown v. Board of Education*, 347 U.S. 483 (1954).

15. Hill, *Keyes*, at 1004.

16. Hill, *Keyes*, at 1004–1005.

17. Hill, *Keyes*, at 1005–1006.

18. Hill, *Keyes*, at 1006–1007.

19. Hill, *Keyes*. At the end of the opinion is appendix I, which shows the racial composition of the affected schools if Resolutions 1520, 1524, and 1531 were to be used and the racial composition if they were not used. Appendix II, Resolution 1562, listed the ways the district would try to improve education in the court-selected core schools. There are also footnotes for data from the Denver public schools.

20. Anon., "GW Teacher Warns against Open Defiance of Law," *Denver Post*, October 20, 1970.

21. Craig Barnes, "A Personal Memoir of Plaintiffs' Co-Counsel in *Keyes v. School District No. 1*," *Denver University Law Review* 90, no. 5 (2013): 1079.

22. "Juanita Gray, Jim Davis, Rachel Bassette Noel: Oral History," October 11, 1973, tape 3, side A, Denver Public Library, Denver, CO.

Chapter 13: The Supreme Court Rules

1. "Denver School Case Slated," *Denver Post*, January 17, 1972, 1.

2. Mary Jean Taylor, "Leadership Responses to Desegregation in the Denver Public Schools: A Historical Study, 1959–1977," PhD thesis, University of Denver, 1990, 182, quoting *Denver Post*, January 17, 1972.

3. Joseph Alsop, "Historic Case on School Busing," *Chicago Sun-Times*, March 14, 1972, 40.

4. "Study Challenges Theory on Integration Benefits; Northern Busing Programs," *Denver Post*, May 25, 1972.

5. "Negroes Defend Busing, Rap Negative Report," *Denver Post*, May 25, 1972.

6. Jack Greenberg, James M. Nabrit III, Charles Stephen Ralston, Norman J. Chachkin, Gordon G. Greiner, Robert T. Connery, and Anthony G. Amsterdam, of Council, "Brief for Petitioners in the Supreme Court of the United States," *Keyes v. School District No. 1*, No. 71–507 (October Term, 1971), 3–4.

7. Greenberg et al., "Brief for Petitioners," 13, quoting Judge William E. Doyle, "Memorandum Opinion and Order," *Keyes v. School District No. 1*, No. C-1499, 303 F. Supp. 279 (D. Colo., July 31, 1969).

8. Greenberg et al. "Brief for Petitioners," 19.

9. Judge Delmas Carl Hill, *Keyes v. School District No. 1*, 445 F. 2d 990 (US Court of Appeals, Tenth Circuit, June 11, 1971), at 1000.

10. Greenberg et al., "Brief for Petitioners," 19, original emphasis.

11. Greenberg et al., "Brief for Petitioners," 19–36.

12. Greenberg et al., "Brief for Petitioners," 38.

13. Greenberg et al., "Brief for Petitioners," 39.

14. Greenberg et al., "Brief for Petitioners," 40.

15. Greenberg et al., "Brief for Petitioners," 45.

16. Greenberg et al., "Brief for Petitioners," 45–46.

17. Greenberg et al., "Brief for Petitioners," 53.

18. Greenberg et al., "Brief for Petitioners," 54, quoting from 313 F. Supp., at 81–82.

19. Greenberg et al., "Brief for Petitioners," 54, quoting 313 F. Supp., at 83.

20. Greenberg et al., "Brief for Petitioners," 57, quoting 313 F. Supp., at 96.

21. Greenberg et al., "Brief for Petitioners," 63, quoting 313 F. Supp., at 8.

22. Greenberg et al., "Brief for Petitioners," 65.

23. Greenberg et al., "Brief for Petitioners," 66.

24. Greenberg et al., "Brief for Petitioners," 66–67.

25. Greenberg et al., "Brief for Petitioners," 67.

26. Greenberg et al., "Brief for Petitioners," 71–72.

27. Greenberg et al., "Brief for Petitioners," 73.

28. Greenberg et al., "Brief for Petitioners," 82, quoting from 313 F. Supp., at 70.

29. Quote from *Swann v. Board of Education*, 402 U.S. 1 (1971), cited in Greenberg et al., "Brief for Petitioners," 84.

30. Greenberg et al., "Brief for Petitioners," 90, from Hill, *Keyes*, at 1005, original emphasis.

31. Greenberg et al., "Brief for Petitioners," 91.

32. Greenberg et al., "Brief for Petitioners," 92–93.

33. Greenberg et al., "Brief for Petitioners," 101.

34. Greenberg et al., "Brief for Petitioners," 102.

35. Greenberg et al., "Brief for Petitioners," 114–115.

36. Greenberg et al., "Brief for Petitioners," 119–120.

37. Greenberg et al., "Brief for Petitioners," 121.

38. Greenberg et al., "Brief for Petitioners," 125–126.

39. *Denver Post*, June 10, 1973, quoted in Taylor, "Leadership Responses," 206.

40. Justices Brennan, Douglas, Stewart, Marshall, and Blackmun, *Keyes v. School District No. 1*, 413 U.S. 189 (June 21, 1973), at 110.

41. Brennan et al., *Keyes*, at 191.

42. Brennan et al., *Keyes*, at 194.

43. Brennan et al., *Keyes*, at 198.

44. Brennan et al., *Keyes*, at 200. In the last sentence Brennan quotes *Brown v. Board of Education*, 349 U.S. 294 (1955) [Brown II], at 301.

45. Brennan et al., *Keyes*, at 203.

46. Brennan et al., *Keyes*, at 204.

47. Brennan et al., *Keyes*, at 207, quoting the Court of Appeals, 445 F. 2d, at 1006.

48. Brennan et al., *Keyes*, at 208.

49. Brennan et al., *Keyes*, at 211.

50. Brennan et al., *Keyes*, at 214.

51. Brennan et al., *Keyes*, at 214.

52. Brennan et al., *Keyes*, at 224.

53. Brennan et al., *Keyes*, at 216.

54. Brennan et al., *Keyes*, at 265.

55. Andy Rogers, "School Case Settlement 'Year of Hassling Away,'" *Denver Post*, July 26, 1973, 28.

Chapter 14: The Finger Plan

1. Mary Jean Taylor, "Leadership Responses to Desegregation in the Denver Public Schools: A Historical Study, 1959–1977," PhD thesis, University of Denver, 1990, profiles at the end of Taylor's thesis.

2. Trial transcript, *Keyes v. School District No. 1*, "Hearing on Remanded Issues" (D. Colo., vol. II, December 5, 1973), 279.

3. Trial transcript, vol. II, 344–345. The transcript for December 6, 1973, is missing at the district court and may not exist. The University of Colorado Archives does not have this transcript either.

4. Judge William E. Doyle, "Memorandum Opinion and Order," *Keyes v. School District No. 1*, No. C-1499, 368 F. Supp. 207 (D. Colo., December 11, 1973), at 209.

5. Doyle, "Memorandum," at 210.

6. Doyle, "Memorandum," at 210.

7. "A Plan for Expanding Educational Opportunity in the Denver Public Schools," Special Report, Denver Public Schools, January 1, 1974, 1.

8. James M. Nabrit III and Gordon Greiner, "Plaintiffs' Proposal for District-Wide Desegregation, Integration and Quality Education, for School District No. 1, Denver, Colorado," *Keyes v. School District No. 1* (US District Court, No. C-1499, January 23, 1974), 2–3.

9. Nabrit and Greiner, "Plaintiffs' Proposal," 6, 8.

10. Nabrit and Greiner, "Plaintiffs' Proposal," 8.

11. Nabrit and Greiner, "Plaintiffs' Proposal," 9–11.

12. Art Branscombe, "School Plaintiffs File Desegregation Plan," *Denver Post*, January 24, 1974, 24; Art Branscombe, "Two Denver Desegregation Plans," *Denver Post*, January 28, 1974.

13. "Plan for Expanding Educational Opportunity in the Denver Public Schools," 3.

14. "Plan for Expanding Educational Opportunity in the Denver Public Schools"; Art Branscombe, "City School Desegregation Plan Adopted," *Denver Post*, January 23, 1974.

15. Trial transcript, *Keyes v. School District No. 1* (D. Colo., vol. I, February 19, 1974), 47–48.

16. Trial transcript, *Keyes v. School District No. 1* (D. Colo., vol. II, February 20, 1974), 267–515. [Exact page number is not available.]

17. Trial transcript, *Keyes v. School District No. 1* (D. Colo., vol. IV, February 22, 1974), 818.

18. Trial transcript, *Keyes v. School District No. 1* (D. Colo., vol. XI, March 27, 1974), 2346. The city of Charlotte and the county in which it was located, Mecklenburg, constituted one school district that permitted a countywide desegregation plan utilizing busing.

19. Trial transcript, vol. XI, 2337.

20. Trial transcript, vol. XI, 2340.

21. Judge William E. Doyle, "Memorandum Opinion and Order," *Keyes v. School District No. 1*, No. C-1499, 380 F. Supp. 673 (D. Colo., April 24, 1974), at 686.

22. Doyle, "Memorandum," at 688.

23. Doyle, "Memorandum," at 687–690.

24. Doyle, "Memorandum," at 691.

25. Doyle, "Memorandum," at 691–692.

26. Doyle, "Memorandum," at 692.

27. Doyle, "Memorandum," at 705.

28. Judge William E. Doyle, "Text of Final Judgment Decree in Denver School Case," *Denver Post*, May 5, 1974, 47. The following summary is from this article.

29. Doyle, "Memorandum," 689–692 and appendix.

30. Doyle, "Text of Final Judgment Decree."

31. Doyle, "Text of Final Judgment Decree."

32. Doyle, "Text of Final Judgment Decree."

Chapter 15: Desegregating Denver "Root and Branch"

1. Mary Jean Taylor, "Leadership Responses to Desegregation in the Denver Public Schools: A Historical Study, 1959–1977," PhD thesis, University of Denver 1990, 220, quoting *Rocky Mountain News*, February 12, 1974.

2. Pat Pascoe's Morey file. The information about Morey in this section comes from this file.

3. Letter from Albert C. Rehmer, principal, to Pat Pascoe, December 6, 1976.

4. *Moore Student Council Newsletter*, November 5, 1974.

5. "The Moore School Dilemma," Pat Pascoe, Spring 1975.

6. *Consolidated Schools Report*, Colorado Department of Education, Denver, 1972[?].

7. Reporter's transcript, "Remarks of Honorable William E. Doyle before the Community Education Council and First Meeting Community Education Council," *Keyes v. School District No. 1* (D. Colo., May 10, 1974), 1–8.

8. Reporter's transcript, "Remarks," 8–12.

9. Judge William E. Doyle, letter to Maurice B. Mitchell, January 27, 1975.

10. Maurice B. Mitchell, letter to Dr. Louis J. Kishkunas, October 7, 1975.

11. Maurice B. Mitchell, letter to Patricia Pascoe, August 12, 1974. Kay Reed was chair and Rhondda Grant was vice chair of that subcommittee. Other members of the subcommittee were Betsy Carey, William Roberts, and Rev. Cruz-Ahedo.

12. Classroom Observation Form for Junior High Schools, Community Education Council, January 1, 1977.

13. Judge Richard P. Matsch, "Order," *Keyes v. School District No. 1*, No. C-1499 (D. Colo., July 13, 1976), 2–3.

14. Pat Pascoe, notes for coordinator report, December 1, 1975.

15. *Denver Post*, May 17, 1975; Superintendent Louis J. Kishkunas, interview, April 8, 1975; Community Education Council report to Judge Doyle, Denver Public School year 1974–1975. All of the sources in this note are quoted in Jessica Pearson and Jeff Pearson, "Litigation and Community Change: The Desegregation of the Denver Public Schools" (Denver: US Commission on Civil Rights, February 1976).

16. Minutes of the Public Relations Committee, Community Education Council, September 14, 1976.

17. Minutes of the Community Education Council regular meeting, October 27, 1976.

18. Report to Judge Richard P. Matsch, Community Education Council, March 1, 1977; minutes of the Community Education Council regular meeting, March 30, 1977.

19. Romel Hernandez, "Judge Richard Matsch, the Man Whose Word Is Law," *Rocky Mountain News*, August 21, 1994, 40A.

20. Jean Bain, letter to Judge Richard P. Matsch, May 20, 1977, 1–2.

21. Report from the Community Education Council Monitoring Committee, March 1977.

22. Report from the Community Education Council Monitoring Committee, June 1, 1977.

23. Martha Radetsky, minutes of the Community Education Council regular meeting, June 20, 1977, 3.

24. Judge Richard P. Matsch, "Memorandum and Order Concerning Community Education Council," *Keyes v. School District No. 1*, No. C-1499 (D. Colo., October 14, 1977).

25. Judge Richard P. Matsch, letter to Patricia Pascoe, November 30, 1977.

Chapter 16: The Tenth Circuit Court Rules Again

1. "Opinion," *Keyes v. School District No. 1*, No. C-1499, 521 F. 2d 465 (D. Colo., 1975).

2. "Opinion," *Keyes*, at 469.

3. "Opinion," *Keyes*, par. 23.

4. "Opinion," *Keyes*, par. 38.

5. "Opinion," *Keyes*, par. 39.

6. "Opinion," *Keyes*, par. 41.

7. "Opinion," *Keyes*, par. 42. The court of appeals described this plan in the future and conditional tenses; I have changed that to past tense because the order was already being implemented in the schools.

8. "Opinion," *Keyes*, par. 50.

9. "Opinion," *Keyes*, par. 62.

10. "Opinion," *Keyes*, par. 66.

11. "Opinion," *Keyes*, par. 70.

12. Art Branscombe, *Denver Post*, March 13, 1976, quoted in Mary Jean Taylor, "Leadership Responses to Desegregation in the Denver Public Schools: A Historical Study, 1959–1977," PhD thesis, University of Denver, 1990, 272.

13. Taylor, "Leadership Responses," profiles at end of dissertation.

Chapter 17: Effects of Desegregation

1. Ian Watt, *Rise of the Novel: Studies in Defoe, Richardson, and Fielding* (Berkeley: University of California Press, [1957] 2001), 186, quoting Mary D. George, *London Life in the 18th Century* (1925), republished Chicago: Academy Chicago Publishing, 1985, 329.

2. Christine H. Rossell, "Desegregation Plans, Racial Isolation, White Flight, and Community Response," in *The Consequences of School Desegregation*, ed. Christine H. Rossell and Willis D. Hawley, chapter 2, 25 (Philadelphia: Temple University Press, 1983).

3. Rossell, "Desegregation Plans," 25.

4. *A New Look in Schools: Who Needs It?* (Denver: League of Women Voters of Denver, July 1969), 3.

5. Tom Boasburg, Superintendent, "Join the Conversation: 20 Years after the End of Busing in DPS," Communications Office, Denver Public Schools, October 9, 2015.

6. Rossell, "Desegregation Plans," 25, 30.

7. Calvin Trillin, *Jackson, 1964* (New York: Random House, 2016), 112. This book contains a reprint of a Trillin article from the *New Yorker* printed on May 31, 1969, with an added commentary at the end.

8. Rossell, "Desegregation Plans," 26–38.

9. Christine Rossell, "The Political and Social Impact of School Desegregation Policy: A Preliminary Report," Paper presented at the Annual Meeting of the American Political Science Association, San Francisco, CA, September 1975, ERIC ED 113 268.

10. Craig Barnes, "The School Board Suit," unpublished memoir, January 6, 2017, 32.

11. Richard Koeppe, interview by Mary Jean Taylor, February 20, 1990, in Mary Jean Taylor, "Leadership Responses to Desegregation in the Denver Public Schools: A Historical Study, 1959–1977," PhD thesis, University of Denver, 1990, 329–330.

12. Richard Koeppe, interview by Pat Pascoe, April 15, 2013.

13. Koeppe interview, April 15, 2013.

14. Koeppe interview, April 15, 2013.

15. Koeppe, interview by Taylor when he was superintendent of the Denver schools, in Taylor, "Leadership Responses," 330.

16. Sheila Macdonald, interview by Pat Pascoe, May 9, 2017.

17. John L. Kane Jr. and Harry F. Tepker Jr., "William E. Doyle," in "Five of the Greatest," *Colorado Lawyer* 21, no. 2, http://doyleinn.com/about-the-william-e-doyle-inn-of-court/about-judge-william-e-doyle/, 7/1/1998.

18. Virginia Culver, "Obituary: Conservative Voted for School Desegregation," *Denver Post*, December 13, 2010, quoting from a 1995 *Denver Post* story.

19. Edgar Benton, interview by Pat Pascoe, January 30, 2012.

20. Edmond Noel, interview by Pat Pascoe, June 6. 2013.

21. Rossell and Hawley, "Introduction," in *The Consequences of School Desegregation*, ed. Christine H. Rossell and Willis D. Hawley, 6 (Philadelphia: Temple University Press, 1983).

22. Benton-Pascoe campaign literature, "Denver Board of Education Election May 20, 1969," Pat Pascoe file.

23. Judge William E. Doyle, "Memorandum Opinion and Order," *Keyes v. School District No. 1*, No. C-1499, 380 F. Supp. 673 (D. Colo., April 24, 1974), at 686.

24. Benton-Pascoe campaign literature. Test scores were not disaggregated by race in 1968.

25. "Composite Percentile Scores of Students in Minority Schools and over 90% Anglo Schools in Denver," in *The Denver Public Schools Look at Themselves, Supplementary Information* (Denver: Denver Public Schools, May 1968). For scores of each school, see appendix I of Judge William Doyle, "Memorandum Opinion and Order," *Keyes v. School District Number 1*, No. C-1499, 313 F. Supp. 61 (D. Colo., March 21, 1970). The tests are usually given in May, the eighth month of the school year, so grade-level achievement should score at the year of the test plus 0.8. Thus, the third grade student achievement would be expected to be 3.8. The expected percentile score would be 50 percent. See also, "An Educated Appraisal" (Denver: Religious Council on Human Relations and over 50 Groups and Agencies in the Denver Area, undated, probably 1968).

26. Rita E. Mahard and Robert L. Crain, "Research on Minority Achievement in Desegregated Schools," in *The Consequences of School Desegregation*, ed. Christine H. Rossell and Willis D. Hawley, 104–111 (Philadelphia: Temple University Press, 1983),.

27. Marshall S. Smith and Jennifer O'Day, "Education Equality: 1966 and Now," in *Spheres of Justice in American Schools*, ed. Deborah Verstegen, 399n (New York: HarperBusiness, 1991), quoting from Jack Greenberg, *Crusaders in the Courts: How a Dedicated Band of Lawyers Fought for the Civil Rights Revolution* (New York: Basic Books, 1994), 399.

28. Melanie Asmar, "Tests Show DPS Achievement Gaps," Chalkbeat Colorado, in *Denver Post*, Your Hub, April 26, 2018.

29. Smith and O'Day, "Education Equality," quoted in Greenberg, *Crusaders in the Courts*, 399.

30. Diane Ravitch, *Reign of Error: The Hoax of the Privatization Movement and the Danger to America's Public Schools* (New York: Alfred A. Knopf, 2013), 51–52, 58, 296. In this paragraph, Ravitch is citing Paul E. Baraton and Richard J. Coley, *The Black-White Achievement Gap: When Progress Stopped* (Princeton, NJ: Educational Testing Service, 2010).

31. Cited in Nikole Hannah-Jones, "Segregation Now . . ." *The Atlantic / Pro-Publica*, April 26, 2014, 15.

32. Ravitch, *Reign of Error*, 296, citing Gary Orfield, John Kucsera, and Genevieve Siegel-Hawley, *E. Pluribus . . . Separation: Deepening Double Segregation for More Students* (Los Angeles: Civil Rights Project, September 19, 2012), civilrightsproject.ucla.edu.

33. "The Problem We All Live With: Prologue," *This American Life*, Episode 562, Ira Glass interviewing Nikole Hannah-Jones of the *New York Times*, National Public Radio, July 31, 2015.

34. Catherine L. Horn and Michal Kurlaender, "The End of Keyes—Resegregation Trends and Achievement in Denver Public Schools," Civil Rights Project, Harvard University, Cambridge, MA, April 2006, 7–8, 11.

35. Horn and Kurlaender, "End of Keyes," 11–12.

36. Horn and Kurlaender, "End of Keyes," 13.

37. Horn and Kurlaender, "End of Keyes," appendix A, 28–29.

38. Horn and Kurlaender, "End of Keyes," 16.

39. Horn and Kurlaender, "End of Keyes," 22–23.

40. Horn and Kurlaender, "End of Keyes," 23.

41. Tom Boasberg, Superintendent, "To Fulfill the Promise of *Brown vs. Board of Education*," Communications Office, Denver Public Schools, May 29, 2014.

Chapter 18: The End of Court Supervision

1. Judge Richard P. Matsch, "Memorandum Opinion and Order," *Keyes v. School District No. 1*, No. C-1499, 902 F. Supp. 1274 (D. Colo., September 12, 1995), at 1274–1275.

2. Matsch, "Memorandum," at 1282.

3. Colorado Constitution, art. IX, sec. 8; Matsch, "Memorandum," at 1276.

4. Matsch, "Memorandum," at 1285.

5. Matsch, "Memorandum," at 1307.

6. Nikole Hannah-Jones, "Segregation Now . . . ," *The Atlantic / ProPublica*, April 26, 2014, 29.

7. Catherine L. Horn and Michal Kurlaender, "The End of Keyes—Resegregation Trends and Achievement in Denver Public Schools," Civil Rights Project, Harvard University, Cambridge, MA, April 2006, 7. Appendix A of their document lists all elementary schools in Denver and the racial percentage changes from 1994 to 1998 in each one, 28–29.

8. *Parents Involved in Community Schools v. Seattle School District No. 1*, 551 U.S. 701 (2007).

9. "K–12 Education: Better Use of Information Could Help Agencies Identify Disparities and Address Racial Discrimination," Report to Congressional Requesters (Washington, DC: United States Government Accountability Office, April 2016), 10–19.

10. "K–12 Education: Better Use of Information," 8–10, 17–19.

11. Gary Orfield, Jongyeon Ee, Erica Frankenberg, and Genevieve Siegel-Hawley, "Brown at 62: School Segregation by Race, Poverty and State," Civil Rights Project, UCLA, May 16, 2016.

12. Orfield et al., "Brown at 62," 1–3.

13. Orfield et al., "Brown at 62," 3.

14. Orfield et al., "Brown at 62," 6–7.

15. Orfield et al., "Brown at 62," 8–9.

16. "Guidance on the Voluntary Use of Race to Achieve Diversity and Avoid Racial Isolation in Elementary and Secondary Schools" (Washington, DC: US Department of Justice, Civil Rights Division, October 28, 2015), 2–5.

17. "Guidance," 4–6.

18. These scores from the Iowa Test of Basic Skills are provided by the Denver Public Schools. I believe they are for the third grade. The national average would be the 50th percentile.

19. "Strengthening Neighborhoods Committee Recommendations," Denver Public Schools, undated, ca. 2017.

20. "Strengthening Neighborhoods," 3.

21. "Strengthening Neighborhoods," 7.

22. "Learn Together, Live Together: A Call to Integrate Denver's Schools," A+ Colorado, www.apluscolorado.org, 2018. Alan Gottlieb, though not listed as the author or editor, was thanked "for his time and thought-leadership" on the report.

23. "Learn Together, Live Together," 5.

24. "Learn Together, Live Together," 8.

25. Nikole Hannah-Jones, "Choosing a School for My Daughter in a Segregated City," *New York Times*, June 12, 2016.

26. "How Racially Diverse Schools and Classrooms Can Benefit All Students," Century Foundation, 2016, quoted in "Learn Together, Live Together," 9.

27. "Learn Together, Live Together," 9, citing C. B. Swanson, *Who Graduates? Who Doesn't? A Statistical Portrait of Public High School Graduation, Class of 2001* (Washington, DC: Urban Institute, February 25, 2004).

28. "Learn Together, Live Together," 11.

29. "Learn Together, Live Together," 11.

30. "Learn Together, Live Together," 12.

31. "Learn Together, Live Together," 12.

32. "Learn Together, Live Together," 13. The sources for these four skills, respectively, are as follows: M. E. Deo, "The Promise of Grutter: Diverse Interactions at the University of Michigan Law School," *Michigan Journal of Race and Law* (2011): 17, 63; Anthony L. Antonio, Mitchell J. Chang, Kenji Hakuta, David A. Kenny, Sharon Levin, and Jeffrey F. Milem, "Effects of Racial Diversity on Complex Thinking in College Students," *Psychological Science* 15, no. 8 (2004): 507–510; Brief of Brown University *et al* in Support of Respondents, *Fisher v. University of Texas*, 570 U.S. (2013), http://www.scotusblog.com/wp-content/uploads/2015/11/14-981-bsac-Brown-University-et-al.pdf; Katherine W. Phillips, "How Diversity Makes Us Smarter," *Scientific American* (October 2014), https://www.scientificamerican.com/article/how-diversity-makes-us-smarter.

33. "Learn Together, Live Together," 14.

34. "Learn Together, Live Together," 16.

35. "Learn Together, Live Together," 17.

36. "Learn Together, Live Together," 18–19.

37. "Learn Together, Live Together," 19.

38. "Learn Together, Live Together," 19–20.

39. "Learn Together, Live Together," 21–23.

Appendix B

1. Edmond (Buddy) F. Noel Jr., interview by Pat Pascoe, June 6, 2013. The information in this section is taken from this interview.

2. Paul Lewis, written interview response provided by Palecia Lewis, July 13, 2017.

3. Sheila Macdonald interview by Pat Pascoe, May 9, 2017.

4. Kadija Haynes, interview by Pat Pascoe, May 18, 2017. All of the quotes from Kadija in this section are from this interview.

5. Mary Haynes, interview by Pat Pascoe, June 1, 2017. The quotes from Mary Haynes are all from this interview.

6. Maegan Parker Brooks, "Schools That Transform Lives: A Lesson from Denver's Integrated Past," *Front Porch*, Stapleton, Denver, CO, January 2015, 2.

7. Brooks, "Schools That Transform Lives," 3.

8. Brooks, "Schools That Transform Lives," 4.

9. E-mail from Connie Platt to Pat Pascoe, date unavailable.

10. Anna Jo Haynes, interview by Pat Pascoe, April 18, 2017. All of her comments are taken from this interview. I interviewed two of her daughters, Mary and Kadija,

but was unable to schedule an interview with Happy Haynes, former city council member and member of the Denver school board.

11. Lorie and Richard Young, interview by Pat Pascoe, May 4, 2017. All of their comments here are from this interview.

12. Palecia Lewis, interview by Pat Pascoe, July 13, 2017. All of her comments in this section are from this interview.

13. Loretta Richardson, written responses to questionnaire provided by Palecia Lewis on July 18, 2017. All of Richardson's comments are from this questionnaire.

Index

Page numbers followed by *f* indicate figures. Page numbers followed by *t* indicate tables.